T0178308

Reactive with ClojureScript Recipes

Functional Programming for the Web

Nicolas Modrzyk

Apress®

Reactive with ClojureScript Recipes: Functional Programming for the Web

Nicolas Modrzyk
Tokyo, Japan

ISBN-13 (pbk): 978-1-4842-3008-4   ISBN-13 (electronic): 978-1-4842-3009-1
DOI 10.1007/978-1-4842-3009-1

Library of Congress Control Number: 2017954495

Cover image designed by Freepik

Managing Director: Welmoed Spahr
Editorial Director: Todd Green
Acquisitions Editor: Pramila Balan
Development Editor: James Markham
Technical Reviewer: Shantanu Kumar
Coordinating Editor: Prachi Mehta
Copy Editor: Brendan Frost
Compositor: SPi Global
Indexer: SPi Global
Artist: SPi Global

Distributed to the book trade worldwide by Springer Science+Business Media New York, 233 Spring Street, 6th Floor, New York, NY 10013. Phone 1-800-SPRINGER, fax (201) 348-4505, e-mail orders-ny@springer-sbm.com, or visit www.springeronline.com. Apress Media, LLC is a California LLC and the sole member (owner) is Springer Science + Business Media Finance Inc (SSBM Finance Inc). SSBM Finance Inc is a **Delaware** corporation.

For information on translations, please e-mail rights@apress.com, or visit http://www.apress.com/rights-permissions.

Apress titles may be purchased in bulk for academic, corporate, or promotional use. eBook versions and licenses are also available for most titles. For more information, reference our Print and eBook Bulk Sales web page at http://www.apress.com/bulk-sales.

Any source code or other supplementary material referenced by the author in this book is available to readers on GitHub via the book's product page, located at www.apress.com/978-1-4842-3008-4. For more detailed information, please visit http://www.apress.com/source-code.

Printed on acid-free paper

Contents at a Glance

About the Author xv

About the Technical Reviewer xvii

Acknowledgments xix

Introduction xxi

■Chapter 1: Using Boot 1

■Chapter 2: ClojureScript 49

■Chapter 3: Working with JavaScript............................. 119

■Chapter 4: Functional Reactive Programming with Reagent...... 199

■Chapter 5: Beyond 303

Index... 361

Contents

About the Author xv

About the Technical Reviewer xvii

Acknowledgments xix

Introduction xxi

■Chapter 1: Using Boot... 1

1-1. Putting On Your Boot... 2

    Problem 2

    Solution... 2

    How It Works... 2

1-2. Writing a First Runnable Application....................................... 7

    Problem 7

    Solution... 7

    How It Works... 8

1-3. Use Boot to Start a REPL.. 12

    Problem 12

    Solution... 12

    How It Works... 12

1-4. Wiring Boot Tasks.. 17

    Problem 17

    Solution... 17

    How It Works... 17

1-5. ClojureScript with Boot 25

Problem 25

Solution 25

How It Works 26

1-6. Your First React-Based Application with Reagent 40

Problem 40

Solution 40

How It Works 40

Summary 47

■Chapter 2: ClojureScript 49

2-1. Reviewing the DOM API 50

Problem 50

Solution 50

How It Works 50

Finding Elements 50

Modifying Elements 51

Creating Elements 51

Removing Elements 53

Events and Event Handlers 53

The JavaScript Window Object 54

2-2. Manipulating DOM with ClojureScript 55

Problem 55

Solution 55

How It Works 55

Preparing the Project 55

Slow Down Running Cat: Accessing Elements and Properties 60

Making the Cat Run Again: Handling Events 62

Access and Modify DOM Nodes: Migrate to a DOM Library 64

CSS Animation Fun: Sliding 69

DOM Creation and DOM Modification 72

2-3. Getting Closer to Async Code with core.async 76

Problem 76

Solution.. 76

How It Works... 76

Core.async Concepts 77

Counting Milk Boxes with core.async.. 78

How Long Has It Been Since the Last Milk Boxes with core.async 80

2-4. Using AJAX along core.async... 82

Problem 82

Solution.. 82

How It Works... 83

What's the Weather?... 83

Quick Trick to Store Data in MongoDB... 87

2-5. Going Back to Function Reactive 93

Problem 93

Solution.. 93

How It Works... 93

Reactive Streams with Beicon... 93

Persistence and Reactive Programming with Google's Firebase 94

Firebase Channels with core.async 99

2-6. Using Rules to Trigger Events and React 101

Problem 101

Solution.. 101

How It Works... 101

2-7. Relax with Quil.. 106

Problem 106

Solution.. 106

How It Works 106

Boot Setup 106

Quilax 1 109

Quilax 2: ColorJoy 114

Quilax 3: Reactive Quil 116

Summary 118

■Chapter 3: Working with JavaScript 119

3-1. Fetching Current Time Across Timezones 119

Problem 119

Solution 120

How It Works 120

jQuery with ClojureScript Setup 120

Toggling Element with jQuery 121

Fetching a JSON File and Adding DOM Elements 122

Event Handling 127

Advanced Compilation Mode Problems 127

3-2. Working with CLJSJS Libraries 130

Problem 130

Solution 130

How It Works 130

Using a the CLJSJS Version of the jQuery Library 130

Creating a CLJSJS Library 133

3-3. Having Fun with JavaScriptProblem 140

Solution 140

How It Works 140

Retrieving a JSON File Asynchronously with oboe 140

Writing Beautiful Charts with ECharts 142

Animation with TweenJS 149

Tame the HTML5 Creation Engine: Pixi 156

What Really Matters: Physics Engine 164

Distributed MQTT Messaging with Paho and Mosquitto 172

Upping Your Game with PhaserJS 176

3-4. ClojureScript on Node.js 189

Problem 189

Solution 189

How It Works 189

Compiling ClojureScript for Node.js 189

ClojureScript REPL on Node.js 191

Compile to Node.js: Back to Boot 191

Using nodejs-Specific Namespaces: fs 192

HTTP Requests with a Third-Party Module 193

A Few Express Notes 194

Auto Reload Express App on Code Change 196

Summary 197

Chapter 4: Functional Reactive Programming with Reagent 199

Level 1 Recipes: Reagent Basics 199

4-1. Creating Reagent Components 201

Problem 201

Solution 201

How It Works 201

4-2. Working with Reagent Atoms 209

Problem 209

Solution 209

How It Works 209

Level 2 Recipes: Reagent Exercises 218

4-3. Creating a Sortable Table 218

Problem 218

Solution 218

How It Works 218

4-4. Using Local Storage 221

Problem 221

Solution 221

How It Works 221

4-5. Single Page Application and Multiple Pages 222

Problem 222

Solution 222

How It Works 223

4-6. Using HTML5 Location 226

Problem 226

Solution 226

How It Works 226

4-7. Animating Components with MOJS 230

Problem 230

Solution 230

How It Works 230

4-8. Creating Dynamic Donut-Shaped Charts 233

Problem 233

Solution 233

How It Works 234

4-9. Using Web Workers with Reagent 238

Problem 238

Solution 238

How It Works 238

4-10. Using the TypeAhead HTML Input Box **245**

Problem 245

Solution.. 245

How It Works... 245

4-11. Using the Mini Audio Player **248**

Problem 248

Solution.. 249

How It Works... 249

4-12. Using the Mini Video Player **253**

Problem 253

Solution.. 254

How It Works... 254

4-13. Generating Scalable Vector Graphics **258**

Problem 258

Solution.. 258

How It Works... 258

4-14. Dragging and Dropping Components **263**

Problem 263

Solution.. 263

How It Works... 263

**4-15. Generating Code on Server-Side Reagent
on Node.js/Express** **266**

Problem 266

Solution.. 266

How It Works... 267

Level 3 Recipes: Writing Reagent Applications 269

4-16. Using a Movie Catalog as a Template 270

Problem 270

Solution... 270

How It Works... 270

4-17. Adding Add and Delete Buttons to the Address Book 274

Problem 274

Solution... 274

How It Works... 275

4-18. Creating a Customized Painting Application 279

Problem 279

Solution... 279

How It Works... 279

Executive-Level Recipes: Advanced Reagent 284

4-19. TODO App Using Reagent/DataScript 284

Problem 284

Solution... 284

How It works... 284

Road to Fame: Beyond Reagent 296

4-20. Using Re-frame 296

Problem 296

Solution... 296

How It Works... 296

Summary... 301

■Chapter 5: Beyond 303

Section 1: Desktop Application with Electron 304

5-1. Modifying the Backend and Frontend 304

Problem 304

Solution 304

How It Works 304

Section 2: Android/iOS Application with Cordova 324

5-2. Building a Bare-Bones Cordova Project 325

Problem 325

Solution 325

How It Works 325

Section 3: Reagent on React-Native 336

5-3. Activating Pure React-Native 336

Problem 336

Solution 336

How It Works 336

5-4. Integrating React-Native with Boot 343

Problem 343

Solution 343

How It Works 344

5-5. Using TextInput, Colors, and Atom 353

Problem 353

Solution 353

How It Works 353

Summary 358

Index 361

About the Author

Nicolas Modrzyk is the technical guru of Karabiner Software and leader of technical development teams. He is also an active contributor to the open source software community in BPM, CMS, and Cloud Computing. As a developer and technical consultant, Nico has been involved over many years in designing large-scale server applications for a video conferencing company, managing enormous clusters of databases through handwritten middleware, enabling Japanese leaders with content management and process management systems, and pushing the boundaries of business processes for leading Asian companies.

Nico is an ardent advocate of Agile methods and is focused on getting the job done right to satisfy clients. He loves to push friends and team members to challenge themselves and define and reach their goals. He has lived by those empowering standards in various countries, including France, America, Ireland, Japan, China, and India. Nico is also the author of books on the programming language Clojure, available in both Engish and Japanese (languages he also speaks fluently). He is currently based in Tokyo, Japan, where he is often found after hours playing soccer, singing with his guitar in bars, and eating, drinking, and enjoying life with friends and colleagues.

About the Technical Reviewer

Shantanu Kumar is a software developer living in Bengaluru, India. He works with Concur Technologies as a principal engineer, building a next-generation stack in Clojure. He started learning computer programming when he was at school and has dabbled in several programming languages and software technologies. Having used Java for a long time, he discovered Clojure in early 2009 and has been a fan of it ever since.

Shantanu is an active participant in The Bangalore Clojure Users Group and contributes to several open source Clojure projects on GitHub. He is also the author of the first and second editions of the book *Clojure High Performance Programming* (Packt Publishing: 2013, 2015).

Acknowledgments

As we express our gratitude, we must never forget that the highest appreciation is not to utter words, but to live by them.

John F. Kennedy

It's been a long road to get this out; there are so many people to be grateful for that it would take another book just to write the list of names. So ...

Thank you to all my family, friends, Abe-san, the Japan awesome party team of Shibaura and Matsuyama, Ludo soccer friends, people still having Guinness pints in Ireland (keep one for me!), the awesome team in America, Sawada-san, Chris and the Biners, Makoto-san, publisher Apress, Prachi for kicking my butt in a timely manner, and ... the other people deep in my heart (you know who you are) for your NEVER-ENDING support. I never could have finished this without you. I appreciate it so much.

Thank you to my two daughters, Mei and Manon, for keeping up even during hard times.

Thank you Minowa-san, Miyazato-san, Greg-san, Waki-san, Kita-san, Erik-san, Yamato-san and all the fantastic people at JPX. The road is sometimes steep, but it is always a pleasure to walk it together.

Thank you Yokohama FC, for giving us so many thrilling games, during relaxing weekends. Thank you Yokohama-san for always staying strong during those games.

Introduction

My father is a dentist. When I was in my early childhood, he used to repeat the same sentence over and over again, which as far as I can remember and translate properly now was something like:

"Son, get the right tool for the job."

And as he was looking at me trying to wash the car with the wrong washing product and spending twice the amount of time that I should have, I knew somewhere deep inside of me that he was right.

He did not use a screwdriver to pull out teeth from his patients, and he had what seemed like twenty different brushes to clean each type of tooth. I even thought it was funny at the time.

But enough of tooth fairy stories.

The main goal of this book is to introduce you to an easy way to write effective and portable web applications using Functional Reactive Programming for the Web with ClojureScript.

This book is also about making your task easier by providing the right tool for the right job, or at the very least, helping you realize you're using the wrong tool for that job.

CHAPTER 1

■ ■ ■

Using Boot

千里之行，始於足下 *(A journey of a thousand miles begins with a single step)*.

Laozi

Good Boot takes you to good places

This first chapter will introduce you to the build tool named Boot. Boot has recently become one of the de facto standards for easy programming with Clojure and ClojureScript. It has become so for a few powerful reasons.

First, the Boot build tool DSL, in other words its syntax, is the same as the main programming language, Clojure. It uses functions such as meaningful data structures for building projects, so you do not have to learn yet another way of doing a loop.

Second, just like Clojure at its core, Boot proposes a few basic concepts like an environment, and some concise tasks that can be composed in multiple ways to make a workflow that is yours and always works the way you expect.

Third, the project definition can be reused both at the command line and through a Read-Eval-Print-Loop environment (REPL). In the latter case, tasks can also be defined and redefined at runtime, usually making it usually a better time-saver than others.

While there are other ways to work with ClojureScript aside from Boot, we think that the facility you will gain after mastering Boot will be a game-changer.

After mastering how Boot and the ClojureScript task work, you will be introduced to simple web examples and slowly work your way toward the core of this book, the use of the library named Reagent which is a ClojureScript wrapper around the Facebook React framework.

The following recipes detail your path to Boot mastery:

- 1-1. Installing the build tool: Boot

- 1-2. Running some very simple Clojure from a file

- 1-3. Using Boot to start a REPL, the Clojure shell

- 1-4. Using Boot tasks, and create a few of your own

- 1-5. Playing with the Boot environment and Clojure dependencies

© Nicolas Modrzyk 2017
N. Modrzyk, *Reactive with ClojureScript Recipes*, DOI 10.1007/978-1-4842-3009-1_1

- 1-6. Building your first reactive application, using only a Boot script, the Reagent library, and just enough code to perform

It is quite a hike, so let's hit the road!

1-1. Putting On Your Boot

Builds are programs. Let's start treating them that way.

```
http://boot-clj.com/
```

Problem

You need to install Boot on different platforms and make sure things are set up properly by starting a REPL, the interactive Clojure environment.

Solution

The solution should not be complicated for regular users, but beginners might be scared by some extra command lines. Just follow around the different examples and you will be on the safe path. No sorcery involved.

At the end of this project, you will be able to have a REPL (i.e., a command prompt) to execute Clojure code from a text editor or from a command line.

How It Works

Nowadays, ClojureScript, just like its target environment, can be compiled and run directly from a JavaScript runtime like node, and does not require a Java Virtual Machine.

That being said, portable file path handling with Java is battle tested and convenient, so the build tool "Boot" itself requires a Java development kit (JDK) to run.

The main drawback of installing Java is the time it takes to download it, but chances are you will be using the development kit for many other development tasks from now on, so this is a good time to install it.

You can download the latest Java installer from the Oracle web site:

```
http://www.oracle.com/technetwork/java/javase/downloads/
```

While Java 9 is probably around the corner at the time this book reaches your hands, we will make use of Java 8.

Now that the base runtime is on your machine, it is time to go and install the Boot script itself. While the procedure is very similar on Linux/OSX and Windows, let's review each one very quickly.

You can understand the main Boot executable to be a thin wrapper that downloads and checks its latest version of the real executable for you. So the core of the install is to download that wrapper and put it in a runnable location on your system and then let that wrapper do the meat of the install for you.

The installation instructions can of course be found on the very well-documented Boot web site:

```
https://github.com/boot-clj/boot#install
```

Installing Boot on Windows, Manually

The boot.exe file can be downloaded from the following github URL:

```
https://github.com/boot-clj/boot-bin/releases/download/latest/boot.exe
```

It is also included in the examples for this book.

Once you have the exe file on your machine, put it somewhere on your path to make it accessible. Regular and easy-to-remember path locations on Windows would be

- C:\Windows

- C:\ProgramData\Oracle\Java\javapath

Copy the boot.exe file there (Figure 1-1); yes, you may need some administrator permissions to copy the file to the Windows folder cited previously. If required, ask your parents to enter the admin password.

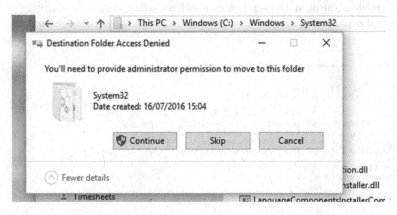

Figure 1-1. *Copy the boot.exe file to the Windows folder*

Once this is done, you can now open a command prompt, using the Windows menu and typing CMD, as shown in Figure 1-2.

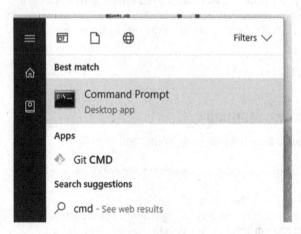

Figure 1-2. Start a command prompt

With the command prompt open, it is high time to enter your first Boot command:

boot

That's it: no parameter needed, just the command name.

This will download the most up-to-date version of Boot, which at the time of writing is 2.7.1. After the download has completed, the versions in use are shown at the prompt, as in Figure 1-3.

```
コマンド プロンプト
Microsoft Windows [Version 10.0.14393]
(c) 2016 Microsoft Corporation. All rights reserved.

C:\Users\hello>boot
Downloading https://github.com/boot-clj/boot/releases/download/2.5.2/boot.jar...
Running for the first time, BOOT_VERSION not set: updating to latest.
[1mRetrieving boot-2.7.1.jar from https://clojars.org/repo/
[m[1mRetrieving clojure-1.7.0.jar from https://repo1.maven.org/maven2/
[m#http://boot-clj.com
#Mon Feb 06 13:05:19 JST 2017
BOOT_CLOJURE_NAME=org.clojure/clojure
BOOT_VERSION=2.7.1
BOOT_CLOJURE_VERSION=1.7.0

C:\Users\hello>
```

Figure 1-3. Finish installing Boot

Once you have gotten this far, you can fire your first Clojure command with Boot. On the same command prompt, type the following warm and welcoming message:

```
echo (println "hello boot") > hello.clj && boot -f hello.clj
```

This writes a file named hello.clj containing a Clojure println statement, then tells Boot to execute this file.

After some serious greetings, let's keep on walking.

Installing Boot on Windows, with Chocolatey

Some of you may have heard of the package manager Chocolatey, which is a very convenient, maybe even the best way to install/upgrade pieces of software on your Windows machine, open source or not.

And when convenience comes to your hand, it's hard to resist. To use Chocolatey, you will need to open a powershell prompt as an administrator this time and type in the following install command:

```
iwr https://chocolatey.org/install.ps1 -UseBasicParsing | iex
```

This is an invoke web request followed by an invoke expression call on the script install.ps1 for Chocolatey installation (Figure 1-4).

Figure 1-4. *Installing Chocolatey*

You can finally put your Boot on. Any package installation with Chocolatey is rather easily done using the following choco install <packagename> to get the package installed.

In this case, the package name for Boot is named boot-clj, following along the package naming for other platforms. This also makes it clear that those are not just any Boots, but Functional Clojure Boots.

The home page for the boot-clj package is hosted on the Chocolatey server:

```
https://chocolatey.org/packages/boot-clj
```

and you can even enjoy virus-free information!

```
choco install boot-clj
```

The output is shown in Figure 1-5.

```
PS C:\WINDOWS\system32> choco install boot-clj
Chocolatey v0.10.3
Installing the following packages:
boot-clj
By installing you accept licenses for the packages.

jdk8 v8.0.121 [Approved]
jdk8 package files install completed. Performing other installation steps.
The package jdk8 wants to run 'chocolateyInstall.ps1'.
Note: If you don't run this script, the installation will fail.
Note: To confirm automatically next time, use '-y' or consider setting
  'allowGlobalConfirmation'. Run 'choco feature -h' for more details.
Do you want to run the script?([Y]es/[N]o/[P]rint): Y

Downloading JDK from http://download.oracle.com/otn-pub/java/jdk/8u121-b13/e9e7ea248e2c4826b92b3f075a80e441/jdk-8u121-wi
ndows-x64.exe
Installing jdk8...
jdk8 has been installed.
PATH environment variable does not have C:\Program Files\Java\jdk1.8.0_121\bin in it. Adding...
Environment Vars (like PATH) have changed. Close/reopen your shell to
see the changes (or in powershell/cmd.exe just type 'refreshenv').
The install of jdk8 was successful.
  Software installed to 'C:\Program Files\Java\jdk1.8.0_121\'

boot-clj v2.6.2 [Approved]
boot-clj package files install completed. Performing other installation steps.
ShimGen has successfully created a shim for boot.exe
The install of boot-clj was successful.
  Software install location not explicitly set, could be in package or
  default install location if installer.

Chocolatey installed 2/2 packages. 0 packages failed.
  See the log for details (C:\ProgramData\chocolatey\logs\chocolatey.log).
PS C:\WINDOWS\system32>
```

Figure 1-5. *Installing Boot package with Chocolatey*

After the installation completes, you can run some Clojure code as was shown in the manual install.

Installing Boot on Linux, OSX

If you have flicked through the install step for Windows, then you would probably get the feel of how things are done on Linux or OSX as well. Basically, a downloaded script or a package manager installs the Boot executable, then the executable installs the required jar file with the current or required version.

The shell one liner to achieve this is

```
sudo bash -c "cd /usr/local/bin && curl -fsSLo boot https://github.com/boot-
clj/boot-bin/releases/download/latest/boot.sh && chmod 755 boot"
```

As you can read, this downloads the boot.sh script and puts it somewhere on your path for execution.

Of course, the first test is always to be polite and say hello, with your new Boot:

```
echo '(println "hello boot world")' > hello.clj && boot -f hello.clj boot -f
hello.clj%
> hello boot world
```

Note that this is also a very simple way to install Boot on your Internet Of Things (IoT) device, like a Raspberry Pi.

So many languages and so many ways to say hello!

Installing Boot OSX with Homebrew

Homebrew, the infamous package manager for OSX, also has a boot-clj package ready to Boot you:

```
https://github.com/Homebrew/homebrew-core/blob/master/Formula/boot-clj.rb
```

And you can install it easily with

```
brew install boot-clj
```

Now whatever your machine, whatever your environment, you can say hello with Boot.

A simple hello could lead to a million things

1-2. Writing a First Runnable Application
Problem

You'd like to write supersimplistic small Java runtime-based applications.

Solution

The idea here is to use Boot to compile and run a very short piece of Java code.

How It Works

We will go over four lines to full Java application but also, two lines less, so two lines to a supersimplistic Clojure application.

A Supersimplistic Java Application

Without getting into details about what a supersimplistic Java application is, and to show the power of Clojure with Boot, you can use the next snippet, which accomplishes the following:

- creates a full Java project from scratch

- adds some Java code to a text file

- compiles

- generates an executable jar file

- executes the stand-alone jar file

It takes more time to describe it than to run it, so here comes the snippet:

```
mkdir -p boot-java/src
cd boot-java
echo 'public class Main{public static void main(String[]args){System.out.
println("hello boot!");}}' > src/Main.java
boot -s src/ javac jar -m Main target
java -jar target/project.jar
> hello boot!
```

On Windows the syntax is only slightly different. So, in a new folder in a command prompt:

```
mkdir src

echo public class Main{public static void main(String[] args)
{System.out.println("hello boot");}} > src/Main.java

boot -s src/ javac jar -m Main target
java -jar target/project.jar
```

Make sure the file Main.java is in UTF-8 if you encounter compilation problems...

If you are from the Java world, probably only the Boot command seems magic. The Boot command executes three built-in tasks one after the other: javac, jar, target, with the extra setting to set a source folder, here src.

The one-line Boot command can be explained as follows:

- the source path is set to the src folder with the -s flag

- javac: compiles the Java code found in the source path

- jar: creates a jar of the files assemble by the javac task

- with the flag -m to the jar task, we tell the jar file that the main Java class is Main.class

- target: takes the file created by the jar task and copies it to the target folder

You should try and play a bit with more Java code at this stage. It does not get much more complicated with Clojure.

A Supersimplistic Clojure Application

You would of course still remember what the simple stand-alone one-liner looks like, where we use standard Clojure to stay hello.

```
echo '(println "hello boot!")' > hello.clj
boot -f hello.clj
> hello boot!
```

This extremely short syntax means a few things for us. First, there was no need to install Clojure apart from the build tool Boot itself. Second, this also turns a file with code into an executable and stand-alone script.

As you may have noticed, the -f flag tells Boot to use the given file and execute the Clojure code found inside it, and this is how you can now create stand-alone Clojure scripting files.

On Linux, the shebang rule applies, and so write a file with the following content:

hello.clj

```
#!/usr/bin/env boot
(println "hello world!")
```

As promised, that means you have a scriptable hello world in Clojure in two lines.

Supersimplistic mp3 Player

Now that we know you have scripting power at hand, let's review a short but refreshing example.

Since the author has been living in Japan for some time now, he has become quite the train otaku, and he cannot get enough of train sounds. Here is a quick list of train sounds for the rest of us:

```
https://www.soundjay.com/train-sound-effect.html
```

While this will assume you have some Clojure knowledge to read the following snippet, let's go over it slowly:

mp3.clj

```
#!/usr/bin/env boot
; play some bell sound

;[1]
(set-env! :dependencies '[[com.googlecode.soundlibs/jlayer "1.0.1.4"]])

;[2]
(def sound "https://www.soundjay.com/transportation/train-pass-by-01.mp3")

;[3]
(with-open [mp3 (clojure.java.io/input-stream sound)]
  (let [player (javazoom.jl.player.Player. mp3)]
    (.play player)))
```

The sheband you know works only on Unix environments, which means that if you are on *ix you can simply execute the preceding code with

```
./mp3.clj
```

If still on Windows, or nomading around with your Surface tablet, you have to use the -f flag to pass in the script as an argument:

```
boot -f mp3.clj
```

You should get a nice train sound that will soothe your mind like a Japanese priest. Let's review the code in detail.

- [1] The set-env! directive tells Boot to include a Java or Clojure dependency, or basically an external library.

The dependency in the script here is named jlayer and has version 1.0.1.4.

There are two main online places to look for third-party dependency that you need to know about for now: one is the mvnrepository and the other one is clojars. You may remember for now that mvnrepository is mostly focused on Java libraries, while clojars is mostly focused on Clojure libraries.

```
https://mvnrepository.com/artifact/com.googlecode.soundlibs/jlayer/1.0.1.4
```

The format used for dependencies here is called Leiningen and looks like this:

```
[com.googlecode.soundlibs/jlayer "1.0.1.4"]
```

set-env! takes a vector of dependencies and makes them available to the classpath, or basically the runtime of the build script.

The rest of the sample reads as follows:

- [2] def: define a variable, here containing a string representing the file path or a URL of the sound to play

- [3] with-open: opens for read the file or the URL

  - javazoom.jl.player.Player. : create a new Player Java object of the jlayer library

  - play: tells the player to play the sound

  - This is Clojure's way of using Java Code using Clojure interop, by the way

This is a portable script that runs on both Windows and Linux/OSX, with the only prerequisite being the Boot installation.

This works very well for one-shot database query, MongoDB client, imaging, Hadoop, and so on, but also to start your own very service.

But let's not rest here; let's walk toward our next example.

Supersimplistic Emergency HTTP Server

On a similar note, you may have to display an emergency message on one of your servers. http-kit being a famous Clojure library for http and websockets server, you can add this library to a short script, then start an http server with the content of any response coming from a simple text message. See the following.

```
#!/usr/bin/env boot

(set-env! :dependencies '[[http-kit "2.2.0"]])
(use 'org.httpkit.server)

(defn app [req]
  {:status 200
   :headers {"Content-Type" "text/html"}
   :body (slurp "message.txt")})

(defn -main [& args]
    (run-server app {:port 8080})
    (while true (do (Thread/sleep 1000))))
```

No need to understand everything here yet, but you would probably get the main idea: Boot allows us to create a long-running executable. In detail, this gives the following:

- Use **set-env!** to update the runtime environment; here, add a dependency on the http server library **http-kit**.

- The Clojure library can now be loaded, but the loading is effectively done through the **use** call.

11

- We define an http application as a function. That function returns a Clojure **hashmap,** specifying http headers and the content of the http body.

- The content of the body itself is read (slurped!) from the content of a file named message.txt.

- Finally, **run-server** starts the http server, on port 8080.

- Also, see that if you change the message.txt file, the content of the response will be updated the next time a request comes.

Again, this is great to use for IoT devices. For example, you could try to get a sensor reading to be stored in a text file, and serve that text file reading through a simple http (or socket-ed) server like the preceding.

1-3. Use Boot to Start a REPL

Problem

Scripting is of course only one side of Boot, and you eventually would like to go back to a more interactive environment where code can be executed one statement at a time; basically you want to have a Clojure shell, as REPL.

Solution

As you know, a REPL is a command prompt where you can issue commands that are compiled, evaluated (eval-ed), and get almost immediate results printed back to the prompt.

This is at the core of any LISP-based language, and in extenso Clojure and ClojureScript.

How It Works

A simple Boot REPL can be started with the Boot built-in task REPL (Figure 1-6).

```
boot repl
```

```
NikoMacBook% boot repl
nREPL server started on port 56859 on host 127.0.0.1 - nrepl://127.0.0.1:56859
REPL-y 0.3.7, nREPL 0.2.12
Clojure 1.8.0
Java HotSpot(TM) 64-Bit Server VM 1.8.0_102-b14
        Exit: Control+D or (exit) or (quit)
    Commands: (user/help)
        Docs: (doc function-name-here)
              (find-doc "part-of-name-here")
Find by Name: (find-name "part-of-name-here")
      Source: (source function-name-here)
     Javadoc: (javadoc java-object-or-class-here)
    Examples from clojuredocs.org: [clojuredocs or cdoc]
              (user/clojuredocs name-here)
              (user/clojuredocs "ns-here" "name-here")
```

Figure 1-6. *Starting a REPL with boot*

The default namespace is the one used for Boot tasks, boot.user, so you can usually switch to another namespace before writing your own code, but the default one is of course usable.

The Sound of Ocean Waves: First Clojure Code on a Boot REPL

So, go ahead and type in a few Clojure lines at this newly started REPL. You may want to reuse the code you have just seen before, and enjoy playing some more relaxing sounds, this time maybe remembering your last summer in paradise, on the beach, far far away from the office and the noisy city life.

The following listing enters the code from the previous script line by line at the started prompt:

```
boot.user=> (set-env! :dependencies '[[com.googlecode.soundlibs/jlayer
"1.0.1.4"]])
nil
boot.user=> (def sound "https://www.soundjay.com/nature/ocean-wave-1.mp3")
#'boot.user/sound
boot.user=> (with-open [mp3 (clojure.java.io/input-stream sound)]
    #_=>    (let [player (javazoom.jl.player.Player. mp3)]
    #_=>       (.play player)))
nil
```

While enjoying the sound of waves, you may also have noticed that the set-env! changes the runtime environment and adds dependencies on the fly to the runtime.

The Boot Environment

If you are curious, you can always check what the current Boot environment is with **get-env:**

```
boot.user=> (clojure.pprint/pprint (get-env))
{:watcher-debounce 10,
 :resource-paths #{},
 :checkout-paths #{},
 :checkouts [],
 :exclusions #{},
 :source-paths #{},
 :repositories
[["clojars" {:url "https://repo.clojars.org/"}]
 ["maven-central" {:url "https://repo1.maven.org/maven2"}]],
 :asset-paths #{},
 :mirrors {},
 :dependencies [[com.googlecode.soundlibs/jlayer "1.0.1.4"]],
 :directories
 ...
```

env is one of the top concepts of Boot, and you will use it all the time. It is represented and can be understood as a watchable hashmap.

All the execution refers to what can be seen as the global state of the runtime.

For your reference, the most common import keys of the environment map are listed in Table 1-1.

Table 1-1. *Environment Map Keys*

Key	Usage
:resource-paths	List of paths that are in the classpath and used when creating a package
:source-paths	List of paths that are in the classpath, but not used when creating a package (meaning compiled artifacts will be used)
:asset-paths	List of paths pointing at resources not on the classpath but will be used when creating a package
:dependencies :exclusions	You have seen this before: Clojure or Java dependencies added to the classpath
:repositories	A list of repositories to retrieve the preceding dependencies from

The full list can be found on the following web site:

```
https://github.com/boot-clj/boot/wiki/Boot-Environment
```

And eventually you may need to add your own!

For now, simply updating the current ones should be enough. To update the Boot environment there are two ways to do this:

```
# reset and write the full list of source-paths at once. Pass-in and use a
vector
(set-env! :source-paths #{"foo" "bar"})

# just add one path to the source-paths key. Pass-in and use a function.
(set-env! :source-paths #(conj % "baz"))
```

Et voila. (That's it!)

Using the Boot REPL over the Network

A Boot REPL is effectively a network REPL, or nREPL, running its own embedded version of nREPL (network-REPL as it stands). The task itself is presented in the online built-in tasks page:

https://github.com/boot-clj/boot/blob/master/doc/boot.task.built-in.md#repl

Like any task, you can also print out the help for it using the autogenerated help document. This is usually a good way to know what parameters can be used for a task.

```
NikoMacBook% boot repl --help
Start a REPL session for the current project.

If no bind/host is specified the REPL server will listen on 127.0.0.1 and
the client will connect to 127.0.0.1.

If no port is specified the server will choose a random one and the client
will read the .nrepl-port file and use that.

The *default-middleware* and *default-dependencies* atoms in the boot.repl
namespace contain vectors of default REPL middleware and REPL dependencies to
be loaded when starting the server. You may modify these in your build.boot
file.

Options:
  -h, --help            Print this help info.
  -s, --server          Start REPL server only.
  -c, --client          Start REPL client only.
  -C, --no-color        Disable colored REPL client output.
  -e, --eval EXPR       EXPR sets the form the client will evaluate in the
                        boot.user ns.
  -b, --bind ADDR       ADDR sets the address server listens on.
  -H, --host HOST       HOST sets the host client connects to.
  -i, --init PATH       PATH sets the file to evaluate in the boot.user ns.
```

```
-I, --skip-init        Skip default client initialization code.
-p, --port PORT        PORT sets the port to listen on and/or connect to.
-P, --pod NAME         NAME sets the name of the pod to start nREPL server
                       in (core).
-n, --init-ns NS       NS sets the initial REPL namespace.
-m, --middleware SYM   Conj SYM onto the REPL middleware vector.
-x, --handler SYM      SYM sets the REPL handler (overrides middleware
                       options).
```

As you have seen, the simplest way to start a REPL is through the Boot REPL task:

```
boot repl
```

Supposing a different command prompt on the same machine, you can connect a client to this REPL by using the -c flag.

```
boot repl -c
```

The first command starts a nREPL (network REPL) server (and connect to it unless you specify the -s flag).

The second command with the -c flag tells the REPL task not to start a REPL server but instead look for an existing one.

This works fine on a single machine, but it is also possible to connect to a remote network REPL, using host and port parameters.

If you have not specified any port when creating the nREPL server, the port will be random, so you must remember it and replace it in the following command, adapting host and port.

```
boot repl -c --host=127.0.0.1 --port 59859
```

You will be welcomed by what looks like a new REPL session but is a common session with the existing server.

```
NikoMacBook% boot repl -c --host=127.0.0.1 -p 3000
REPL-y 0.3.7, nREPL 0.2.12
Clojure 1.8.0
...
```

To check that no one is faking it, let's create a simple binding with def in this new REPL:

```
boot.user=> (def message "Someone was booting here")
#'boot.user/message
```

Since it is the same REPL, it will also be in the first REPL, which you can check by coming back to the first prompt and typing

```
boot.user=> message
"Someone was booting here"
```

This is actually a fantastic way to remotely command an IoT device as well and can be used to pick up info from the remote device.

Obviously, on a trusted network, this is barely OK to have access to an opened REPL without security, so you would normally use an SSH tunnel for this; while much discussion of this topic is beyond the scope of this book, the following shows how an SSH tunnel can be created with a command similar to this one:

```
ssh -L 3000:localhost:59859 niko@remote
```

Where remote is the remote device where the nREPL server is running, 59859 is the port of that nREPL, and 3000 is the new port assigned to our local machine used to do the tunneling.

So now that you have completed a distributed REPL task, it is time to start writing a few easy Boot tasks and start creating your own workflow.

1-4. Wiring Boot Tasks
Problem

Boot task are built in a way so that they can be used either from the command line, from a REPL, or from regular Clojure namespaces.

Boot tasks are fundamentally meant to be able to interact with each other. This interaction is done through updating a virtual set of files that is derived step by step from the original set of directories.

Solution

The goal of this section is to slowly walk toward a simple boot-based workflow to compile and run Clojure(Script) code and get it refreshed in real time on file save.

How It Works

Tasks are defined using the deftask macro from the **boot.core** namespace, which is already included for your convenience when running Boot. deftask is very like the common defn standard macro, and in its shortest version looks very much the same as the following:

```
(deftask                      ; macro
  hello                       ; task name
  "Say hello"                 ; task description
  []                          ; task parameters (empty for now)
  (println "hello boot."))    ; task body
```

17

If you have a boot-based REPL started already, you can define the task by copying and pasting the preceding, and you can call it like a regular Clojure function:

```
boot.user=> (hello)
hello boot.
```

Now obviously just like a regular function, sometimes you want to make use of parameters. The following enhances the hello task with a message parameter.

```
(deftask hello
  "Say hello with a message"
  [
  m                            ; parameter short name
  message                      ; parameter name
  nil                          ; default value
  str                          ; parameter type
  "A custom message"           ; parameter description.
  ]
  (if message
    (println message)
    (println "hello boot.")))
```

This time the task can now take the parameter named message as input:

```
boot.user=> (hello :message "I have a message")
I have a message
```

It is also nice to know that doc and help are automatically generated:

```
boot.user=> (doc hello)
-------------------------
boot.user/hello
([& {:as *opts*, :keys [help message]}])
  Say hello with a message

  Keyword Args:
    :help      bool  Print this help info.
    :message   str   A custom message
```

Now, in the scope of a build, you may also want to set the default value for message throughout so you do not need to repeat it. This can be done with the use of task-options!

```
(task-options!
    hello
    {:message "I have been set before"})
(hello)

; I have been set before
```

This is often used in Boot build, so it's best to get used to it early.

Setting Up the Boot Environment

As you have seen, one of the core concepts of Boot is the notion of environment. The environment is basically a global map used throughout the build.

For example, to set the resource path to the folder rsc, you would use set-env! in the following way:

```
(set-env!
  :resource-paths #{"rsc"})
```

In the same build file, or still at the REPL, if you then define a task named print-env, you could use the task to see the current resolved map.

```
(deftask print-env
  "Print Environment variables"
  []
(println (get-env)))
```

Here, you could also remember how in the mp3 sound sample, the updated environment was also triggering an update of the project dependencies.

Defining and Using Dependencies

Say you want to compute the sha value of a string in during your build. You would

- Add an external dependency to the build; here we will use a third-party library named pandect.

- Require the namespace to be included in the build runtime, just like regular Clojure.

- Define the task that makes use of the sha1 function.

Now that you have all the required steps... let's write the Boot build file accordingly!

```
(set-env!
  :dependencies '[[pandect "0.5.4"]])

(require '[pandect.algo.sha1 :refer [sha1]])

(deftask sha-me
  "Sha me"
  []
  (println (sha1 "Hello World!")))
```

Again, you could type all the preceding at the REPL, or write it in a build.boot file and run Boot in the same folder.

```
boot sha-me
; 2ef7bde608ce5404e97d5f042f95f89f1c232871
```

19

Composing Tasks

In most builds, a main task is usually made of a set of subtasks reused and composed to produce the final build result.

In Boot, composition is done through standard Clojure using the **comp** function. Extending the preceding sha example, we can define a second sha-ing task. The following example shows a second Boot task composed with the first to be run together:

```
(set-env!
 :dependencies '[[pandect "0.5.4"]])

(require '[pandect.algo.sha1 :refer [sha1]])

(deftask sha-me-1 "Sha me 1" []
  (println (sha1 "I need red wine!")))

(deftask sha-me-2 "Sha me 2" []
  (println (sha1 "I need white wine!")))

(deftask sha-me-sen "Sha me all" []
    (comp
          (sha-me-1)
          (sha-me-2)))
```

This gives a good idea of how to compose tasks together. Calling (sha-me-sen) at the REPL works, but using it from the command line **or** using the Boot directive (which is equivalent!) gives some trouble:

```
boot.user=> (boot (sha-me-sen))
85324fb3c4edb26d91b4f5a7a1e7bc9894a92608
0f209505ac9364f73cd5f2cd5af1603533a02991
java.lang.NullPointerException:
```

The NullPointerException comes from the fact that tasks are meant to work on filesets and pass filesets around so that the next task can pick them up.

Noting that we could have used a parameter instead of two completely different tasks, let's rewrite the two tasks in a more concise manner:

```
(deftask sha-me "Sha me" [m message nil str "A custom message"]
  (fn [fileset]
      (println (sha1 message))
      fileset))

(deftask sha-me-sen "Sha me all" []
    (comp
      (sha-me :message "I need red wine")
        (sha-me :message "I need white wine")))
```

This works better and is close to what you would see in a regular Boot build.

20

Now in all honesty, you have seen task composition, but the tasks defined so far have been a bit naïve and have not really shown how to handle, transform, or compile files.

Let's work on that!

Writing a Task That Computes sha of Text Files

This is going to get slightly advanced, and is not directly needed in the first project examples.

While on the one hand, you would mostly reuse preexisting Boot tasks, you could decide to skip this small section for now and come back later when you have seen the project examples.

On the other hand, writing your own processing task makes you understand pretty much everything there is to learn about writing builds with Boot, so now is as a good time as ever.

If you have chosen to keep going and read, welcome! The first step is always the hardest; just be sure to grab a nice cup of coffee before going on to the next line.

To make task composition easy, Boot defines tasks as middleware. In Boot terms, a middleware is a module that queries an in-memory set of files, executes an action, performs a commit (e.g., for adding compiled files to the fileset), and then passes it on to the next middleware.

The next middleware does not know anything about the previous or the next middleware, and just keeps on doing what its good at doing, which is performing actions on files.

Figure 1-7 shows how the files coming from a set of directories are being turned into a temporary file system and then each task is taking a subset of the whole fileset to perform its action.

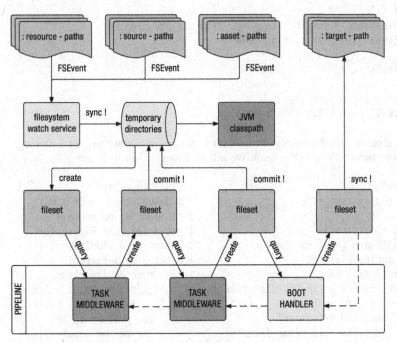

Figure 1-7. In-memory filesystem flow in Boot

Note also how, as a side effect, the JavaVirtualMachine classpath (i.e., where the code and third-party library reside) is dynamically constructed from the temporary set of files and directories.

The great sha example starts as a usual Boot build, by setting the path, the classpath, and the required namespaces.

The source files will be coming from a src-txt folder, and we will make use of the clojure.java.io namespace to handle files, as well as the pandect library to compute sha from the text content of the files. In a new directory, create a build.boot file with the following content:

```
(set-env!
  :dependencies '[[pandect "0.5.4"]]
  :resource-paths #{"src-txt"})

(require
  '[pandect.algo.sha1 :refer [sha1]]
  '[clojure.java.io :as io])
```

Then comes two standard Clojure methods to

- compute the sha from a file

- get the name of the file to store the computed sha

```
(defn- sha-txt!
  [in-file out-file]
  (doto out-file
    io/make-parents ; remember io comes from clojure.java.io
    (spit (sha1 (slurp in-file)))))

(defn- txt->sha
  [path]
  ; this is using a java regexp
  (.replaceAll path "\\.txt$" ".sha"))
```

Following comes the sha task itself. Stay with us. If you can understand the following, you can understand anything in this book. We will go through it line by line.

```
(deftask sha                               ;1 usual task def
  "Compute sha of .txt files."             ;2 a description doesn't hurt
  []                                       ;3 no need for parameters
  (let [tmp (tmp-dir!)]                    ;4 get a ref temp filesystem
    (fn middleware [next-handler]          ;5 a task is a middleware
      (fn handler [fileset]                ;6 working on a fileset
        (empty-dir! tmp)                   ;7 make sure we are clean
        (let [in-files (input-files fileset)        ;8 ref on input files
              txt-files (by-ext [".txt"] in-files)] ;9 filter *.txt files
          (doseq [in txt-files]            ;10 process in seq
            (let [in-file  (tmp-file in)   ;11 ref on input file
```

```
            in-path  (tmp-path in)              ;12 ref on input path
            out-path (txt->sha in-path)         ;13 convert the path
            out-file (io/file tmp out-path)]    ;14 out file in tmp
         (sha-txt! in-file out-file)))          ;15 compute the sha
     (-> fileset                                ;16 work on fileset
         (add-resource tmp)                     ;17 add all new out
         commit!                                ;18 must be called
         next-handler))))))                     ;19 pass it on !
```

Whew... That was a long piece of code, but here you go: with this in a build file, you are ready to sha!

Put some text files in a src-txt folder and run the following:

```
boot sha target
Writing target dir(s)...
```

And now we can inspect the two folders, src-text target:
This is where the original text files were:

```
src-txt
└── thisisatextfile.txt
```

And the generated files are stored in the target folders:

```
target
├── thisisatextfile.sha
└── thisisatextfile.txt
```

Note that if you do not call the target task, then the files are processed but not stored physically on the filesystem, so you would not be able to see the beautiful shas; that why it is included in the preceding command.

Reacting to File Changes with Watch

Wouldn't it be great to have your shas being generated automatically every time you add a file or edit an existing one?

This is used all the time in builds, and this is done using the provided watch task. Now we are back to regular easy-to-look-at code.

If you look again at the preceding diagram, you would notice where the watch service is located. It *listens* to file changes, and then triggers the composed pipeline. You also remember that comp is used to compose Boot tasks, and this is how the build pipeline is created.

So, let's create a new **build** task that will listen for file updates on the set of directories defined in the environment, and then trigger sha computation.

It's probably easy for you to look at this simple code now:

```
(deftask build []
  (comp
    (watch)
    (sha)
    (target)))
```

You can now call the task from the command line with

```
boot build
# or
# export BOOT_FILE=build.boot && boot build
```

And see the output:

```
Starting file watcher (CTRL-C to quit)...

Writing target dir(s)...
Elapsed time: 0.088 sec
```

Now go ahead and add a new file in the src-txt folder. You will notice the build is triggered, and the writing target dir message appears again.

And a new beautiful sha file has been generated in the target folder.

The Sound

I still love the whole history of jazz. The old things sound better than ever.

Steve Lacy

To conclude this section, let's add the relaxing sound of ocean waves as our build is running.

First, let's turn the ocean sound–playing code, which you have written at the REPL earlier, into a task. Try to write it yourself before looking at the following code.

```
(deftask train[]
  (let [sound "https://www.soundjay.com/nature/ocean-wave-1.mp3"]
    (fn [next-task]
      (fn [fileset]
        (future
          (with-open [mp3 (clojure.java.io/input-stream sound)]
          (let [player (javazoom.jl.player.Player. mp3)]
            (.play player))))
          (next-task fileset)))))
```

Notice how Clojure's future function makes the sound to be played in the background of the build, and the pipeline moves on to the next task before the sound has finished playing.

Obviously before all that, you need to import the require library into the environment:

```
(set-env!
  :dependencies '[
  [pandect "0.5.4"]
  [com.googlecode.soundlibs/jlayer "1.0.1.4"]]
  :resource-paths #{"src-txt"})
```

Finally, the previous build comp task, our build workflow, gets a new task:

```
(deftask build []
  (comp
    (watch)
    (train)
    (sha)
    (target)))
```

And now, each time a text file is changed, the noisy sound of the build is covered by the soothing sound of ocean waves.

Note that this can be enhanced for IoT, to trigger a sound each time a file has been updated on the device, and play a different sound depending on the content of the file. Say the room temperature becomes greater than a given value, then the sound of the waves could become more agitated, or if the room temperature becomes too low, you could have an icy sound of a snowstorm.

1-5. ClojureScript with Boot

Problem

So now that you have Boot in your hands, or at your feet, you want to work on your first ClojureScript project.

Solution

For a simple ClojureScript project, just about four text files are required:

- an html file

- a ClojureScript file

- a descriptor file containing the compilation settings

- the Boot file

A typical structure is shown in the following small diagram:

```
.
├── build.boot
├── html
│   └── index.html
└── src
    ├── main.cljs.edn
    └── mycljs
        └── first.cljs
```

How It Works

The Boot file is now a formality. A Boot task named cljs will do the compilation, meaning converting the ClojureScript file to JavaScript code.

There is also a need for ClojureScript itself. Current versions are shown in the following build.boot file.

```
(set-env!
 :resource-paths #{"src" "html"}
 :dependencies '[[adzerk/boot-cljs "1.7.228-2"]
                 [org.clojure/clojurescript "1.9.456"]])

(require '[adzerk.boot-cljs :refer [cljs]])
```

The index.html file is simple-looking:

```
<!doctype html>
<html>
    <body>
    <script type="text/javascript" src="../target/main.js"></script>
    </body>
</html>
```

It has a reference on the to-be-generated main.js file. That JavaScript file will be generated from the following src/mycljs/first.cljs ClojureScript file.

```
(ns mycljs.first) ;1

(defn main [] ;2
   (js/alert "It is time for a break...")) ;3
```

The ClojureScript file is about three lines; since those are the first ones, let's review them one by one.

1. The ClojureScript file needs a namespace definition; it can be anything Clojure usually accepts for namespace, but it needs to be specified later, so let's remember it.

2. This looks like, and in fact is, a regular ClojureScript function definition.

3. This is code to display a standard JavaScript dialog using the alert function.

Note the js/ here. The js namespace is always included for you, and refers to calls to existing JavaScript objects. You will be introduced to more of this JavaScript interop shortly, but for now let's assume it works and focus on the example.

Last, we need a binding file, which for now essentially tells ClojureScript which function in which namespace is the actual entry point seen from JavaScript. This is the main method that will be executed.

This is placed in an src/main.cljs.edn file, which contains a Clojure data structure, here a standard Clojure map.

```
{
    :init-fns [mycljs.first/main]
}
```

The map has a key :init-fns which turns mycljs.first/main into the point of entry of this example.

Everything is in place; let's use Boot to compile JavaScript for us. As you remember, there are two ways to do this. One is from the command line:

```
boot cljs target
```

And enjoy the output:

```
Writing main.cljs.edn...
Compiling ClojureScript...
• main.js
Writing target dir(s)...
```

The other way is to start a Boot REPL with

```
boot repl
```

Then type in the tasks in the REPL:

```
boot.user=> (boot (comp (cljs) (target)))
Writing main.cljs.edn...
Compiling ClojureScript...
• main.js
Writing target dir(s)...
```

Whichever way you chose to do the compilation, you will have noticed that files were generated in the target folder.

Talking about the target folder, resources have been copied to it, so the file index.html can also be found there.

Figure 1-8 shows the content of the browser Window when you open the file.

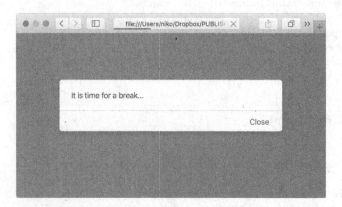

Figure 1-8. *Maybe it's time for a break?*

While indeed great for your first testing, opening the html file directly from the file system is rarely the recommended way, so you would usually go over to HTTP.

There is an existing Boot task, boot-http, that can serve HTTP content from folders, so let's use it with the following command:

```
boot -d pandeiro/boot-http:0.7.3 serve -d . -p 3000 wait
```

the -d parameter of Boot adds a dependency to the runtime (instead of defining it from the command line) here:

```
pandeiro/boot-http:0.7.3
```

Unfortunately, at the time of writing, the latest boot-http is missing a dependency on nrepl, when called from the command line.

Fortunately, we can go around the limitation by using the previous version, here 0.7.3.

We also just read it had be fixed, so by the time you read the book it may not be needed anymore, but this is beyond the author insurance policy.

Now, the following two Boot tasks used are serve and wait, one to start the http server (with the root directory specified by '-d '. pointing to the local directory) and the wait task that prevents the script from shutting down by waiting like a patient lover, forever.

After running the command, point your favorite browser to

```
http://localhost:3000/target/index.html
```

And enjoy another much-needed coffee break.

Building Up a Simple Workflow

The previous example was nice for a one-off build, turning the ClojureScript into JavaScript and then reloading the page.

Eventually you would like to get something more dynamic, like automatic reloading when you are changing code and saving a file.

In this new development workflow, the boot-http task is included in the pipeline directly and will be the first task.

Then comes the watch task that listens for file change on the environment folders.

Finally, reload and cljs come, telling the pipeline to reload cljs file when triggered from upstream.

Note that the reload option needs a parameter point to the namespace(s) to reload.

In a new folder, create (a new) updated build.boot file, as follows:

```
; set up the environment
(set-env!
 :source-paths    #{"src/cljs"}
 :resource-paths  #{"resources"}
 :dependencies '[[adzerk/boot-cljs    "1.7.228-2"      :scope "test"]
                 [adzerk/boot-reload "0.5.1"          :scope "test"]
                 [pandeiro/boot-http "0.7.3"          :scope "test"]
                 [org.clojure/clojurescript "1.9.456"]]])
; get the tasks in the build
(require
 '[adzerk.boot-cljs      :refer [cljs]]
 '[adzerk.boot-reload    :refer [reload]]
 '[pandeiro.boot-http    :refer [serve]])
```

```
; setup the global options
(task-options!
    reload {:on-jsload 'boot-03.app/main})

; composed main dev task
(deftask dev []
  (comp (serve) (watch) (reload) (cljs)))
```

While we're at it, let's update the folder structure a little bit:

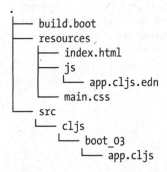

```
├── build.boot
├── resources
│   ├── index.html
│   ├── js
│   │   └── app.cljs.edn
│   └── main.css
└── src
    └── cljs
        └── boot_03
            └── app.cljs
```

5 directories, 5 files

Some ClojureScript compile options can be set in either the build.boot file or the app.cljs.edn file.

It is usually easier to have them in the edn file, so you just need to include a different folder for development and for production.

```
{:init-fns [boot-03.app/main]
 :compiler-options {
     :output-to "js/app.js"
     :optimizations :whitespace
     :asset-path "js/app.out"}}
```

For your reference, all the Compiler options are listed on the ClojureScript wiki and shown in Table 1-2 (https://github.com/clojure/clojurescript/wiki/Compiler-Options).

Table 1-2. *Compilation Options Summary*

Option Name	What It Does
:output-to	The top JavaScript file being outputted by the Compiler. This is the file that needs to be referenced and will be loaded from the html file.
:output-dir	The folder where all the assets will be generated.
:optimizations	While default is :none, where the JavaScript is outputted as is, you may want to use :whitespace, to remove whitespace, and :simple to compact the generated JavaScript just enough to make it smaller.
:asset-path	Depending on the top webserver configuration, you may want to have subfiles loaded from a different URL path.
:main	This is the main ClojureScript namespace; it will also be required by default.
:parallel	Setting this to true, allows for parallel compilation which may speed up things by splitting small compilation tasks across cores.

Once you have found settings that rock for you, let's Boot.

```
boot dev
```

This command will be the new mantra for the many pages to come. A regular, working, output would be like the following:

Starting reload server on ws://localhost:61345
```
2017-02-16 10:33:16.026:INFO::clojure-agent-send-off-pool-0: Logging
initialized @26456ms
2017-02-16 10:33:16.185:INFO:oejs.Server:clojure-agent-send-off-pool-0:
jetty-9.2.10.v20150310
2017-02-16 10:33:16.256:INFO:oejs.ServerConnector:clojure-agent-send-off-
pool-0: Started ServerConnector@729ad67{HTTP/1.1}{0.0.0.0:3000}
2017-02-16 10:33:16.273:INFO:oejs.Server:clojure-agent-send-off-pool-0:
Started @26703ms
```
Started Jetty on http://localhost:3000

Starting file watcher (CTRL-C to quit)...

Writing adzerk/boot_reload/js/app.cljs to connect to ws://localhost:61345...
Adding :require adzerk.boot-reload.js.app to js/app.cljs.edn...
Compiling ClojureScript...
• js/app.js
Elapsed time: 20.307 sec

As wanted, in the current build workflow

- An HTTP Server is started on port 3000.

- A file watcher is started to listen to file changes on directories.

- A websocket is also started by the reload task. This websocket is used to send the updated compiled ClojureScript to the browser. This is how reloading code works.

- ClojureScript code is compiled from the specified namespace.

- Then, waiting ...

When opening the page from the browser, you can see a simple JavaScript dialog shown in Figure 1-9.

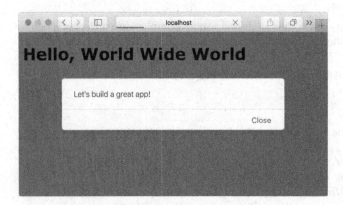

Figure 1-9. *Real-time compilation: first page load*

Now after clicking close (otherwise the browser is stuck), edit the ClojureScript code. Let's change from

```
(defn main []
  (js/alert "Let's build a great app!"))
```

To

```
(defn main []
  (js/alert "But first .. a small break!"))
```

Then, you will notice that the Boot command is recompiling code, and after merely a few seconds, your code is reloaded directly in the browser, so without a browser refresh the dialog shown in Figure 1-10 is now nicely showing up.

Figure 1-10. *Real-time compilation: page autorefresh*

Our project structure is ready; we are one step closer to browser heaven.

Where in the World Is the ClojureScript REPL?

> *Well they never Arkansas her steal the Mekong from the delta, Tell me where in the world is Carmen Sandiego?*

With your firm command of a build tool that reloads code from text editor updates, you are now wondering if you could get something closer to a command prompt that emits ClojureScript code directly to the browser... or... where is the ClojureScript REPL. This is a valid question.

In the ClojureScript world, there are two renowned projects bringing support to package all this together.

- PiggieBack (https://github.com/cemerick/piggieback)
  allows you to start a ClojureScript REPL on top of an nREPL
  environment, so that functions like eval or load-file can still be
  used, while being in a JavaScript runtime. This is used on the
  REPL side that writes code.

- Weasel (https://github.com/tomjakubowski/weasel) is
  websocket-based middleware that receives compiled code from a
  remote REPL (here PiggieBack) and executes it in an environment
  that can execute compiled ClojureScript, most of the time a
  browser, but any JavaScript runtime (Node.js, etc.) would do.

Let's add the dependencies to the build.boot file and require the extra namespace and function.

```
(set-env!
 ...
 :dependencies '[...
                 ; REPL
                 [adzerk/boot-cljs-repl    "0.3.3"  :scope "test"]
                 [com.cemerick/piggieback "0.2.1"  :scope "test"]
                 [weasel                   "0.7.0"  :scope "test"]
                 [org.clojure/tools.nrepl "0.2.12" :scope "test"]
])

(require
 ...
 '[adzerk.boot-cljs-repl :refer [cljs-repl start-repl]]
 ])
```

And finally, let's update the Boot build pipeline to include the new cljs-repl task:

```
(deftask dev []
  (comp (serve)
        (watch)
        (reload)
        (cljs-repl)
        (cljs)))
```

With the build file updated, you can make use of the new pipeline with the same command:

```
boot dev
```

Let's leave this building Boot walking its route while we grab a new command prompt and start a REPL client to connect to the nREPL that was just opened:

```
boot repl -c
```

This is the REPL you will be writing ClojureScript code in. If you remember in the build.boot, we also required the *start-repl* function. This is the function starting the ClojureScript mode, and the require call in the build.boot makes that function available in the boot.user namespace in the REPL. How lucky.

So now in this newly connected REPL:

```
NikoMacBook% boot repl -c
REPL-y 0.3.7, nREPL 0.2.12
...
boot.user=> (start-repl)
<< started Weasel server on ws://127.0.0.1:52080 >>
<< waiting for client to connect ... Connection is ws://localhost:52080
Writing boot_cljs_repl.cljs...
```

Uh-oh. It seems that the start-repl function is stuck and is waiting for something. At this stage, it is waiting for the browser to connect to it via the newly created websocket.

The necessary code that opens a websocket has already been sent to the browser via the Boot build, so if you open the page at http://localhost:3000, you can see a screen like in Figure 1-11.

Figure 1-11. Programming with the REPL: connect

And the ClojureScript REPL is finishing loading:

```
connected! >>
To quit, type: :cljs/quit
nil
cljs.user=>
```

At this stage, all your ClojureScript code has also been loaded, including of course the main ClojureScript namespace.

In this example, the ClojureScript code in the cljs file is simply directly updating the loaded Document Object Model (DOM).

```
(ns boot-04.app)

(defn set-container-html [msg]
  (let [ container (.getElementById js/document "container")]
  (set! (.-innerHTML container) msg)))

(defn init[]
    (set-container-html "I am a super exciting container!"))
```

The ClojureScript init function is called on refresh, so the HTML div with id *container* has its innerHTML property updated with the new string.

The next chapter will review ClojureScript-specific syntax, especially how to convert JavaScript code to ClojureScript syntax, but let's review the preceding code quickly now.

```
(defn set-container-html [msg]      ; using clojure defn, to define a
                                      function
  (let [                            ; standard clojure let for local
                                      bindings
   container                        ; a binding named container
   (.getElementById                 ; the javascript getElementById function
     js/document                    ; javascript document object.
     "container")                   ; parameter of getElementById
  ]
  (set!                             ; set a property on the coming object
    (.-innerHTML container)         ; .- denotes a JS property(. a JS
                                      function)
    msg)))                          ; the parameter to set
```

The equivalent JavaScript would be ... have you guessed it?

```
function set-container-html(msg) {
   var container = document.getElementById("container");
   container.innerHTML = msg;
}
```

OK, so playing with the new REPL a bit, you now have godlike powers to directly change the DOM in the browser (Figure 1-12).

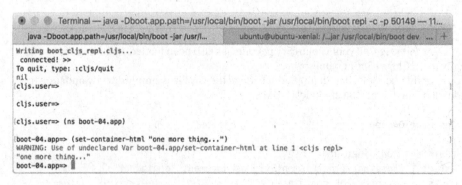

Figure 1-12. *Programming with the REPL: updating the DOM*

```
(set-container-html "one more thing")
```

And the updated browser page is shown in Figure 1-13 (remember, no page refresh has been harmed or involved in this sequence ...).

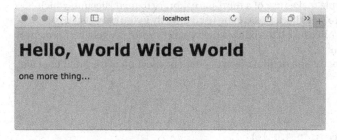

Figure 1-13. *Programming with the REPL: updated DOM*

Try to change the method so it can change the text of an arbitrary HTML element. Should not be too hard for you at this stage ...

You could quickly add a container div to the index.html page, so that now it looks like the following:

```
<body id="bodyid">
    <h1>Hello, World Wide World</h1>
    <div id="container">I am a boring html container</div>
    <div id="container2"></div>
    <script type="text/javascript" src="js/app.js"></script>
</body>
```

And back to the REPL, we can define a new ClojureScript function:

```
(defn set-container-msg [container msg]
  (let [ container (.getElementById js/document container)]
    (set! (.-innerHTML container) msg)))
```

And set the inner HTML of the new div with

```
(set-container-msg "container2" "the more the merrier")
```

Again, no page refresh necessary; even the HTML code has been updated directly in the browser. (Try to update the Cascading Style Sheet (CSS) as well and see what happens)

A Hiccup Before Turning Reactive...

You are almost to the point where you can develop creative applications using ClojureScript. We understand how you cannot hold yourself still anymore, but let's take a small sidestep.

The library that will be introduced shortly, Reagent the ReactJS wrapper, **mounts** components in a copy of the HTML DOM.

While we're not into mounting functional components into the DOM just yet, we can get a first impression by **mounting** functions that render to html somewhere into the real DOM.

The next small example makes use of a third-party library named Hiccups, which turns arrays and maps into valid html that can be used directly in the browser.

Why would we use it? Because it introduces the syntax to write Reagent component that we will adjust later on.

Let's add a dependency at the bottom of the dependency section of the build.boot file:

```
(set-env!
 ...
 :dependencies '[...
                 [hiccups "0.3.0"]])
```

Now back to the example: we declare a function my-component returning an html string by parsing the enclosed data structure and converting it to standard HTML.

```
(ns boot-05.app
  (:require-macros [hiccups.core :as hiccups :refer [html]])
  (:require [hiccups.runtime]))

(defn my-component [txt]
  (html
    [:div
     [:label {:for :input} txt]
     [:input#input]]))

(defn init[]
  (set!
    (.-innerHTML (.getElementById js/document "container"))
    (my-component "not much here yet...")))
```

The component is using a hiccup-based syntax.

The Hiccup syntax is something like markdown syntax in that some simple text is converted to HTML mostly by avoiding tag repetition. It is also much easier to read.

A few examples of Hiccup syntax are shown in Table 1-3.

Table 1-3. Hiccup Syntax Summary

Hiccup	HTML Equivalent
[:div]	<div></div>
[:div#myid]	<div id="myid"></div>
[:div {:class "klass"} "sometext"]	<div class="klass">sometext</div>
[:div#id1 [:div#id2]]	<div id="id1"><div id="id2"/></div>
[:ul (for [x (range 1 3)] [:li x])]	<ul><li>1</li><li>2</li><li>3</li></ul>
[:div#divid.klass "hello"]	<div id="divid" class="klass">hello</div>

This is usually nice and easy to grasp, and by this time you will have guessed what the following snippet gets generated to:

```
[:div
 [:label {:for :input} txt]
 [:input#input]]
```

Once you have figured it out, you can look at the following result:

```
<div><label for="input">txt</label><input id="input"/></div>
```

The component, represented as a function, is inserted somewhere in the page's DOM. The component was asked to *render* itself before being mounted in the DOM. In this case, the life cycle of the component itself is to be rendered once.

It is also possible to use the defhtml macro that does the same, expands to a def and a call to html.

```
(hiccups/defhtml div-link [link-string]
  [:div
   [:a {:href "https://github.com/weavejester/hiccup"}
     link-string]])
```

Mounting the component into the DOM is done in a similar way from the init function.

```
(defn init[]
  (set!
    (.-innerHTML (.getElementById js/document "container"))
    (my-template "Hiccup")))
```

You could try a few more things at this stage, like adding images or even video tags to impress your coworkers.

1-6. Your First React-Based Application with Reagent

Problem

You want to write a dynamic application.

Solution

We'll introduce the Reagent library, which wraps the React JavaScript framework with ClojureScript, and a syntax to write components similar to the Hiccup library you just have been introduced to.

To quickly migrate from Hiccup to Reagent, you need a minimal update to the latest build.boot file, so let's start from there.

How It Works

Let's begin by adding the current dancing version of Reagent (0.6.0) to the project file in the dependencies array:

```
:dependencies '[
          ...
          [org.clojure/clojurescript "1.9.456"]
          [reagent "0.6.0"]]
```

You need to restart the boot dev command so the Boot project properly picks up the new library.

Our namespace definition needs only the Reagent library at this stage, so let's remove the other ones and only keep the minimal:

```
(ns boot-06.app
    (:require [reagent.core :as reagent]))
```

Do not forget to update the namespace definition where needed if you change the namespace as is done here. If you kept the same project moving along, no need to worry.

Otherwise, there is a need to update the build.boot file and app.cljs.edn with the new namespace name, here boot-06.app.

The library is now in the namespace, so it is now possible to create a static Reagent component. The syntax used here is just like the Hiccup library.

```
(defn static-component []
  [:a {:href "http://www.apress.com"} "Get me to Apress please"])
```

Well ... hmm ... This component is not making any use of Reagent yet. The component is defined as a function returning an array of html elements: here a link to everyone's favorite publisher.

In a similar way as we have done up to now, let's update the init function to mount the Reagent/React component:

```
(defn init[]
  (let [ container (.getElementById js/document "container")]
    (reagent/render-component
            [static-component]
        container))
```

Mounting makes use of Reagent's render-component. It takes a Reagent component and a mount point of the DOM.

Of course you would need a corresponding div element, like <div id="container"> </div> somewhere in your index.html file.

The result is surprisingly pleasant, as shown in Figure 1-14.

Hello, World Wide World

Get me to Apress please

Figure 1-14. *Mounting a Reagent/React component*

This is all shiny but we feel a need for a bit more dynamism here.

A First Look at Reagent and States

Just like Clojure and ClojureScript can create atoms, variables that can be updated asynchronously in a thread-safe way, Reagent also proposes own version of atoms, which respond to the same ClojureScript functions on atoms, and are also defined in a similar way.

The core feature we are interested in an atom is the fact that they can only be updated from inside a transaction and that transactions are watchable. Whenever an update is made, some feedback is generated before and after the atom changes value.

The following snippet defines the Reagent atom with an initial string value, and the dynamic-component gets to read the current value of that atom:

```
(def my-text
  (reagent/atom "I really am an atomized reagent component"))

(defn dynamic-component []
  [:p @my-text ])
```

You can now mount the dynamic-component from the familiar init method:

```
(defn init[]
  (let [ container (.getElementById js/document "container")]
        (reagent/render-component [dynamic-component] container))
```

The output is like the previous screenshot, so you might be wondering what this was all about.

Now, you can update the text of that paragraph, not by acting directly on the component, but by changing the value of the bound atom. This is just like a Clojure atom so of course the reset! method works here.

To remember a bit what was done a few pages ago, let's try to do this from a ClojureScript REPL.

In a different command prompt or terminal, let's start a REPL with

```
boot repl -c
```

And let's connect the REPL to the websocket running in the browser with

```
(start-repl)
```

Since the atom was defined in the boot-06.app namespace, you will need to either switch namespace with (ns boot-06.app) or reference the atom with its namespace prefix. Let's say we want to try the second option:

```
(reset! boot-06.app/my-text "It's my life!")
```

The message of the div has been updated in the browser (Figure 1-15).

Figure 1-15. *Updating the state of a Reagent component*

Now some more fun. That atom value change does not have to be done straightaway; it is possible to mix pure JavaScript timer events and delay the rendering asynchronously:

```
(js/setTimeout #(do
    (reset!
            boot-06.app/my-text
            "this is the story of my life ..."))
    2000)
```

The setTimeout method is a pure JavaScript function so it needs to be prefixed with js/.

In JavaScript, setTimeout usually takes a JavaScript function as a parameter; see how an anonymous ClojureScript function, prefixed with #, can be used in this case nicely. The last parameter, 2000, is the timeout value in milliseconds; the anonymous will be executed after that amount of time.

This could all be done in real time as well, in the file containing the boot-06.app namespace. Have a try.

```
(defn init[]
  (let [ container (.getElementById js/document "container")]
    (reagent/render-component [dynamic-component] container))

  (js/setTimeout
    #(reset! my-text "this is the story of my life ...")
    2000))
```

Now, let's package all this knowledge into a simple Celsius-to-Fahrenheit application.

Celsius to Fahrenheit

It doesn't matter what temperature the room is, it's always room temperature.

Steven Wright

With all this globalization going on, why is it always so hard to understand what the temperature it is in some American cities? While it would be easier for everyone to start using Celsius nowadays, let's write a small application to help that world transition going forward.

So, to get things straight out of the way, let's just say someone knows how to convert from Celsius to Fahrenheit and has written a ClojureScript function for it.

```
(defn c-to-f [myc]
  (+ (* myc 1.8) 32))
```

Our application will be made of a temperature component, and this temperature component itself will be composed of two components, one input field for Celsius and one input field for Fahrenheit, preceded by a simple html heading.

Code-wise, the temperature component should probably come just before the init method, so toward the end of the file, but let's write it first. It is usually a nice way to start working from top to bottom, so write the top component first and slowly work on its inside.

A bit new for the reader at this stage is that a component can ask custom subcomponents to be mounted inside this top element. This is done through square brackets, which denote either a regular HTML component or a custom one you have defined. As proposed, the top temperature component is made of a div surrounding the Celsius input and the Fahrenheit input. Note this is still in the Hiccup markup style.

```
(defn temperature []
  [:div
   [:h3 "Temperature Converter"]
   [celsius]
   [fahrenheit]]])
```

We will make use of an atom to hold the Celsius value. You have seen this before; let's make the starting value at a nice summer of 30 degrees Celsius.

```
(def celsius-v
  (reagent/atom 30))
```

The Celsius component will be made of an html div, a label, and an input field. The input field value will be bound to the atom's value. The Celsius component comes to

```
(defn celsius []
  [:div
   [:label "celsius"]
   [:input {:value @celsius-v } ]])
```

The Fahrenheit component is just like the Celsius component, except its value is derived from the Celsius-v atom.

You want here that the Fahrenheit field gets its value from the converted Celsius value.

```
(defn fahrenheit []
  [:div
   [:label "fahrenheit"]
   [:input {:value (c-to-f @celsius-v)}]])
```

In the init method, we finally mount the top temperature component as you have seen before:

```
(defn init []
  (reagent/render-component [temperature]
    (.getElementById js/document "container")))
```

Time to enjoy the summer in Fahrenheit values too (Figure 1-16)!

Temperature Converter

celsius

30

fahrenheit

86

Figure 1-16. *Reagent temperature converter*

Of course, you could start the ClojureScript REPL and update the Celsius atom... (Figure 1-17).

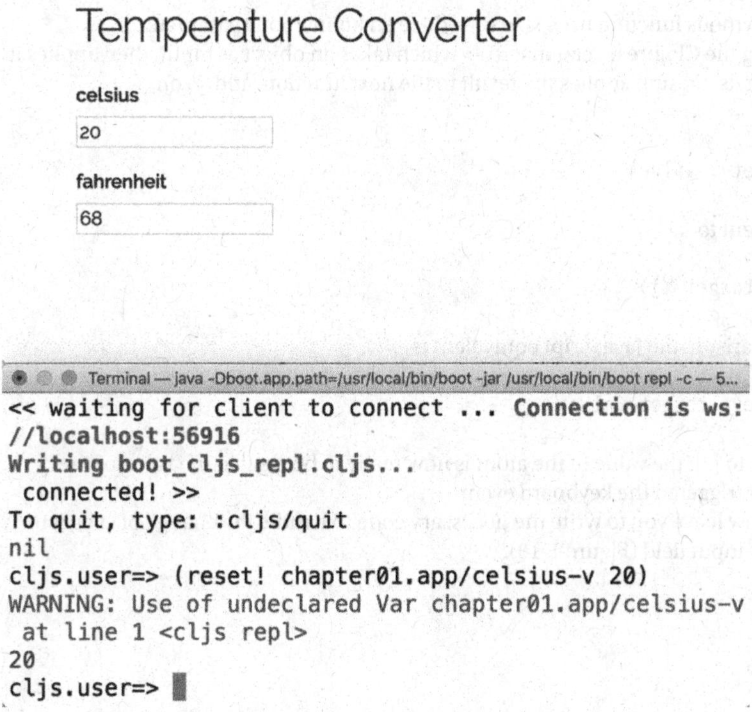

Temperature Converter

celsius

20

fahrenheit

68

```
Terminal — java -Dboot.app.path=/usr/local/bin/boot -jar /usr/local/bin/boot repl -c — 5...
<< waiting for client to connect ... Connection is ws:
//localhost:56916
Writing boot_cljs_repl.cljs...
 connected! >>
To quit, type: :cljs/quit
nil
cljs.user=> (reset! chapter01.app/celsius-v 20)
WARNING: Use of undeclared Var chapter01.app/celsius-v
 at line 1 <cljs repl>
20
cljs.user=> ▋
```

Figure 1-17. *Reagent temperature converter, at the REPL*

But, wouldn't it be also nice to have the temperature being computed while typing at the keyboard?

Let's rewrite the input field of the Celsius component with an added extra on-change attribute so the component can get an event when its value has been changed, for example via the keyboard.

This gives the update inner code for the Celsius component:

```
[:input {
:value (c-to-f @celsius-v)
:on-change
          #(reset!                    ; [1]
            celsius-v                 ; [2]
            (-> % .-target .-value)) ; [3]
          }]])}]
```

Hmm ... This works! Promise. Now, let's review this piece of Clojure code in the middle.

On-change takes a function with an event parameter. You could write it like a regular function, (fn[event] ...); also, most of the time, Reagent can also be used with anonymous function #(..). [1]

The anonymous function uses % to introduce an anonymous parameter.

[3] is using the Clojure thread macro -> which takes an object as input, then applies it to a function, gets a result, applies the result to the next function, and so on.

So:

```
(-> % .-target .-value)
```

is equivalent to

```
(.-value (.-target %))
```

For comparison, the JavaScript equivalent is

```
var value = evt.target.value;
```

Now back to [2]: the value of the atom is now ready to be reset to the value of the input field that triggered the keyboard event.

We will now leave you to write the necessary code to handle the change of events in the Fahrenheit input field (Figure 1-18).

Figure 1-18. Handle input field updates

Summary

This first chapter comes to an end. It was fast-paced, and you have been introduced to many bits of the puzzle already.

You have seen how to install Boot and script some portable ClojureCode, sometimes even playing music, on the fly.

Then, you were introduced to playing with a Boot REPL and remotely running code instantly on other machines.

Next was defining and writing Boot task, which make up the core of the workflow of a ClojureScript project.

Finally, bringing all the pieces together, you have created a small temperature converter application written in the ClojureScript wrapper for React. You have seen how to use components to bring an application alive and how to use atoms to interact with stateful components.

The following chapters will take it from here and make you more familiar with the ClojureScript environment and its ecosystem.

CHAPTER 2

■ ■ ■

ClojureScript

You do what you have to do to give people closure; it makes them feel better and it doesn't cost you much to do it.

John Scalzi, *Old Man's War*

In Chapter 1, you learned how to use Reagent and React ClojureScript to build a frontend application.

Now, let's step back a bit, breathe, and delve a bit more into the ClojureScript specifics to build a strong base to move forward on the quest of the ultimate Single Page Application (SPA).

This chapter slowly introduces ClojureScript features one by one, through a Single Page Application named Neko, the Japanese for cat. At its core, Neko is a simple application of a graphically running cat but when milk starts going missing, the cat stops running.

In this chapter, you will

- Review the DOM API

- Manipulate the DOM, first using simple code, then using a core library

- Use Clojure's core async to perform asynchronous-like tasks

- Perform AJAX requests alongside core async

- Delve deep into the Reactive-ness of an SPA, using Clojure atoms and event streams

- Write rules to React on events and streams

- Work with code in the graphic world with Quil

A Single Page Application, at its core, avoids any page reloads through direct manipulation of the document loaded in the browser, the DOM. External data is fetched through AJAX requests or websockets, based on timers, server updates, or direct user interaction.

With the JavaScript runtime now able to handle most of the computation-heavy details, server-computed rendering and visual updates are now completely offloaded to the client rendering side.

© Nicolas Modrzyk 2017
N. Modrzyk, *Reactive with ClojureScript Recipes*, DOI 10.1007/978-1-4842-3009-1_2

TODO list applications, because they match the underlying needs nicely, nowadays make heavy use of SPAs, as seen in Figure 2-1.

Figure 2-1. *TODO list, example of an SPA*

A ClojureScript SPA starts the same as a standard JavaScript one, with an HTML skeleton page first loaded; then, most of the application rendering is done on the client side. To this, the ClojureScript coding experience adds that the coding itself is also done directly on the DOM, and compiled code is directly updated onto the Client side; thus, visual impacts on the application can be viewed instantly.

2-1. Reviewing the DOM API

Problem

You want to find, update, and delete elements and listen for events on of the tree using the DOM API.

Solution

We are going to rely on the DOM API almost transparently from ClojureScript; let's review the main areas of the API and how they work. Tables 2-1 through 2-3 are provided as helpers to navigate later in the ClojureScript code interacting with the DOM.

How It Works

The following sections map out the solution for this recipe.

Finding Elements

Finding nodes is probably the first need when interacting with the tree. Table 2-1 presents the main JavaScript functions that can query the DOM for elements.

Table 2-1. *Core DOM Manipulating JavaScript Functions*

Method	Usage
getElementById	Returns 0 or 1 element. If there was an ID on a tag, and the ID matches, return that element.
getElementsByTagName	Returns a list of elements, where the tag name matches.
getElementsByClassName	Returns a list of elements, where the element is assigned the required class.

Modifying Elements

A DOM element has a set of children nodes and some properties to itself. Also, the CSS-based style of an element is done through either the style or the class property.

Assigning or reassigning a property of an element is done through the getAttribute or setAttribute functions. In ClojureScript, this is done with the following:

```
; set the node's propertyName to value; propertyValue
(aset node propertyName propertyValue)

; get the value of node's property propertyName
(aget node propertyName)

; same as above
(.- node propertyName)
```

Creating Elements

Creating a new element can be achieved using one of the three methods listed in Table 2-2.

Table 2-2. *JavaScript Functions to Create DOM Elements*

Method	Usage
document.createElement(name)	Creates a new node of name.
document.createTextNode(text)	Creates a new text-only node.
node.cloneNode(shallow?)	Creates a copy of the given node, by either performing a simple copy or also cloning all the children of node.

■ **Note** that whichever function you use to create a new node, the newly created node is not attached to the DOM tree yet.

You need to call a second function to insert the node at a location of your choice.

The Special Case of innerHTML

While innerHTML was not part of the DOM API at first, it is now supported by pretty much all standard browsers, so it is safe to use it. innerHTML is a property on a node that takes a string as input parameter and effectively renders the children of the given node as a set of nodes.

So, the following ClojureScript code will be rendered in the DOM tree as shown in Figure 2-2.

```
(asset
    (.getElementById js/document "button-slide")
    "innerHTML"
    "<img height=16 width=16 src=\"/imgs/milk.png\"/>")
```

```
▼ <button id="button-slide"> = $0
    <img height="16" width="16" src="/imgs/milk.png">
  </button>
```

Figure 2-2. *DOM equivalent of ClojureScript code*

The button appears as an image on the browser screen, as shown in Figure 2-3.

Figure 2-3. *Button insertion via the DOM*

Attaching to the DOM

If innerHTML is not usable, use one of the functions listed in Table 2-3.

Table 2-3. *JavaScript Functions to Insert Nodes in the DOM*

Method	Usage
node.appendChild(child)	Insert child as the last subnodes of node.
node.insertBefore(child, sibling)	Insert child, as a subnode of node; insert it before the sibling node.
node.replaceChild(newnode,oldnode)	Replace child of node oldnode with newnode.

Your new DOM node is now in the live DOM tree.

Removing Elements

Removing a node is done through the removeChild function, but note that you need to indicate both the parent node of the node to be removed, and the node itself. So, in ClojureScript, without using libraries, this would give the following:

```
(.removeChild
  ; parent of the node to remove
  (.getElementById js/document "div1")
  ; the node to remove
  (.getElementById js/document "button-slide") )
```

Events and Event Handlers

Mozilla keeps a nice list of the different events being generated in Firefox when something of importance occurs in the loaded DOM. It is highly recommended to have a look at the following exhaustive list and keep it for further reference:

https://developer.mozilla.org/en-US/docs/Web/Events

In practice, the events you are most likely to use are shown in the following two lists. The input events:

- blur

- change

- focus

- submit

- reset

- keypress

And the mouse events:

- click

- dbclick

- mousedown

- mousemove

- mouseover

Those event names are used as is in native JavaScript and in ClojureScript interop as well.

Most of the time, events are attached through the addEventListener function. For example, to add a mouse listener to an image with id neko-gif, you could write the following ClojureScript code.

```
(.addEventListener
 (.getElementById js/document "neko-gif")
 "mouseover"
 #(println "the mouse is over the cat")
  false)
```

Hovering the mouse over the image will print out messages in the console.

The JavaScript Window Object

The Window object is the link between the DOM world and the JavaScript world. It is a global object, and every tab or Window in your browser has a Window object. A frame also has its own Window object.

Functions like alert, confirm, prompt, setTimeout, and setInterval are all DOM API functions that can be accessed through the JavaScript's Window object.

In ClojureScript, that JavaScript's Window object can be accessed through js/window. Expanding on the preceding small listener example, you could use a JavaScript alert on mouseover using the following snippet:

```
(.addEventListener
 (.getElementById js/document "neko-gif")
 "mouseover"
 #(.alert js/window "mouse detected")
  false)
```

The result of the snippet is shown in Figure 2-4.

Figure 2-4. *Mouse event detection*

That is mostly it for a brief reminder of what the different DOM APIs are. Now you are ready to tackle the real stuff with ClojureScript.

2-2. Manipulating DOM with ClojureScript

Problem

You want to play with the DOM in ClojureScript through an SPA using pure JavaScript interop or a ClojureScript library.

Solution

The following examples will bind components directly together directly, which works best on small projects.

How It Works

You will need a few files organized in a project folder. Let's review the file layout of the base project that will be used throughout this chapter...

Preparing the Project

The file layout is kept close to the minimum, and is based on what was seen in Chapter 1. We prepare a simple project structure with a set of defined files as shown in Figure 2-5.

Figure 2-5. Project structure for a simple ClojureScript project

55

Most of those files feel familiar, with a few newcomers. Let's go through the list slowly again:

- html > imgs > neko.gif: a running cat animated gif. You always need one.
- html > js > app.cljs.edn: the descriptor file for the ClojureScript Compiler.
- html > index.html: the skeleton html file.
- src > frontend > app.cljs: the top ClojureScript file containing the init method, called when the application starts.
- src > frontend > utils.cljs: a helper file, with some functions to access the DOM easily in the first examples.
- styles > styles.clj: a set of CSS directives written in Clojure, which will be compiled to CSS.
- build.boot: your favorite build script!

The HTML page, being more of a skeleton, is compact. We insert here two HTML divs element, ready to mount dynamic-components from ClojureScript code. Also, a Google font is added so to make the page looks a little bit nicer than usual.

```
<!doctype html>
<html>
  <!-- Headers -->
  <head>
    <meta charset="utf-8">
    <title></title>
     <!-- Google Fonts -->
    <link href="https://fonts.googleapis.com/css?family=PT+Sans|Pangolin"
    rel="stylesheet">
    <link href="styles.css" rel="stylesheet">
</head>

<!-- Body with html div elements -->
  <body>
    <h1>Today is a gift.</h1>
    <div id="div1">
      <p>That's why it is called the present</p>
    </div>
    <div id="div2">
      <img id="neko-gif" src="imgs/neko.gif"/>
    </div>
  </body>

  <!-- File compiled from ClojureScript -->
  <script src="js/app.js"></script>
</html>
```

Note the insertion of the ClojureScript compiled file, js/app.js. The file, generated by Boot, contains code that is executed directly when loaded.

The source of the js/app.js file, the frontend/app.cljs file, is currently as succinct as possible, except for a console print preliminary statement.

```
(ns frontend.app)
(enable-console-print!)
(defn init []
  (println "Where a new adventure starts ...")
  (newline))
```

This console print setting sets a binding named *print-fn* to the JavaScript console. log. Here is also an equivalent for Node.js that we will see later. This helps making logging from within ClojureScript easy.

In the browser, this prints to the browser's console; in a node environment, it prints to the runtime console.

Many functions are using this binding internally. For example, newline will also output a new line in the browser console.

Finally, the Boot script itself. This is a simple version of what was used in Chapter 1, with source-paths, resources-path, and dependencies set in the environment.

Next comes a main Boot task named dev, containing the http server to hold files, the automated reloading with watch, compilation of ClojureScript files, and a new task for compilation of Clojure files contained in the style folder to style.css. The file style.css referenced from the HTML file is actually the one coming from this compilation circle.

```
(set-env!
 :source-paths    #{"src" "styles"}
 :resource-paths  #{"html" "build"}
 :dependencies    '[ [adzerk/boot-cljs "1.7.228-2"]
                     [adzerk/boot-reload "0.4.13"]
                     [org.martinklepsch/boot-garden "1.3.2-0"]
                     [pandeiro/boot-http "0.7.5"]

                     [org.clojure/clojurescript "1.9.456"]
                     [org.clojure/core.async "0.2.395"]])

(require
 '[org.martinklepsch.boot-garden :refer [garden]]
 '[adzerk.boot-cljs    :refer [cljs]]
 '[adzerk.boot-reload :refer [reload]]
 '[pandeiro.boot-http :refer [serve]])

(task-options!
 garden {:styles-var 'styles/base :output-to "styles.css" :pretty-print true}
 cljs      {:optimizations :none :source-map true}
 reload {:on-jsload 'frontend.app/init}
 garden {:styles-var 'styles/screen})
```

57

```
(deftask dev []
  (comp
   (serve)
   (watch)
   (reload)
   (garden)
   (cljs)
   (target)))
```

And the source file styles.clj used to generate css code from Clojure code:

```
(ns styles
  (:require [garden.def :refer [defrule defstyles]]
            [garden.stylesheet :refer [rule]]))

(def main-color "#55bbff")

(defstyles screen
  (let [h1 (rule :h1) body (rule :body)]
    [(h1 {
        :font-size   "14px"
        :color main-color
        :line-height 1.5})
     (body
      {:background-color "#C2DFFF"
       :height 400
       :padding-left "20%"
       :font-family "Pangolin, cursive"
       :font-size   "12px"})]))
```

Garden is the Boot task and the Compiler used to generate CSS code from Clojure code. Garden in a sense is similar to SASS and other stylesheet generators. The selectors used by Garden are close to standard:

- a colon : marking the start of a keyword, used for the selector

- a tag name: for example, :h1 or :body

- or a class name: for example, :.first, :.myclass

- or both: for example, :h1.first, :div.myclass

The defstyles macro returns a list of pairs selector/map where the selector is one of the preceding, and the map describes familiar css attributes.

From the preceding Clojure code, the following CSS code is being generated by the Garden task:

```
h1 {
  font-size: 14px;
  color: #55bbff;
```

```
  line-height: 1.9;
}

body {
  background-color: #C2DFFF;
  height: 400;
  padding-left: 20%;
  font-family: Pangolin, cursive;
  font-size: 12px;
}
```

This can be checked later, by accessing the stylesheet directly through its http URL:

```
http://localhost:3000/styles.css
```

Talking about http, it is high time to kick the boot dev task from a command prompt or a shell and start the server along with ClojureScript code generation.

After accessing the main page URL at

```
http://localhost:3000
```

You finally get to see the energetic and running cat (Figure 2-6).

Figure 2-6. *The energetic and running cat*

Everything is wired simply though text files, and we are pretty set to work off this Boot project layout for a while.

Slow Down Running Cat: Accessing Elements and Properties

Now that we have a first template, we can clone it and be ready to move on the cat's next adventure.

This time, we would like to simulate the cat stopping, by setting the src property of the html img element containing the running cat, and replacing it with a static version, namely the first frame of the animated gif.

We need a few things to achieve this. First we need a way to find an html element by id in the DOM; then, we need to set an attribute, src, to a new value.

We will define methods in a separate utils namespace. This namespace will be handmade with functions to help manipulate the DOM easily by calling ClojureScript interop with JavaScript.

In the src/frontend folder, we start by creating a new file utils.cljs. The first method, by-id, will be a helper function to help in the finding.

```
(ns frontend.utils)

(defn by-id         ; define a new function named by-id
  [id]                      ; needs one parameter, here a keyword or a string
  (.getElementById ; the getElementById is called on next param
    js/document               ; the document object from js
    (name id)))               ; turn a keyword into a string
```

The equivalent JavaScript code would be

```
function by-id(id) {
    return document.getElementById(id);
}
```

Now you can access the cat's image dom element by using

```
(by-id "neko-gif")
```

This will find whatever tag in the DOM with an id set to neko-gif. To check that this works, in the app.cljs file, we will access the src attribute of the img element. We update the app.cljs file with a require to get the functions from the utils namespace in the app namespace.

Then we call following code:

```
(ns frontend.app
    (:require [frontend.utils :as utils]))
...
(defn init []                ;
  (println              ; println prints tothe console
    (aget                    ; get from a map, or a JS object
      (utils/by-id ; function by-id from utils namespace
        "neko-gif")          ; the id of the element in the DOM
        "src")))             ; the attribute
```

On save, Boot recompiles the ClojureScript code and the browser's console prints the content of the src element of the image.

```
http://localhost:3000/imgs/neko.png
```

To be able to change the cat image's src attribute, we will now see how to change an attribute on a DOM element in ClojureScript. We will define a new function in the utils namespace that does just that.

The set-attribute function takes three parameters:

- dom, the element in the DOM retrieved from

- attr, the attribute of the element

- value, the new value of the attribute

This translates in the following function in the utils namespace:

```
(defn set-attribute          ; new function set-attribute
    [dom attr value]              ; the three parameters
    (aset dom attr value)) ; ClojureScript aset does map assignment.
```

The function is imported in the frontend.app namespace and is ready for usage to update the src attribute of the target img element.

```
(defn init []                ;
  (utils/set-attribute        ; the new function
    (utils/by-id "neko-gif")     ; the DOM element with id: neko-gif
    "src"                     ; the attribute of neko-gif
    "/imgs/neko.png"))        ; the new value
```

On saving the file, the init function is called, as per the Boot task reload settings, and the cat is now having a small running break, as can be seen in Figure 2-7.

Figure 2-7. *Stopping the gif animation*

Making the Cat Run Again: Handling Events

In this next section, we want to use a button to act on the cat image. We would like to create a function that adds a listener on a dom element and triggers a ClojureScript function being called when the event is triggered.

We prepare two functions in the utils namespace: the first, add-listener-old-skool, uses the old-skool way of setting a property on the JavaScript object.

```
(defn add-listener-old-skool    ; old-skool naming
    [dom event function]        ; three paremeters
    (aset                       ; using set on a map or js object
     dom                        ; the dom element
     (str "on" event)           ; the old skool event naming
     function))                 ; the callback function
```

The second function, add-listener, uses the (now) recommended way of adding a listener to an element of the DOM.

```
(defn add-listener              ; recommended naming
    [dom event function]        ; three parameters
    (.addEventListener          ; the recommended way of adding
     dom
     event
     function
     false))
```

We then need a button to receive click events. In the HTML page, let's add a simple HTML button. The button will be assigned the id neko-button, so it is simple to reference it.

```
<body>
  ...
  <div id="div2">
    <button id="neko-button">Neko Dash</button>
    <img id="neko-gif" src="imgs/neko.gif"/>
  </div>
  ...
</body>
```

Now that the button is showing in the browser, in the main ClojureScript namespace, in the init method, you can now use either event listener method to React on a click on the button.

We'll go for old-skool first:

```
(defn init []
  ...
  (utils/add-listener-old-skool
      (utils/by-id "neko-button")
      "click"
      #(println "Clicked"))
  ...)
```

Clicking the button will print in the console, which is one step closer to the running cat, but still some more efforts are needed.

Let's write a bit of ClojureScript. We want to have a Clojure atom that holds a value on the running or not-running status of the cat.

Related to that atom, we also want a swap-cat function that switch both the running status of the cat, the atom, and the src of the img as well.

```
(def cat-running                      ; the atom knowing if the cat
  (atom true))                        ; is running or not

(defn change-cat-img                  ; update the img src attribute
  [img-file]                          ; needs the filename of image
  (utils/set-attribute               ;
      (utils/by-id "neko-gif")        ; as seen, sets the src
      "src"                           ; attribute of the image
      (str "/imgs/" img-file)))       ;

(defn make-cat-run[]                  ; make the cat runs means
  (change-cat-img "neko.gif"))        ; use animated gif as src

(defn make-cat-stop[]                 ; make the car stops means
  (change-cat-img "neko.png"))        ; use the static png
```

```
(defn swap-cat[]                                ; swap cat function
    (reset! cat-running (not @cat-running)) ; negate the value of the atom
    (if @cat-running                            ; if atom is true
            (make-cat-run)                      ; make cat run
            (make-cat-stop)))                   ; make cat stop
```

It is hard to get a moving feeling simply by reading the book, so at this stage, we hope you were typing running cat code all the time. By click the "Neko Dash" button in **your** browser you should have nice feeling of action, as seen in Figure 2-8.

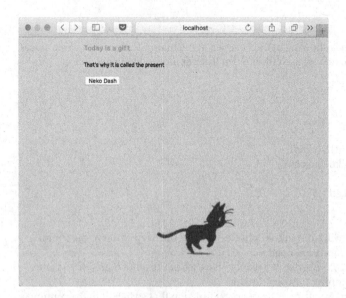

Figure 2-8. *Atom-based event handling*

Access and Modify DOM Nodes: Migrate to a DOM Library

It is possible to write your own utility functions to retrieve sequence of nodes from tags or classnames. The two functions are very similar and make use of the glue-ing function as-seq.

```
(defn as-seq
  "Convert a set of DOM node to a ClojureScript sequence"
  [nodes]
  (let[ length (fn [nodes] (. nodes -length))
        item (fn [nodes n]  (.item nodes n))]
    (for [i (range (length nodes))]
      (item nodes i))))
```

```
(defn by-tag [tag]
  (as-seq
    (.getElementsByTagName js/document (name tag))))

(defn by-class [klass]
  (as-seq
    (.getElementsByClassName js/document klass)))
```

It is probably also time to use a library that will cover the full DOM API for us. Here we introduce one of them, named Dommy. There are a few others (like domina) but Dommy is very stable after reaching version 1.0 and has been getting a good bug-free reputation so far.

The Dommy library gives you all the DOM API through ClojureScript-like functions and macros. It also gets you covered with DOM events handling.

Since we will be creating new DOM nodes in ClojureScript as well, let's add the html library that you used in Chapter 1, Hiccups, at the same time.

You add the Dommy and the Hiccups libraries to your build.boot file in the dependencies section with the following two lines:

```
[prismatic/dommy "1.1.0"]
[hiccups "0.3.0"]
```

This needs a reboot of the boot dev task that, if you haven't done it yet, you should do now.

The namespace of frontend.app should be updated to require the new libraries functions so we can refer to them in the code.

Following indications from the respective documentation about the namespace to import, we require them in the namespace definition of the frontend.app namespace:

```
(ns frontend.app
  (:require-macros
   [hiccups.core :as hiccups :refer [html]])
  (:require
   [hiccups.runtime]
   [dommy.core :as dommy :refer-macros [sel sel1]]
   [frontend.utils :as utils]))
```

We can immediately use dommy to update from the hand-coded selector written previously with the given selector.

The init method now becomes

```
(defn init []
  (utils/add-listener-old-skool
    (sel1 :#neko-button)
    "click"
    swap-cat))
```

Note how the utils/by-id has been replaced by the use of sel1 to select the neko-button. sel1 stands for selector-returns-one-element, so that the query does not return a sequence but only one element.

Old-skool jQuery inspired, dommy also helps with registering event handler on DOM elements using the listen! function. listen! takes three parameters:

- a node, selected with sel1

- a keyword of the event name

- a ClojureScript function

The init method also becomes easier to read:

```
(defn init []
  (dommy/listen!
    (sel1 :#neko-button)
    :click
    swap-cat))
```

Behind doors, dommy uses the JavaScript methods to interface with the DOM as we have used them before.

While we are in jQuery land, a good old way to show and hide elements is with the show! and hide! dommy function. If we now want to completely show and hide the cat, we can do it by writing a new swap-cat-dommy function and the corresponding init function:

```
(defn swap-cat-dommy[]
  (reset! cat-running (not @cat-running))
  (println "Running:" @cat-running)
  (let[cat (sel1 :#neko-gif)]
  (if @cat-running
    (dommy/show! cat)
    (dommy/hide! cat)))
...

(defn init []
  (dommy/listen! (sel1 :#neko-button) :click swap-cat-dommy))
```

Nicely enough in this case, you can use dommy's toggle function:

```
(defn swap-cat-dommy[]
  (reset! cat-running (not @cat-running))
  (let[cat (sel1 :#neko-gif)]
    (dommy/toggle! cat)))
```

■ **Note** As a preview of what is coming when using ReactJS and Reagent, you can see neatly in the preceding toggle version that there is a link between the way the image of the cat is rendering on the screen and the state of the atom cat-running.

Eventually, you will see how Reagent directly links the atom and the rendering of the image using functional components. During the rendering phase of a component, rendering will access the value of the atom to decide on whether the cat is running/showing or not.

In the swap-cat-dommy function, the state and the rendering are done at the same time, which is kind of misleading. Using a ReactJS/Reagent component, you would update the value of the atom in the callback, and any component having a binding on that atom would be redrawn, using its rendering function.

This allows decoupling of concerns, and also allows for more modular ways of building an application.

This is for the next chapter though … we will get back to this shortly.

A few other methods worth knowing to access and modify elements with the dommy library are shown in Tables 2-4 and 2-5.

Table 2-4. Dommy Functions to Access DOM Elements

Function	Example	Usage
text	(text el)	Retrieve the inner text from element el
html	(html el)	Retrieve the inner html from element el
value	(value el)	Retrieve the value of element el
class	(class el)	Retrieve all the classes as a string of element el
attr	(attr el :key)	Retrieve the value of the attribute :key on element el

Table 2-5. Dommy Functions to Modify DOM Element

Function	Example	Usage
set-text!	(set-text! el "text")	Update the text of the element el with "text", by updating its internal text
set-html!	(set-html! el "<span>hello </spam>")	Update the innerHTML of the element el with "<span>hello </span>", by updating its internal HTML property
set-value!	(set-value! el "value")	Update the value of the component el to "value"
set-class!	(set-class! el "klass")	Replace the class field of element el with "klass"
set-attr!	(set-attr! elem :disabled) (set-attr! elem :attr-name "value")	Update the attribute of an element
remove-attr!	(remote-attr! elem :attr-name)	Remove attribute attr-name from element el
add-class!	(add-class! elem "klass")	Add a class "klass" to element el
remove-class!	(remove-class! elem "klass")	Remove class "klass" from element el
toggle-class!	(toggle-class! elem "klass")	Add or remove the class "klass" on element el
toggle!	(toggle! el)	Toggle the visibility of element el
show!	(show! el)	Turn on visibility of element el
hide!	(hide! el)	Turn off visibility of element el
scroll-into-view!	(scroll-into-view! el)	Make sure element el is showing on the screen by scrolling the view port up or down if needed

Note that toggling class on an element in jQuery would be similar to the following:

```
$(document).ready(function(){
  $('a#click-a').click(function(){
    $('.nav').toggleClass('nav-view');
  });
});
```

So if you were used to jQuery before, you should get close to realizing that the ClojureScript version is easier to read and write.

CSS Animation Fun: Sliding

With a simple CSS animation definition and dommy, we can expand on the toggle a class example, and do some transition animation. We would like to move a text paragraph from top left to the center of the screen.

You will need a few things for this CSS-based transition example:

- In the HTML page: add a button to trigger a click starting the transition.

- In the styles.clj file: add an animation and create a class definition using the CSS transition.

- In the ClojureScript init function: add a dommy listener on the new button, and toggle the class with the animation.

The HTML code is only slightly modified; let's add a button before the paragraph p in the div1 section:

index.html file

```
<div id="div1">
    <button id="button-slide">Slide</button>
    <p id="slide">That's why it is called the present</p>
</div>
```

The CSS animation slide needs to be defined to do a simple transition. We expect some CSS code like the following where the slide @keyframes takes from/to keys with start position, final position. Then a .slide class makes use of the animation and of a start position. If you are not familiar with animation,

```
@keyframes slide {
  from {
    left: 0px;
    top: 0px;
  }
  to {
    left: 300px;
    top: 300px;
  }
}

.slide {
  position: absolute;
  left: -100px;
  width: 100px;
  height: 100px;
  z-index: -10;
  animation: slide 0.5s forwards;
  animation-delay: 0s;
}
```

While you could insert this CSS directly in the HTML and it would still work, the Garden library to generate CSS code also works very well and keeps the syntax unified. Updating the CSS now turns into translation CSS code to Clojure.

defkeyframes is added to the namespace, and used to create the definition for the CSS animation. Then, the slide animation converted, and the .slide class definition is added to the styles.clj file.

```
(ns styles
  (:require [garden.def :refer [defrule defkeyframes defstyles]]
            [garden.stylesheet :refer [rule]]))

...

; from and to each takes a maps of CSS properties,
; :from for the start of the animation, and
; :to for the css when the animation ends.

(defkeyframes slide
  [:from
   {:left "0px" :top "0px"}]
  [:to
   {:left "300px" :top "300px"}])

; the screen styles create a rule for CSS class .slide
; including animation and animation-delay properties
; the slide animation itself is added at the top of the array.

(defstyles screen
(let [...]

   [ slide
   ( (rule :.slide) {
   :position "absolute"
   :left "-100px"
   :width "100px"
   :height "100px"
   :z-index -10
   :animation "slide 0.5s forwards"
   :animation-delay "0s"})
   ...
]))
```

The CSS definition is set up, on save Garden generates the resulting CSS, which you can see at

```
http://localhost:3000/styles.css
```

Finally, the init function in the frontend.app namespace needs a new listener on the button with id #button-slide. When clicked, the button should toggle the class "slide" of the #slide element.

This is pretty much a rehash of what was done in the previous example and that gives

```
(dommy/listen!
```

```
(sel1 :#button-slide)
:click #(dommy/toggle-class! (sel1 :#slide) "slide"))
```

If all works well, you can trigger the CSS animation clicking the slide button, as shown in Figure 2-9.

Figure 2-9. Triggering animation with dommy

DOM Creation and DOM Modification

Dommy has helped to target the DOM with quite some ease, but sliding and changing class and properties definitions are surely not enough all the time.

There are times when you need to insert new or remote present elements, and so basically modify the structure of the document.

The DOM API supports this very well, and you probably have seen code like this to add new elements using standard JavaScript:

Add Element to the DOM using JavaScript

```
<div id="div1">
  <p id="p1">This is a paragraph.</p>
</div>

<script>
  var p2 = document.createElement("p2");
  var node = document.createTextNode("This is new.");
  p2.appendChild(node);

  var div1= document.getElementById("div1");
  div1.appendChild(p2);
</script>
```

Dommy has two standard methods to create nodes in the DOM:

- (create-element tag)
- (create-text-node text)

However, even though they do the job, it is a bit hard to use them as is, so we will reuse it and write a small ClojureScript function, taking a tag name, an id, and a Hiccup data structure as parameter to create a node. Think about it just a little bit yourself before looking at the following.

The frontend.app namespace needs the html function from the Hiccups library. Those are the same imports that were used in Chapter 1.

```
(:require-macros
    [hiccups.core :as hiccups :refer [html]])
  (:require
    [hiccups.runtime]
    ...))
```

Then comes the custom-made enhanced create-element function. Comments are inlined.

```
(defn create-element                            ; the new method
    [tag id & [nodes]]                          ; tag, id and hiccup
                                                  nodes
    (let [el (dommy/create-element tag)]  ; create the top tag
      (aset el "id" id)                         ; assign it an id
      (when nodes                               ; if nodes are specified
        (dommy/set-html! el (html nodes))) ; convert to html and add them
      el))                                      ; return the parent node
```

dommy/set-html! takes a string, and that works well with hiccups/html, which itself returns a string.

Our cat is probably getting tired with all this running on the screen, so it is high time to give it some milk to get refreshed.

Using the create-element function, we can now create a div node with a milk image using the following code:

```
(create-element :div
      "newdiv"
      [:img {.:class "milk" :src "/imgs/milk.png"}]))
```

This generates the following HTML code:

```
<div id="newdiv">
  <img class="milk" src="/imgs/milk.png"/>
</div>
```

Adding the milk itself, actually adding an img node in the DOM tree, is done via the dommy/append! function, which takes an existing DOM node to attach the new node to, and the new node to be attached, as parameters.

```
(defn more-milk []
  (dommy/append!  (sel1 :#div1)
    (create-element :div
      "newdiv"
      [:img {:class "milk" :src "/imgs/milk.png"}])))
```

To finish putting things together, let's add a new milk button that will be listening for click events.

index.html

```
<button id="button-milk">milk</button>
```

And a bit of CSS magic, by adding one more rule in the styles.clj file to style the new coming image via the .milk CSS class. Here we set the size and the float positioning to left.

73

```
( (rule :.milk)
 {:height "32px"
  :width "32px"
  :float "left"
 })
```

Listening to events from the main frontend.app namespace, you know how to do it:

```
(defn init []
  ...
  (dommy/listen!
    (sel1 :#button-milk)
    :click more-milk))
```

Clicking the milk button can bring an insane amount of milk on the screen, so let's use it with caution.

All in all, Figure 2-10 shows the milk icons piling up on the screen above the cat.

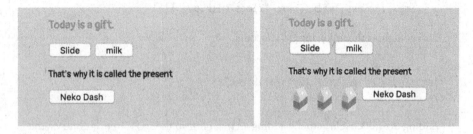

Figure 2-10. *Adding milk boxes with dommy/append*

If you open your browser developer tools, you can also see the new nodes being added to the DOM tree, as shown in Figure 2-11.

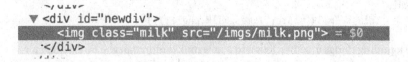

Figure 2-11. *DOM equivalent of the milk boxes*

Since dommy extensively supports the DOM API, adding elements to the DOM with dommy can be done with one of the methods from Table 2-6.

Table 2-6. *Ovewview of Dommy Functions*

Function	Example	Usage
append!	(append! el node)	As we have just seen, appends node to existing DOM element el
clear!	(clear! el)	Removes all elements inside el
prepend!	(prepend! el node)	Companion of append!, but puts node as first of children of el
insert-before!	(insert-before! el node)	At parent node of el level, adds node before el
insert-after!	(insert-after! el node)	At parent node of el level, adds node after el
replace!	(replace! el node)	In the DOM, replaces el with node
replace-contents!	(replace-contents! el node)	Replaces contents of el with node
remove!	(remove! el)	Removes el from the DOM tree

So, to take one more example, let's add a button that when pressed, drinks all the milk, and remove all the milk div nodes from the DOM.

One more button in index.html is needed:

```
<button id="button-drink">drink</button>
```

And frontend.app namespace needs a new listener using dommy/clear!. Since, clear! only takes one node, we need to loop through the sequence returned from calling sel on the added nodes:

```
(dommy/listen!                    ; new listener
  (sel1 :#button-drink)           ; selector on the new button
  :click                          ; the event type
  #(doseq [d (sel :#newdiv)]      ; sel returns a sequence,
    (dommy/clear! d )))           ; clear/remove one node at a time
```

And see in Figure 2-12 how the browser application is adding and removing milk like it's on a dairy diet.

Figure 2-12. Adding/removing milk boxes with milk and drink button

2-3. Getting Closer to Async Code with core.async

Problem

In the browser JavaScript runtime, the JavaScript engine is by default limited to a single thread. Core.async for ClojureScript does not go around this limitation.

Solution

Remove any couplings and use queues or channel of events to bind your project's components.

How It Works

The following sections will show you how to create and handle events internal to your application.

Core.async Concepts

Core.async introduces the concept of channel, and the ability to write code in sequential manner using those channels. core.async has APIs to read and write messages to channels, in other word blocking queues, and communication between different parts of the code is done through those channels. Each side of the sending or receiving end does not know about the other side. This allows for decoupling and reducing overall complexity in your application.

Everything is easier to understand with less text and more pictures; that's of course why you bought this book. Figure 2-13 shows how the channel interaction is done between the sender and the reader.

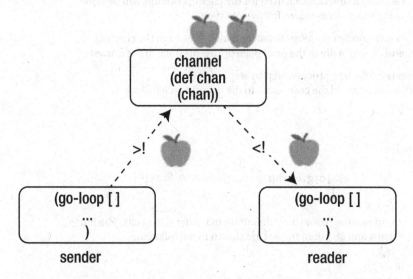

Figure 2-13. *Channel interaction between sender and receiver in core.async*

A channel is created using the chan function from core.async. The channel is the mean of communication between readers and receivers, in the simplest case, one sender and one receiver.

go-loop is the ClojureScript macro telling the coming code block to interact with a channel, either for read, or for write.

A message is sent to the channel using >! In Clojure code, it can be any kind of message.

A message is read from the channel using <! The read part is blocking, so code after a <! statement will only be executed once a message is received from the channel.

Counting Milk Boxes with core.async

In the cat application, you would like to know how many boxes of milk have been delivered in total, regardless of whether they have been drunk or not.

We will now implement this in the Neko application. The plan is to

- add the core.async library to the application dependencies

- add the needed require statement in the frontend.app namespace

- create a channel

- send a message on the channel when the milk button is pressed (actually in the callback used for the click event); this will be done using the go-loop macro from core.async

- create another go-loop- to listen to messages from the channel and change a div in the html page print a message in the browser.

The plan is made; let's proceed step by step.

In build.boot, let's add the core async to the dependencies section:

```
(set-env!
 ...
 :dependencies    '[
                    ...
                    [org.clojure/core.async "0.3.441"]
                    ])
```

Then, let's update the namespace definition in frontend/app.cljs. The full namespace macros and standard import are shown in the following:

```
(ns frontend.app
  (:require-macros
   [cljs.core.async.macros :refer [go go-loop]]
   [hiccups.core :as hiccups :refer [html]])
  (:require
   [cljs.core.async :refer [put! chan <! >! timeout close!]]
   [hiccups.runtime]
   [dommy.core :as dommy :refer-macros [sel sel1]]
   [frontend.utils :as utils]))
```

In the frontend/app.cljs file again, you can now add a milk-counter and a milk-channel.

```
(def milk-counter (atom 0))
(def milk-channel (chan))
```

The milk-counter will hold the total number of milk boxes, while the milk-channel will receive a message when a new milk box is coming.

The more-milk handler for the click event is getting a milky upgrade. Whenever it is called, it will increase the atom counter, and then send a message to the milk-channel. The message will simply be the value of the milk-counter itself.

```
(defn more-milk []
  (go
    (swap! milk-counter inc)
    (>! milk-channel @milk-counter ))

  (dommy/append!  (sel1 :#div1)
    (create-element :div
      "newdiv"
      [:img {:class "milk" :src "/imgs/milk.png"}])))
```

Note how the message-sending part is done in a go block.

Finally, we would like to set the text content of a DOM element of the application to show the number of boxes. In the namespace's init function, let's add the following go-loop:

```
(go                                            ; start a new go block
    (loop []                                   ; this will loop forever
      (let [v (<! milk-channel)]               ; wait for a message from chan
        (dommy/set-text!                       ; when a message comes
          (sel1 "#slide")                      ; update the text of #slide
          (str "Boxes of Milk delivered:" v))  ; the message
        (recur))))                             ; go back at beginning of loop
```

If no typos and no bad copy-and-paste were involved, you should be able to play with the milk and the drink buttons and see the counter increasing accordingly, as shown in Figure 2-14.

Figure 2-14. *Core.async channels coupled with button events*

How Long Has It Been Since the Last Milk Boxes with core.async

The first example of core.async seemed almost natural because it was reacting to a user click, and propagating an event throughout the code.

In this second example, we would like to measure the time spent since the last box of milk was delivered.

The idea is to have a core.async loop send a message every one second on a channel, then display the waited time on the screen.

When delivering a new box of milk by clicking the milk button, the timer will be reset to 0, and waited time should show accordingly.

To display the message, a new paragraph element needs to be added in the index. html file:

```
<p id="nomilk"></p>
```

The rest of the action takes place directly in the frontend/app.cljs file.

First let's create a new atom, nomilk-counter, which counts seconds since the last delivered milk. The nomilk-counter will be sent through the nomilk-channel. Even though we use the value of nomilk-counter as a message, it would be also possible to just send a token message to simply say the atom was updated.

```
(def nomilk-counter (atom 0))
(def nomilk-channel (chan))
```

The more-milk from the previous example is slightly enhanced with a first resetting the nomilk-counter to a no-wait-time value of –1. The rest of the function is left as before.

```
(defn more-milk []
  (reset! nomilk-counter -1)
  (go (swap! milk-counter inc) (>! milk-channel @milk-counter ))
  (dommy/append!  (sel1 :#div1)
    (create-element :div
      "newdiv"
      [:img {:class "milk" :src "/imgs/milk.png"}])))
```

Finally, in the init function or outside in the namespace, let's create the two go blocks sending and receiving messages. The first go block reads from the nomilk-channel and updates the paragraph #nomilk with the number of seconds waited.

```
(go
  (while true
    (let [v (<! nomilk-channel)]
      (dommy/set-text!
        (sel1 "#nomilk")
        (str "Time without fresh milk:" v " s")))))
```

The second go block uses a new function named timeout, which acts like the JavaScript setTimeout function, except the callback is replaced by linear code. The timeout function spawns a short-lived channel that will send one message after the number of milliseconds specified. The <! code blocks on timeout for 1000 milliseconds.

Once the timeout value is read (and discarded), next is to increasing the value of the atom nomilk-counter using the clojure.core's swap! function. swap! replaces the counter with the returned value of the function applied to the counter, here inc.

Finally, the new value of the milk-counter atom is sent in the nomilk-channel. And then loop back again to wait one more second...

```
(go
  (loop []
    (<! (timeout 1000))
    (swap! nomilk-counter inc)
    (>! nomilk-channel @nomilk-counter)
    (recur)))
```

After a bit of pressing buttons and waiting, counters are increased, and milk is appearing on the screen (Figure 2-15).

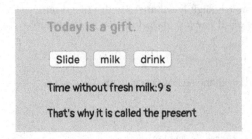

Figure 2-15. *Elasped time updates*

It is important to notice the decoupling between user events and internal events in this application (Figure 2-16).

Figure 2-16. *Increasing counters*

2-4. Using AJAX along core.async

Problem

AJAX in JavaScript can rapidly turn into a monster of piling callbacks.

Solution

Plug core.asyc with remote AJAX calls.

How It Works

Using a remote webservice with an AJAX call in ClojureScript will keep code linear, functional, and simple. Obviously, the cat in the Neko application will refuse to run if the weather is rainy, so let's check the weather before it is too late.

What's the Weather?

At the start of the application, we would like to check the weather and set the running state of the cat depending on the weather itself.

We will call on the OpenWeatherMap service to check on the local Tokyo weather and retrieve a JSON object from the service. After checking the result from the AJAX call, we will first display an icon representing the current weather.

The current frontend.app namespace is getting a bit crowded at this stage, so let's create a new namespace named weather, with the code related to perform the ajax code and retrieve remote data.

The OpenWeatherMap API when called returns a JSON object. When queried for the city of Tokyo, something like the following JSON object is returned:

```
{
    "coord": {
        "lon": 139.69,
        "lat": 35.69
    },
    "weather": [
        {
            "id": 701,
            "main": "Mist",
            "description": "mist",
            "icon": "50n"
        },
        {
            "id": 520,
            "main": "Rain",
            "description": "light intensity shower rain",
            "icon": "09n"
        }
    ],
    "base": "stations",
    "main": {
        "temp": 7.4,
        "pressure": 1002,
        "humidity": 87,
        "temp_min": 6,
        "temp_max": 9
    },
```

```
"visibility": 10000,
"wind": {
    "speed": 1.5,
    "deg": 300
},
"clouds": {
    "all": 75
},
"dt": 1488461460,
"sys": {
    "type": 1,
    "id": 7619,
    "message": 0.0218,
    "country": "JP",
    "sunrise": 1488402571,
    "sunset": 1488443853
},
"id": 1850147,
"name": "Tokyo",
"cod": 200
}
```

In the preceding map, we are interested into showing the icon of the weather element:

```
{   "id": 701,
    "main": "Mist",
    "description": "mist",
    "icon": "50n"}
```

The icon code can be used to retrieve an icon visually describing the weather.

Before starting, you will need an API key for the OpenWeatherMap web site (Figure 2-17).

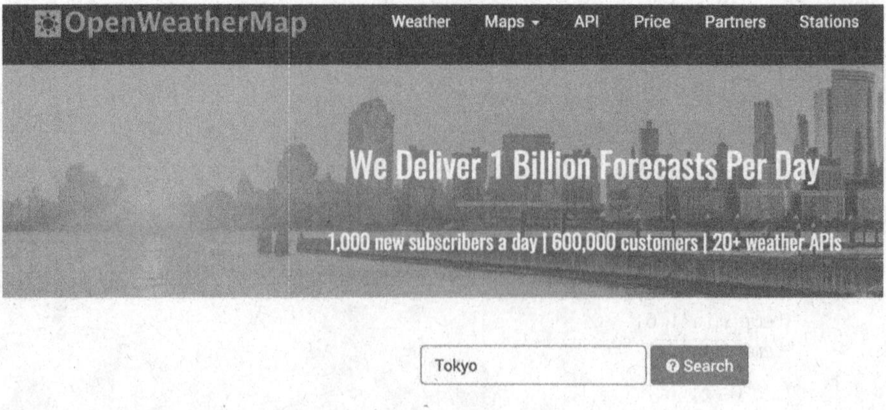

Figure 2-17. *OpenWeatherMap home page*

While the full instructions are not included here, signing up and getting an API key is quite straightforward. After signing up, your key is available in the API keys section (Figure 2-18).

API keys

| Setup | **API keys** | My Services | My Payments | Billing plans | Map editor | Blc |

Activation of an API key for **Free** and **Startup accounts** takes **10 minutes**. For **other accounts** it take
You can generate as many API keys as needed for your subscription. We accumulate the total load

Key		Name		
9▮▮▮▮▮▮▮▮▮▮▮▮efb		Default	☑	✕

Figure 2-18. *Get your OpenWeatherMap API key*

To execute AJAX queries, we will be using a library named cljs-ajax, which offers easy AJAX requests.

It is time to add a new dependency to the build.boot file, and restart the boot dev task:

```
[cljs-ajax "0.5.3"]
```

The code to do the AJAX request will be done in the new weather namespace. It has a bit more code than usual, but it should be rather straightforward to go along and read at this stage.

```
; the namespace definition gets the ajax.core/GET function
(ns frontend.weather
    (:require-macros [cljs.core.async.macros :refer [go go-loop]])
    (:require        [ajax.core :refer [GET]]
                     [cljs.core.async :refer [chan <! >! timeout]]))

; this is the channel used to post returned values
; from the ajax GET request
(def weather-handler-chan
    (chan))

; Add your own API key here, retrieve from the OpenWeatherMap website
(def api-key
    "...")
```

```clojure
; the endpoint is constructed from the base openweathermap URL
; the city and the API key
(defn endpoint [city]
    (str    http://api.openweathermap.org/data/2.5/weather?
            "units=metric&"
            "q=" city "&"
            "APPID=" api-key))

; extract the icon from the returned weather section
(defn get-icon [weather]
    (str "http://openweathermap.org/img/w/"
       (get weather "icon") ".png"))

; convert the JSON object to a ClojureScript structure using js->clj
; if you look at the map back again, there may be more than one element
; in the weather section, so let's only look at the first one
(defn read-weather [weather]
    (first (get-in (js->clj weather) ["weather"])))

; an error handler, contains a status code and status text
(defn error-handler [{:keys [status status-text]}]
  (prn (str "something bad happened: " status " " status-text)))

; meat of this namespace
; GET is a method from the new ajax library.
; GET takes an endpoint, here constructed from the city name
; and a map of two handlers, one success handler and one error handler
;
; see how the success handler post a message onto weather-handler-chan.
(defn get-weather [city]
    (prn "Fetching Weather for:" city)
    (GET (endpoint city)
      {    :handler #(go (>! weather-handler-chan %))
           :error-handler error-handler}))
```

This weather namespace is then included in the main frontend.app namespace, and the weather information will be done on page load, from inside the init function.

The namespace definition now includes a require for the new weather namespace:

```clojure
(ns frontend.app
   ...
   (:require
   ...
   [frontend.weather :as weather]
   ))
```

The code in the app namespace consists of two parts. The first is to fetch the weather using the get-weather function from the weather namespace. The second is a go-loop block. The go-loop block listens for messages coming from the weather-handler-chan, which, you would remember, gets value when the AJAX call has been successfully executed and a value, a JSON object, has been returned from the call.

Here again, let's use the dommy library to add a new element to the DOM tree: an image containing the icon visually describing the weather.

```
(defn init []
...
  (weather/get-weather "Tokyo")

  (go-loop []
    (when-let [msg (<! weather/weather-handler-chan)]
        (dommy/append!  (sel1 :#div1)
        (create-element :div
        "weather"
        [:img
            {:class "weather"
             :src (weather/get-icon (weather/read-weather msg)) }]))))
...
```

Currently, the weather here in midnight Tokyo is quite a futuristic mist, and it shows well while using the OpenWeatherMap API (Figure 2-19).

Figure 2-19. *Misty Tokyo icon from OpenWeatherMap*

Obviously, it would be also possible to not retrieve the weather information directly, but maybe on a button click. This is left as an exercise for the reader.

Quick Trick to Store Data in MongoDB

We have seen how to perform an AJAX GET request to retrieve the weather. Now we would like to store in a persistent NoSQL database values retrieved from the previous GET request. MongoDB may be one of the easiest NoSQL databases to use, which allows various objects to be stored; this makes it very nice to use for IoT projects.

This second part of the AJAX workout will be focusing on quickly setting up MongoDB to receive HTTP Post requests, including CORS setup (Cross Origin Resource Sharing; we will look into that in a minute), preparing the data, and sending it using an AJAX POST request.

Downloading, installing, and running the MongoDB daemon itself can be done through using your favorite package provider as shown in Table 2-7.

Table 2-7. *Quick MongoDB Install per Platform*

Platform	Command
Redhat/CentOS	yum install MongoDB
Debian/Ubuntu	apt install MongoDB
OSX	brew install MongoDB
Windows	`https://chocolatey.org/packages/mongodb`

Even easier, you can download a portable install from

`https://www.mongodb.com/download-center#community`

Then, unzip the content of the archive from the download page (Figure 2-20).

Figure 2-20. *MongoDB download page*

Whatever the platform, you get an executable, mongod, and you can start it with the HTTP interface enabled with the following command:

`./bin/mongod -dbpath data --rest`

The folder used for data is named here data folder, and the --rest flag tells the server to spawn an HTTP interface.

To be able to send a request from a JavaScript browser application to a service or server running on a different host (or port), you need to have some special settings done at the HTTP level.

Effectively, there is a need for the server to tell the client it accepts cross-domain requests. This is done through setting HTTP headers on prerequest, the option request.

In its simplest form, this gives the diagram in Figure 2-21.

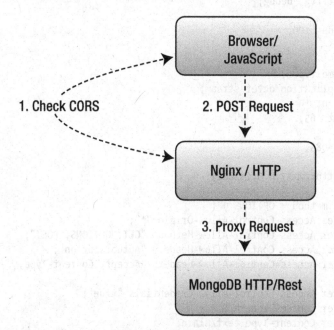

Figure 2-21. *CORS setup with Nginx as an http proxy*

The first request is an HTTP OPTION request, which checks that the HTTP headers are present so that the cross-domain request can be done.

Since MongoDB has no settings to do that, we will quickly set up a Nginx server with minimal configuration to act as a proxy and return the CORS headers as expected when an OPTION request is sent from the client.

The proxy setup is mostly a pass-through proxy, with the added OPTION request handling, which sets up the CORS headers properly and directly returns the required headers to the JavaScript client:

```
if ($request_method = OPTIONS ) {
  add_header Access-Control-Allow-Origin "*";
  add_header Access-Control-Allow-Methods "GET, OPTIONS, POST";
  add_header Access-Control-Allow-Headers "Authorization";
  add_header Access-Control-Allow-Headers "Accept, Content-Type, Origin";
  add_header Access-Control-Allow-Credentials "true";
  add_header Content-Type text/plain;
  return 200;
}
```

The full Nginx configuration is shown in the following:

```
worker_processes  1;
error_log  /tmp/error.log  debug;
events {
    worker_connections  100;
}
http {
    include       mime.types;
    default_type  application/octet-stream;
    sendfile          on;
    keepalive_timeout  65;
    server {
        listen          8085;
        location / {
        proxy_pass http://127.0.0.1:28017;

        if ($request_method = OPTIONS ) {
            add_header Access-Control-Allow-Origin "*";
            add_header Access-Control-Allow-Methods "GET, OPTIONS, POST";
            add_header Access-Control-Allow-Headers "Authorization";
            add_header Access-Control-Allow-Headers "Accept, Content-Type,
            Origin";
            add_header Access-Control-Allow-Credentials "true";
            add_header Content-Length 0;
            add_header Content-Type text/plain;
            return 200;
        }

        add_header Access-Control-Allow-Origin "*";
        add_header Access-Control-Allow-Methods "GET, OPTIONS, POST";
        add_header Cache-Control no-cache;

        proxy_buffer_size          4k;
        proxy_buffers              4 32k;
        proxy_busy_buffers_size    64k;
        proxy_temp_file_write_size 64k;

        }
    }
}
```

While obviously this is not recommended in production for security reasons, this Nginx configuration allows us to store data directly for easy prototyping.

From the previous example, we will add a new method in the weather namespace, which can send a POST request to MongoDB.

The namespace require should be in place. Make sure you have this namespace require section included:

```
(ns frontend.weather
  ...
  (:require
          [ajax.core :refer [GET POST]]
          ...
  ))
```

The request itself is quite similar to the GET request. We specify a collection to the endpoint, and supposing the mongodb+nginx combo is running on the same machine as the SPA, this gives the following function:

```
(defn store-in-mongo[collection msg]
    (POST (str "http://localhost:8085/local/" collection "/")
    { :body msg
      :handler #(prn "OK")
      :error-handler #(prn "ERROR:" %1 %2)}))
```

Performing the AJAX request using the newly created function is then a matter of passing the collection and the JSON message you would like to store.

```
(weather/store-in-mongo
  "messages"
  (str
"{'language':''ClojureScript',"
"'message':'the cat is inside mongo.''}") )
```

Upon sending the request, this shows up in the MongoDB messages collection, as shown in Figure 2-22.

▢ messages		
_id	language	message
▤ 58b8f37dc7...	▢ ClojureScript	▢ the cat is inside mongo.
▤ 58b8f38cc7...	▢ ClojureScript	▢ the cat is inside mongo.
▤ 58b8f3bcc7...	▢ ClojureScript	▢ the cat is inside mongo.
▤ 58b8fbeec7...	▢ ClojureScript	▢ the cat is inside mongo.

Figure 2-22. Messages from a ClojureScript application to MongoDB

For this minimal setup, stringified JSON, so plain text, is expected to be sent. In the first insert in MongoDB, straight text was inserted, so there was no problem.

But maybe you want to store the weather object that was returned from the OpenWeatherMap request.

To do this, you can use the following snippet, which turns any ClojureScript data structure to JavaScript, first using the core function clj->js, converting a Clojure data structure to its JavaScript equivalent, and then calling stringify using the JavaScript's JSON object.

```
(defn clj->json [ds]
  (.stringify js/JSON (clj->js ds)))
```

In pure JavaScript, as you remember, this would be

```
var stringJSON = JSON.stringify(ds);
```

Supposing the preceding method were added to the utils namespace, the msg retrieved from the channel could now be stored almost directly into MongoDB.

```
(go-loop []
  (when-let [msg (<! weather/weather-handler-chan)]
    (weather/store-in-mongo
      "weather"
        (utils/clj->json (weather/read-weather msg) ))
      ...
      ))
```

This new weather object shows well in MongoDB and in Figure 2-23.

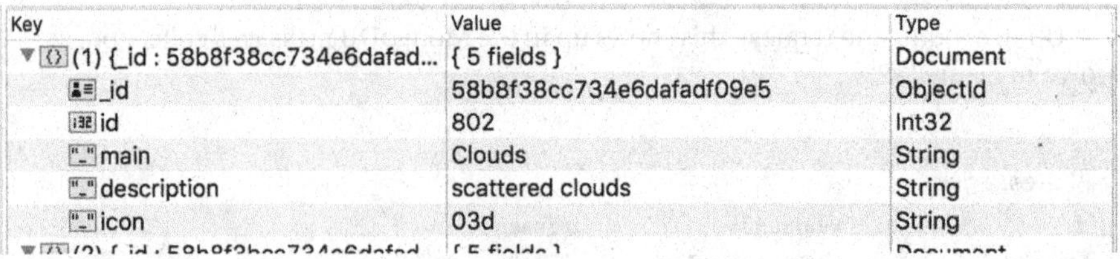

Key	Value	Type
▼ {} (1) {_id : 58b8f38cc734e6dafad...	{ 5 fields }	Document
🔢 _id	58b8f38cc734e6dafadf09e5	ObjectId
🔢 id	802	Int32
🔤 main	Clouds	String
🔤 description	scattered clouds	String
🔤 icon	03d	String
▼ {} (2) { id : 58b8f3bcc734e6dafad	{ 5 fields }	Document

Figure 2-23. *OpenWeatherMap object into MongoDB*

2-5. Going Back to Function Reactive

Problem

On our mission to creative reactivity, we actually strayed a bit away from reactive in the last few pages, so it's probably time to get back on track and put in some more reactivity.

Solution

We will look at two main pieces of reactive middleware. One, named Beicon, is to handle stream of events and allow reactive principle to be put in action on those events. The other middleware will be Firebase, which brings reactive persistence to your ClojureScript application.

How It Works

Being Reactive can be applied at different layers of your application, whether the event part or the persistence part.

Beicon creates streams, made from atoms, that can create events based on thresholds, or different external conditions. The streams are created based on atoms and produce events based on those atoms' values and some predefined conditions.

After mastering Beicon, we will switch to persisted data with Firebase, where the persisted data acts as the distributed source of reactiveness.

Reactive Streams with Beicon

When using Reagent in the next chapters, we will see how changes of values in atoms are reflected directly at the UI level through a clever watch mechanism.

This is done through something similar to core.async channel but directly listening to changes made on atoms.

For example, let's say the cat in the application should not run if there has been no fresh milk for the last 10 seconds.

Remember, in the application we currently count the number of seconds elapsed since the last fresh box of milk with the nomilk-counter atom.

```
(def nomilk-counter (atom 0))
```

Wouldn't it be great to have something listening to change of values on that atom, and triggering an action if the value of that atom is greater than, say, 10 seconds.

Beicon is a ClojureScript library that provides just that. It introduces reactive streams from which instant decisions and actions can be taken.

Beicon is currently at version 3.1.1 and can be added to the Boot file with

```
[funcool/beicon "3.1.1"]
```

Beicon makes it straightforward to implement such a check on an atom using streams, via the s/from-atom function:

```
(def nomilk-counter (atom 0))
(def nomilk-stream
  (->>
    (s/from-atom nomilk-counter)
    (s/filter #(> % 10))))

(s/on-value nomilk-stream #(make-cat-stop))
```

In this case, the stream is created from changes on the atom, and the stream also filters values of the atom that are under 10.

Any value coming out of that stream is being listened to by the s/on-value function which has two parameters. One is the stream to listen to, and the other a function to call when the stream produces a new value.

In general, a core.async channel may be more versatile because the message on the channel could be anything, and the go-loop provides channel interaction block at first glance.

Beicon streams, however, allow for chain of events based on atom's value change, and some extra rules made on the stream itself.

With this simple example, the cat stops running once the number of seconds without milk goes beyond 10 seconds. So, don't forget the milk!

Persistence and Reactive Programming with Google's Firebase

While Beicon makes it easy to React on atom value changes locally, Google's Firebase, a distributed database, brings that to the next level by having what is needed for distributed atoms and distributed reactive streams.

Firebase has been recently acquired by Google, and the database has gained in fame and scale.

Basically, Firebase is a NoSQL database in the cloud, which means you cannot install it on premises, unfortunately. On the other hand, if you need something to scale rapidly in case of emergency or server-less architecture, this is probably a fantastic choice of a database.

Signing up and registering your first project should be straightforward; probably the most difficult part is to go and browse to the following URL:

```
https://console.firebase.google.com
```

With Google leading the database now, you can simply sign up and sign in using your Google account, as shown in Figure 2-24.

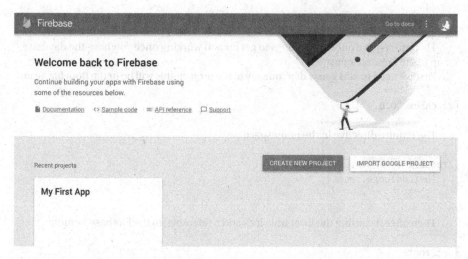

Figure 2-24. *Your Firebase dashboard*

After creating a new project in the region of your choice, you should be able to see the web Firebase console, as in Figure 2-25.

Figure 2-25. *Firebase application content*

This is where you can find the ProjectId and the API key used in the example to come.

To interface with Firebase, we will use the ClojureScript client named Matchbox. Matchbox not only proposes to connect to Firebase but also has atoms, cursors on Firebase objects. Clojure database structures are stored and retrieved directly; no need for JSON or plain text conversion before storage. It also has async callback and can optionally be plugged in your now-favorite async library, core.async.

To get started gently, the first example will be to log a message when the Neko application was last loaded/reloaded.

This will require only a few things to get up and working once you have the database set up in the Firebase console.

First we need to add a new dependency to the project; this will be in the Boot file again:

```
[matchbox "0.0.9"]
```

The require directive in the namespace is

```
(:require
    [beicon.core :as s]
    ...)
```

Then after restarting the Boot task, let's add a reference to the Firebase Remote:

```
(def root
  (m/connect "https://blistering-inferno-558.firebaseio.com"))

(m/auth-anon root)
```

This updates the content of your remote Firebase instance, as shown in Figure 2-26.

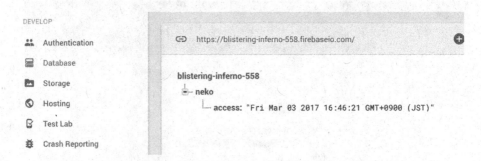

Figure 2-26. *Your own custom data in your own Firebase project*

Note also that updates can be viewed in real time already in the UI (Figure 2-27).

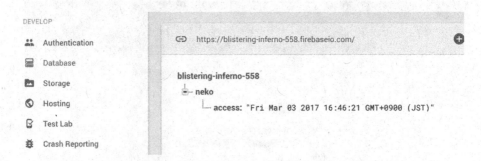

Figure 2-27. *In-browser real-time Firebase updates*

Rereading the value that as stored is done using m/deref. So, the last date the application was opened can be printed or shown in the browser's console.

```
(m/deref root #(prn "Previous Date Was:" %))
```

Using dommy plugs in nicely here too, and the function used for callback can be used to directly create a new node in the DOM:

```
(m/deref root
    #(dommy/append!  (sel1 :#div1)
    (create-element :div
      "lastdate"
      [:p (str "Last Neko Access: " (get-in % [:neko :access]))] )))
```

The root node can be assigned a keyspace, for example to store a separate user account in a single database. To set the current root node to a more cat base, you can pass in a parameter when connecting to Firebase.

```
(def root
  (m/connect "https://blistering-inferno-558.firebaseio.com" "neko"))
```

Getting a child reference from the root node is done using the function get-in:

```
(def child (m/get-in root [:neko :milk]))
(m/deref child prn)
```

And the child can be updated just like the root, using the m/reset! function. Now this is starting to get really interesting because you can now combine regular atoms, Beicon streams, and Matchbox storage in only a few lines.

You obviously would like to know how much milk is currently available for the cat, not in the current application but say in another SPA. The following three lines create a stream from the milk-counter atom, and on value change update the value in Firebase:

```
(s/on-value
    (s/from-atom milk-counter)
    #(m/reset! milk @milk-counter))
```

Looking at the UI and the Firebase console at the same time, it is possible to check the count on the UI and the remote database (Figure 2-28).

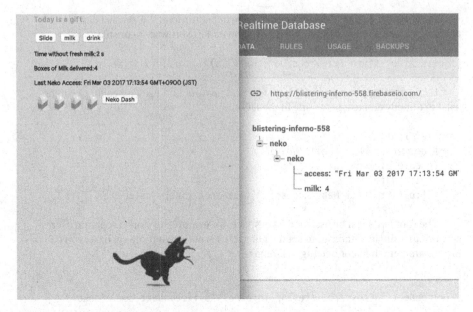

Figure 2-28. *Synchronized app state and remote Firebase content*

Figure 2-29 shows the reactive flow that was gone through just now after clicking the milk button.

Figure 2-29. *Reactive flow*

Listener and callbacks are integrated in the Matchbox library; this is done using the function listen-children, so in a different application to get updates on the amount of milk currently available you would use the following callback:

```
(m/listen-children
  root [:neko]
  (fn [[_ val]] (prn ">" val)))
```

This offers your application distributed persistence and a distributed event listener mechanism, as shown in Figure 2-30.

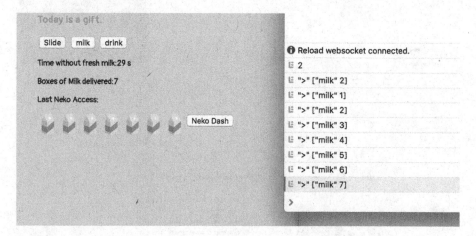

Figure 2-30. *Distributed application persistence*

Firebase Channels with core.async

This final section in the Firebase challenge lets you have the best of both worlds, with listeners on value in the database returning core.async channels.

The plug with core async is done through a variant of the listener, returning a channel, the method coming from the matchbox.async namespace:

```
[matchbox.async :as ma]
```

The preceding simple listener version can now be replaced with a channel instead of a callback:

```
(def neko-chan
  (ma/listen-to< root [:neko :milk] :value))
```

The rest is a simple core async channel, so to retrieve messages from it, you can use a regular go-loop macro:

```
(go-loop []
 (when-let [msg (<! neko-chan)]
  (prn "Milk from channel:" msg))
 (recur))
```

The result is shown in Figure 2-31.

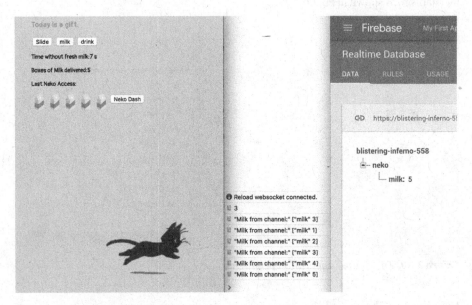

Figure 2-31. *Firebase and core.async*

Matchbox is a great library: it brings the different good parts of ClojureScript in action:

– Transactional Atoms

– Channels

– Async-like code

It also abstracts the need of custom AJAX requests to store values remotely.

2-6. Using Rules to Trigger Events and React

Problem

Sometimes the logic gets a bit complicated to be just included in just a pipeline of streams.

Solution

Use a few strong ClojureScript libraries to help you form sets of rules to organize your code accordingly.

How It Works

Clara used to be a Clojure-only forward rule engine, but is now ported to the ClojureScript environment, and it is possible to use those rules from within your code.

Clara has a bit of a steep learning curve, so we will start with a rather simple example. We want to check if the current time waited since the last box of milk is greater than a given short limit. If the time waited by the cat is reached, the rule should trigger an event, to alert us. With Clara, a triggered rule can be forwarded to a standard ClojureScript function, which will then be called.

At its most basic level, Clara needs a set of fact definitions, rules, and a session to insert new facts as they are coming along.

In the following example, we will create a dumb simple fact, which is the amount of time without milk. We will also write a Clara rule that checks the value against a given threshold, and trigger a simple message on the console alerting us when the time waited for milk has gone beyond the threshold.

The rules will be defined in a new namespace, frontend.rules. The session and the facts definition will also be done in that namespace for convenience.

```
; the new namespace with the required clara namespaces
(ns frontend.rules
(:require
    [clara.rules :refer [defsession defrule insert fire-rules]]))

; a Clara Fact, is a simple ClojureScript record.
; a ClojureScript record can be seen as a mini class
(defrecord MilkTime [value])

; a simple binding for the time threshold.
(def high-threshold 10)

; this is a simple function called when the rule has "fired"
; meaning the check was validated
(defn cannot-run-anymore [i]
  (prn "The cat will stop running ... no fresh milk for " i " seconds"))
```

```
; the rule itself is created using the Clara macro defrule
; The [] before the => describe the rule check
; This firt check is done on the Fact table MilkTime.
; Any entry in the MilkTime table with a value bigger than the threadshold ;
  will trigger.
; (= ?value value) describes a binding ?value that can be reused in the
; triggered section
; Code after the => is the code block executed if the rule triggers.
(defrule too-long-without-milk
  [MilkTime (> value high-threshold)  (= ?value value)]
  =>
  (cannot-run-anymore ?value))

; lastly, Clara requires a session. The macro defsession creates a clara
; session made from rules contained this namespace
(defsession session 'frontend.rules)

; since session is immutable, we wrap it around an atom so as to update it
(def global-session (atom session))

; this method will be called from other namespaces to insert milk and fire ;
the rules
; A new record is created with (-> MilkTime i) which
; effectively creates a new object, and assigned the MilkTime's value to i
; at the same time we update the atom's session with a new session,
; containing the new fact and a call to trigger the rules.
(defn new-milk-time[i]
    (reset!
      global-session
      (-> @global-session (insert (->MilkTime i)) (fire-rules))))
```

The Clara code is now in place. It is now possible to insert a new fact from a different namespace. Here we would like to insert a new fact, MilkTime, every second to track the total number of time waited.

From the app namespace, let's require the new milk namespace.

```
[frontend.rules :as rules]
```

Remember there was a core.async loop triggered every second to count the number of seconds without milk. We will update the go-loop to insert a new fact at the same time as the rest of the work.

```
(go
  (loop []
    (<! (timeout 1000))
    (swap! nomilk-counter inc)
    (rules/new-milk-time @nomilk-counter) ; rule inserted
    (>! nomilk-channel @nomilk-counter)
    (recur)))
```

And the cat will probably stop running soon enough (Figure 2-32).

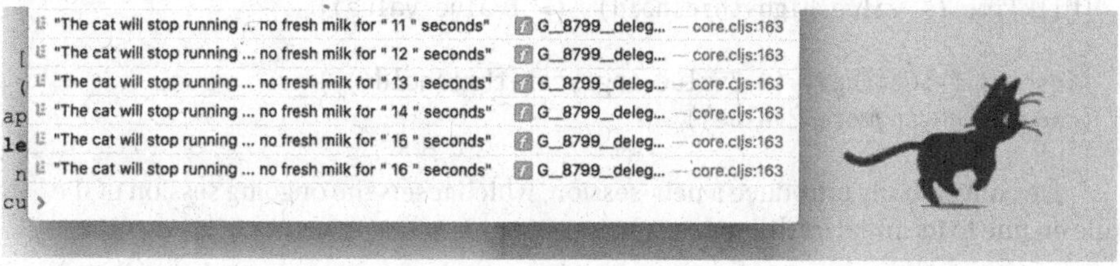

Figure 2-32. *No milk, and the cat stops running*

Note that the rule fires as long as no milk is added with the milk button. Indeed, the rule checks if the time elapsed is longer than ten seconds, so it will keep on printing for some time.

Queries can also be used between Clara and standard code by using the defquery macro. The query works just like a condition inside a rule but can be used in other parts of the code.

Improving on the last example, we will introduce a CatAngry fact, along with a threshold.

We will also create a Clara accumulator to count the level of cat angriness. This is done by performing the equivalent of a reduce function on a fact table.

```
; namespace gains some more refers and a reference to the accumulators
namespace.
(ns frontend.rules
  (:require
    [clara.rules.accumulators :as acc]
    [clara.rules :refer
      [defsession defrule defquery query insert! insert fire-rules]]))

(defrecord MilkTime [value])
; the new fact, insert Angry cats and not so angry cats
(defrecord CatAngry [yesno])

(def high-threshold 10)
; the cat becomes angry after 15 seconds ...
(def angrycat-threshold 15)

; same as before
(defn cannot-run-anymore [i]
  (prn "The cat will stop running ... no fresh milk for " i " seconds"))

; when the rule is triggered, ie, when the threshold is reached for milk
; time, we insert an angry cat with a yes no value corresponding to its
; own threshold. The new insert is done with insert!.
```

103

```
; note in that case, the same session is reused.
(defrule too-long-without-milk
  [MilkTime (> value high-threshold)  (= ?value value)]
  =>
  (insert! (->CatAngry (> ?value angrycat-threshold )))
  (cannot-run-anymore ?value))
```

We conveniently introduce a new-session, which resets the ongoing session of the rule engine to its initial fresh state.

```
(defsession session 'frontend.rules)
(def global-session (atom session))

(defn new-session[]
    (reset! global-session session))
```

After session definition, the rest of the code follows by query for angry cats.

```
(defn new-milk-time[i]
    (reset!
        global-session
        (-> @global-session (insert (->MilkTime i)) (fire-rules))))

; this gets a list of CatAngry facts where the yesno parameter
; is set to yes.
; this returns a list of facts
(defquery angry-cat[]
  [?angry_cats <- CatAngry (= yesno true)])

; this used the above query and counts the number of results
(defn is-cat-angry?[]
  (> (count (query @global-session angry-cat)) 1))
```

To measure anger level, we can also make use of an accumulator. Here we define a my-count accumulator, which counts the number of really angry cats. Accumulators always work on a fact collection.

It takes an initial value and three functions. Note how you can get values for each value going through each of the supplied function. Also note that the accumulator is a function itself.

```
(defn my-count []
  (acc/accum
    {:initial-value 0
     :reduce-fn
        (fn [count value] (if (get value :yesno) (inc count) count))
     :retract-fn
        (fn [count retracted] (dec count))
     :combine-fn +}))
```

Now the new accumulator can be used in a query (or a rule). When used, the query will return a list of one single element, a map, with a key of ? level and a value corresponding to the result of the accumulator.

```
(defquery angriness-level[]
  [?level <- (my-count) :from [CatAngry]])

(defn angry-level[]
  (:?level (first (query @global-session angriness-level))))
```

In the app namespace, we can now refer to the new query, so in the init function, let's add a new dommy listener that shows the level of cat angriness:

```
(dommy/listen!
    (sel1 :#button-angry) :click
    #(.alert js/window (if (rules/is-cat-angry?)
      (str "The cat is angry:[lvl " (rules/angry-level) "]")
        "The cat is not angry yet")))
```

And as we can see in Figure 2-33, I think it is time to give some milk to a few cats around …

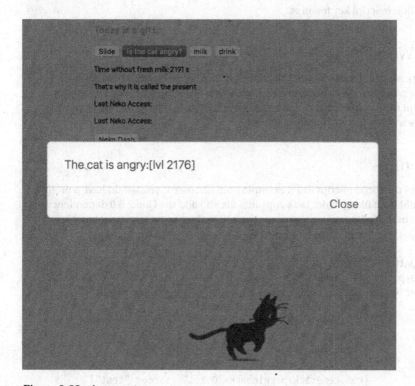

Figure 2-33. Angry cat

Obviously you could write rules that update atoms when they are triggers, and those atoms could change visuals on your UI.

Instead of having to click to check if the cat is angry or not, you could introduce and update the cat-angry atom, which will show up on the screen. Binding values directly to UI element is easily done with Reagent, so do keep this rule engine thing in mind for when we will tackle Reagent later.

For more info on Clara Rules, you can refer to the extensive online documentation:

```
http://www.clara-rules.org/
```

2-7. Relax with Quil

Problem

You would like to bring reactive programming concepts to interactive art and visual compositions.

Solution

Quil brings the power of processing and processing.js to Clojure and ClojureScript. While not easy to integrate with other framework useful, it actually works quite well with atoms and other ClojureScript key features.

How It Works

Quil is very easy to get started with a boot-based setup, and to start drawing and getting your cat imagination free by using Quil. Using the setup that was done to start a ClojureScript REPL, you can also change drawing code on a remote browser using that REPL, so we will briefly have a look at this too.

Boot Setup

If you copied the ClojureScript REPL example from Chapter 1, you would have a pretty genuine build.boot file at hand. Let's copy that file and add the Quil 2.6.0 dependency to it, as shown in the following:

```
(set-env!
 :source-paths   #{"src/cljs"}
 :resource-paths #{"resources"}
 :dependencies '[[adzerk/boot-cljs    "1.7.228-2"   :scope "test"]
                 [adzerk/boot-reload "0.4.11"         :scope "test"]
                 [pandeiro/boot-http "0.7.3"          :scope "test"]
                 [quil                        "2.6.0"]
                 ; REPL
                 [adzerk/boot-cljs-repl   "0.3.3"] ;; latest release
                 [com.cemerick/piggieback "0.2.1"  :scope "test"]
```

```
                   [weasel                  "0.7.0"  :scope "test"]
                   [org.clojure/tools.nrepl "0.2.12" :scope "test"]
                   [org.clojure/clojurescript "1.9.456"]
                   ])

(require
 '[adzerk.boot-cljs      :refer [cljs]]
 '[adzerk.boot-reload    :refer [reload]]
 '[adzerk.boot-cljs-repl :refer [cljs-repl start-repl]]
 '[pandeiro.boot-http    :refer [serve]])

(task-options!
    reload {:on-jsload 'frontend.app/init})

(deftask dev []
  (comp (serve)
        (watch)
        (reload)
        (cljs-repl)
        (cljs)))
```

The index.html file goes back to being simple again. The only thing you need to work with Quil is a canvas with an id.

```html
<!doctype html>
<html>
  <head>
    <meta charset="utf-8">
    <title>hi, world!</title>
    <link rel=styleSheet href="main.css" type="text/css" media=screen>
  </head>
  <body id="bodyid">
    <h1>Hello, QUIL World</h1>
    <canvas id="quil"></canvas>
    <script type="text/javascript" src="js/app.js"></script>
  </body>
</html>
```

That's it. Now let's go to work with Quil in the frontend.app namespace.

Quil works with the concept of sketch. A sketch starts with an initial state, has an update function to update an internal state, and has a draw function to draw things onscreen depending on data from the state, and possibly events.

We will look at events later; for now, let's review a minimal sketch setup.

```clojure
(ns frontend.app
     (:require
        [quil.core :as q :include-macros true]
        [quil.middleware :as m]))

; kept here so the compiler does not get exited with current setup
(defn init[])

; a setup function.
; in functional mode (see below)
; the initial state is the value returned by this setup function
(defn setup []
    ; this change the per second frame rate
    ; obviously higher is faster, and lower is slower
    (q/frame-rate 5)
    ; the state in this example is composed of a color entry
    {:color 255})

; the state update function, is called once before draw
(defn update-fn [state]
    ; at each iteration, we set the color in state to a new
    ; random value
    ; standard ClojureScript can be used here.
    {:color (rand-int 255)})

; the refresh on screen function.
; this draws things.
; here, we set the RGB background color value to
; a set of 3 values, one depending on the value of the state
(defn draw [state]
  (q/background 128 128 (:color state)))

; the sketch setup
; host needs a canvas id in the index.html page
; the other functions have been defined above
; fun-mode is for functional mode (but fun as well!)
; it makes it more functional but also easier
; to update the state
(q/defsketch hello-quil
  :host "quil"
  :size [200 200]
  :setup setup
  :update update-fn
  :draw draw
:middleware [m/fun-mode])
```

After boot dev on this newly set-up project, a few dependencies are downloaded:

```
Retrieving quil-2.6.0.pom from https://repo.clojars.org/ (6k)
Retrieving processing-core-3.2.4.pom from https://repo.clojars.org/ (1k)
...
Retrieving processing-core-3.2.4.jar from https://repo.clojars.org/ (990k)
Retrieving quil-2.6.0.jar from https://repo.clojars.org/ (246k)
Retrieving processing-js-1.6.4.0.jar from https://repo.clojars.org/ (235k)
```

After the http server is ready, loading the usual development URL in the browser results in Figure 2-34.

Hello, QUIL World

Figure 2-34. First Quil sketch

Quilax 1

The Boot setup worked great! Now on to functional and fun Quil art. This second example is a close copy of the example from the Quil web site.

This time the setup takes a color and an angle to create the state. The frame rate is also slightly increased. The update method slowly goes through the different shares of color using mod to keep the value between 0 and 255.

The draw function itself:

```
(defn setup []
  (q/background 255)
  (q/frame-rate 60)
  {:color 0 :angle 0})

(defn update-fn [state]
  {:color (mod (+ (:color state) 0.7) 255)
   :angle (+ (:angle state) 0.1)})
```

The draw function will draw a circle, using the q/ellipse function from Quil, which is just the same function as exposed with standard processing.

The position of the circle will be computed from the cosines and sines of the current angle as defined in the state.

```
(defn draw [state]
  (q/background 255)
(q/fill (:color state) 128 255)

  (let [angle (:angle state)
        x (* 100 (q/cos angle))
        y (* 100 (q/sin angle))]
    (q/with-translation [(/ (q/width) 2) (/ (q/height) 2)]
      (q/ellipse x y 50 50))))
```

Just updating the code from the frontend.app namespace and saving will refresh your sketch (Figure 2-35); again, no need to refresh the browser page at this time.

Hello, QUIL World

Figure 2-35. *Real-time coding a Quil sketch*

This is quite refreshing.

You may have noticed that you actually do not need to redefine the sketch each time. For example, let's say you update code in the file, but leave the defsketch section commented out; only the update-fn and draw function will be updated and will affect the currently drawing sketch.

The setup function itself will be updated too, but is only called at sketch creation and thus does not affect the currently running one.

The q/background Quil function forces a refresh of the canvas at each draw iteration.

It does not have to be so, and commenting it out leaves a nice trailing effect on the screen (Figure 2-36).

```
(defn draw [state]
  ; (q/background 255)
  (q/fill (:color state) 128 255)
  (let [angle (:angle state)
        x (* 100 (q/cos angle))
```

```
      y (* 100 (q/sin angle)))]
  (q/with-translation [(/ (q/width) 2)
                       (/ (q/height) 2)]
    (q/ellipse x y 50 50))))
```

Figure 2-36. *Easy trailing effect*

Now playing with the position of the circle, still without redrawing, you can create a superposition effect (Figure 2-37).

```
(defn draw [state]
  (q/fill (:color state) 128 255)
  (let [angle (:angle state)
        x (* 10 (q/cos angle))
        y (* 10 (q/sin angle))]
    (q/with-translation [(/ (q/width) 2)
                         (/ (q/height) 2)]
      (q/ellipse x y 50 50))))
```

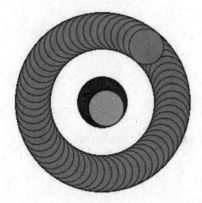

Figure 2-37. *Superposition effect*

111

And then again after updating the x and y values (Figure 2-38).

Figure 2-38. *Multiple superposition effects*

Of course, you can also play with the position of the circle as well, this time updating the translation settings.

Note that the following is still the one and same sketch. The background not cleaned up, and gives this new superposition effect (Figure 2-39).

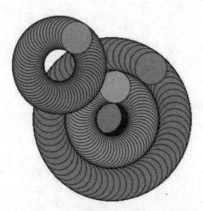

Figure 2-39. *Updating the object base rendering location*

On our quest to ever-better-looking donuts, we will now take into account mouse input to get the center position of the circle.

This needs to be added to the sketch definition in the key :mouse-moved.

```
(defn setup []
  (q/background 255)
  (q/frame-rate 30)
  {:color 0 :angle 0 :x (/ (q/width) 2) :y (/ (q/height) 2) })

(defn update-fn [state]
  {:color (mod (+ (:color state) 0.7) 255)
   :angle (+ (:angle state) 0.1)
   :x (state :x)
   :y (state :y)
   })

(defn draw [state]
  (q/fill (:color state) 128 255)
  (let [angle (:angle state)
        x (* 50 (q/cos angle))
        y (* 50 (q/sin angle))]
    (q/with-translation [ (:x state) (:y state)]
      (q/ellipse x y 50 50))))

(defn mouse-moved [state event]
  (-> state
      ; set circle position to mouse position
      (assoc :x (:x event) :y (:y event))))

(q/defsketch hello-quil
  :host "quil"
  :size [500 500]
  :setup setup
  :mouse-moved mouse-moved
  :update update-fn
  :draw draw
  :middleware [m/fun-mode])
```

Somehow, with Figure 2-40, it feels like donut time ...

Figure 2-40. *Donuts everywhere*

By the way, the cheat sheet is always a welcome addition to have at hand:

https://raw.githubusercontent.com/quil/quil/master/docs/cheatsheet/ cheat-sheet.pdf

Quilax 2: ColorJoy

To conclude this recipe, we will go over the code of one of the author's favorite ClojureScript/Quil sketch examples (Figure 2-41).

Author: Abe Pazos

```
(defn setup []
  ; sets a high frame rate of 60 refresh per seconds
  (q/frame-rate 60)
  ; change the color mode to HSB.
  ; (which hue,saturation,brightness) with a max value of 1
  (q/color-mode :hsb 1)

  ; background uses the new color mode
  (q/background 0.05)
  )
```

```clojure
(defn draw []
  ; 0.12, F is a small enough value as suggested by the algorithm
  ; used in q/noise
  (let [F (/ (q/frame-count) 500.0)]
    ; for each vertical line of the canvas
    (doseq [x (range 0 (q/width))]
      (let [
              ; 1/6 of the canvas is used for margin at top and bottom
              margin (/ (q/height) 6.0)
              ;l
              ; values for HSB color, randomized with q/noise
              i (/ x (q/width))
              sat (+ 0.5 (* 0.4 (Math/sin (* 14 (q/noise i 5 F)))))
              bri (+ 0.5 (* 0.4 (Math/sin (* 21 (q/noise 6 (- F) (* i 5))))))
              ]
        ; the stroke sets the HSB color to use when the drawing
        (q/stroke (mod (+ i F) 1.0) sat bri)
        ; the line from
        (q/line x margin x (- (q/height) margin)))
      )
    )
  )
; the sketch setup itself is simple, not needed a state nor an update
function.
(q/defsketch colorjoy
  :host "quil"
  :size [500 500]
  :setup setup
  :draw draw)
```

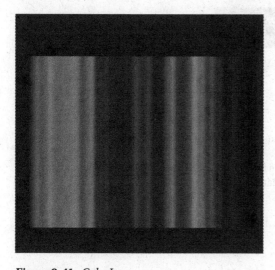

Figure 2-41. *ColorJoy*

A simpler draw function that, while quite less outstanding than the original, is quite enjoyable, and also brighter (Figure 2-42):

```
(defn draw []
  (let [F (/ (q/frame-count) 500.0)]
    (doseq [x (range 0 (q/width))]
      (let [
            margin (/ (q/height) 6.0)
            i (/ x (q/width))
            sat (q/noise i 5 F)
            bri (+ 0.5 (q/noise 6 (- F) (* i 5)))
            ]
        (q/stroke (mod (+ i F) 1.0) sat bri)
        (q/line x margin x (- (q/height) margin))))))
```

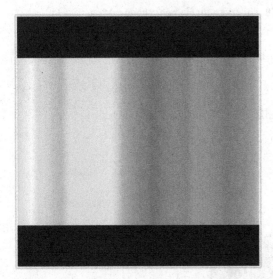

Figure 2-42. *Brighter ColorJoy*

Quilax 3: Reactive Quil

Basically, we would like to get the value of the color of the canvas to be set via the value stored in the remote database.

A listener is set up to get the value from Firebase, via Matchbox, then on update, an atom holding the value of color is updated.

When the atom is updated, the value of the atom is taken into account directly from the draw function, although it would also work to go through an update function.

```
(def color (atom 255))

(def root
  (match/connect "https://blistering-inferno-558.firebaseio.com"))

(match/auth-anon root)
(match/listen-to
  (match/get-in root [:color])
  :value
  #(reset! color (second %)))

(defn draw [state]
  (q/background 128 128 @color))

(q/defsketch hello-quil
  :host "quil"
  :size [200 200]
  :draw draw
  :middleware [m/fun-mode])
```

The result is in Figure 2-43.

Hello, QUIL World

Figure 2-43. *Bringing Firebase to Quil*

Think about changing the value of the color of this application from the other application, in which the cat would be out of milk and stop running. Having two ClojureScript applications also does not seem difficult anymore.

The reader could also now get his Raspberry Pi to read and update the temperature of the room value somewhere in the Firebase database, then similarly use a ClojureScript/Quil-based app to update the color palette of your application depending on the temperature.

Summary

Going back over this chapter, you have seen how to

- Update elements directly into the DOM, using pure JavaScript and then pure ClojureScript.

- Migrate to a library to update the DOM tree but also register events.

- Use core async and streams to propagate data throughout a cat application. (Maybe the cat is still running.)

- Studied a bit of remote persistence and plugged in streams and core.async to seamlessly connect to different set of remote data.

- Played with Clara rules to validate rules and triggered actions based on those rules.

- Relaxed with Quil, drawing on the screen but still remembering how to connect to Firebase to update the drawing using external inputs.

In the next chapter, you'll learn how to integrate ClojureScript with pure JavaScript libraries and work around basic difficulties.

Keep your Boot on and let's run with the cat!

■ ■ ■

## CHAPTER 3

Working with JavaScript

What is there more kindly than the feeling between host and guest?

Aeschylus

The last chapter targeted almost pure ClojureScript code and useful ClojureScript libraries to swiftly build Single Page Applications. While this is ideal, it's not always possible, and sometimes you really need to use a JavaScript library that has been helping you for months on another project, or you may also have developed a library yourself and you would like to reuse it as is from ClojureScript.

This chapter consists of four recipes and focuses on the linking parts between ClojureScript and the JavaScript runtime:

- The first two recipes will show different ways to use JavaScript libraries, first directly, then how to prepackage them to make them easier to use throughout different projects.

- The third recipe will go through a few different small concept applications, to show the fun parts of the JavaScript runtime using ClojureScript.

- The final recipe will look at how to write code in ClojureScript targeting not the browser but instead the Node.js runtime.

3-1. Fetching Current Time Across Timezones
Problem

You want to use standard JavaScript libraries and perform AJAX queries to retrieve remote data and insert results directly into the DOM.

© Nicolas Modrzyk 2017

N. Modrzyk, *Reactive with ClojureScript Recipes*, DOI 10.1007/978-1-4842-3009-1_3

Solution

jQuery gives programmers the power to play with the DOM in an easy and cross-browser-compatible way and has put quick animations, toggling elements, event handling, and AJAX into the mainstream. In a small set of exercises, we are going to go back and see how to use standard jQuery from ClojureScript.

How It Works

The setup for the first exercise is simply to copy the template that was created in Chapter 2, to which we will add some jQuery and bootstrap standard CSS and JavaScript files. The application we want to develop will have a button that, when clicked, will trigger and query to retrieve the time in a given timezone. The timezone will be picked up from an autocomplete input field.

jQuery with ClojureScript Setup

There is actually nothing ClojureScript-specific to start using jQuery. Keeping the build. boot and other files as originally done in the project template, the setup to include jQuery; bootstrap is entirely done in the index.html only.

```
<!doctype html>
<html>

<head>
  <meta charset="utf-8">
  <title></title>
  <link rel="stylesheet" href="https://maxcdn.bootstrapcdn.com/
  bootstrap/3.3.7/css/bootstrap.min.css">
  <link href="styles.css" rel="stylesheet">
  <link rel="stylesheet" href="//code.jquery.com/ui/1.12.1/themes/base/
  jquery-ui.css">
  <link rel="stylesheet" href="https://maxcdn.bootstrapcdn.com/
  bootstrap/3.3.7/css/bootstrap-theme.min.css">
  <script type="text/javascript" src="https://code.jquery.com/jquery-
  3.1.1.min.js"></script>
  <script src="https://code.jquery.com/ui/1.12.1/jquery-ui.js"></script>
  <script src="https://maxcdn.bootstrapcdn.com/bootstrap/3.3.7/js/bootstrap.
  min.js"></script>
</head>
```

```
<body>
  <h1>Today is a wonderful day!</h1>
  <div class="col-sm-5">
  <input class="col-sm-2 form-control" type="text" id="foo"/>
  <button id="toggle" class="btn btn-info"></button>
  <button id="btn-date" class="btn btn-info">get date</button>
  <div id="banner-message">hidden message</div>
  </div>
  <script src="main.js"></script>
</body>

</html>
```

To make the example easier to start with, the scripts are included using their hosted versions. The loading of the compiled ClojureScript code is done at the bottom part of the body element.

Toggling Element with jQuery

In its simplest form, our copied-over ClojureScript namespace is pretty basic, and it does ... nothing (obvious for now).

```
(ns frontend.app)
(enable-console-print!)
(defn init [])
```

The init method is kept there to keep the reload plugin happy. The ClojureScript setup is actually done.

Then on to executing some jQuery code. In jQuery, a selector is usually created with the dollar symbol ($). So, to replace the html content of an element, you would use the html method on the result of the jQuery selector, as shown in the following.

```
$("#toggle").html("jquery toggle...")
```

The $ is a function defined in JavaScript land. If you remember from previous chapters, any JavaScript variable can be accessed in ClojureScript using the prefix js/, so let's try to port the preceding example to ClojureScript:

```
(.html (js/$ "#toggle") "jquery toggle")
```

Or you can achieve similar result by using the Clojure threading macro:

```
(-> (js/$ "#toggle")
  (.html "jquery toggle"))
```

Since the button with id #toggle is present in the HTML page, once you've added the code and waited for the usual autorefresh, the page will then show the button with the updated text, as shown in Figure 3-1.

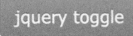

Figure 3-1. *jQuery toggle button*

If you remember the setup for the ClojureScript REPL you did before, it is actually a good time to put it in practice again.

Fetching a JSON File and Adding DOM Elements

In this new example, the JavaScript code fetches a json file and creates new elements with jQuery.

```
$.getJSON( "/sample.json", function( data ) {
  var items = [];
  $.each( data, function( key, val ) {
    items.push( "<li id='" + key + "'>" + val + "</li>" );
  });

  $( "<ul/>", {
    "class": "my-new-list",
    html: items.join( "" )
  }).appendTo( "body" );
});
```

Given that the sample.json file is

```
{
  "one": "Singular sensation",
  "two": "Beady little eyes",
  "three": "Little birds pitch by my doorstep"
}
```

This code can be converted directly to ClojureScript using code similar to the following:

```
(defn json-callback[data]                        ; callback function
  (.append (js/$ "#banner-message")                      ; append to
                                                          ;   element
    (str                                         ;
      "<ul>"                                     ;
      (apply str                                 ;
        (map                                  ; loop through elements
          #(str "<li id=" (first %) ">" (second %) "</li>")   ; anonymous fn
          (js->clj data)))                       ; to use map,
                                                 ;   convert
        "</ul>")))                               ;

(.getJSON js/$ "/sample.json" json-callback)         ; call jQuery getJSON
```

The latest getJSON jQuery method called from a ClojureScript can also update the DOM in real time and then add nodes to the given div element. This can be a useful technique to bulk insert test nodes from test data into the page (Figure 3-2).

| jquery toggle | get date |

- Multiple sensation
- Beady little eyes
- Little birds pitch by my doorstep

- Multiple sensation
- Beady little eyes
- Little birds pitch by my doorstep

Figure 3-2. *Dynamically inserted list*

At this point, remember it is also useful to do a mix of file-based and REPL development. For example, you could write a new callback in the frontend.app namespace:

```
(defn json-callback-2[data]
  (.append (js/$ "#banner-message")
    (str
      "<b>" (js/Date.) "</b><ul>"                  ; NEW insert a header
      (apply str
        (map
          #(str "<li id=" (first %) ">" (second %) "</li>")
          (js->clj data)))
        "</ul>")))
```

Then, from the ClojureScript REPL, you already have access to the new function just by making sure the REPL is in the same namespace as the one used in the file. So executing the following snippet creates a new list as shown in Figure 3-3.

```
frontend.app=> (ns frontend.app)
frontend.app=> (.getJSON js/$ "/sample.json" json-callback-2)
```

hidden message**Mon Mar 13 2017 15:28:02 GMT+0900 (JST)**
- Multiple sensation
- Beady little eyes
- Little birds pitch by my doorstep

Mon Mar 13 2017 15:28:14 GMT+0900 (JST)
- Multiple sensation
- Beady little eyes
- Little birds pitch by my doorstep

Figure 3-3. *Inserting multiple lists in the DOM*

A few more ideas for you to try:

- Add images from URLs stored in the json file

- Prepare different json files to add different nodes to the page

- Choose a random quote message from a list stored in the json file

- ...

To finish this short jQuery section, we will now show how to use the autocomplete plugin of jQuery UI and send a generic AJAX request.

The autocomplete part is easy to set up. In its basic form, the autocomplete widget takes possible values from a list. The list is based on a sequence, and the autocomplete method is called on an input field.

```
(def tz [ "Europe/Paris" "Asia/Tokyo" "US/Eastern" "US/Pacific" "UTC"])

(.autocomplete                    ; from jQuery UI plugin
    (js/$ "#foo")                 ; jQuery selector
    (clj->js {:source tz}))       ; parameter is a javascript map
```

Since the jQuery script itself has been included in the page using the script directive from the HTML page, the new methods are already properly bound, and if your setup is correct you should be able to see the autocomplete in action, like in Figure 3-4.

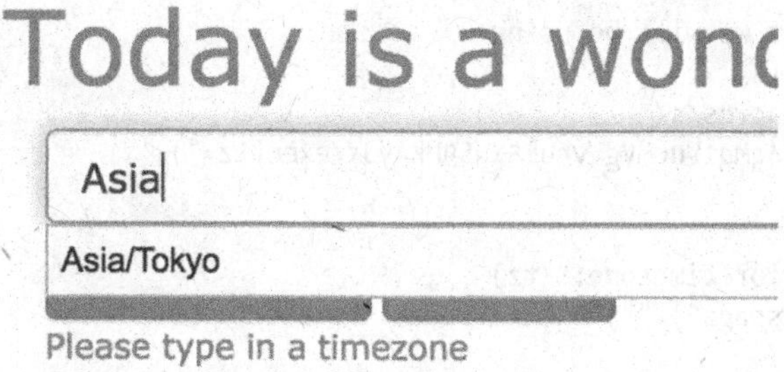

Today is a wonc

Asia
Asia/Tokyo

Please type in a timezone

Figure 3-4. Autocomplete with jQuery

Now, from the value of this drop-down box, we would like to send an AJAX request to retrieve the time. The time API service that will be used is running directly from script. google.com, and the web site is located as in the following:

http://davidayala.eu/current-time/

Using the proposed API, you can find the time given a timezone. If you try one of the available timezones, you can query directly from the browser and expect a response like the following:

```
{
    "day": 13,
    "dayofweek": 1,
    "dayofweekName": "Monday",
    "fulldate": "Mon, 13 Mar 2017 16:11:37 +0300",
    "hours": 16,
    "millis": 721,
    "minutes": 11,
    "month": 3,
    "monthName": "March",
    "seconds": 37,
    "status": "ok",
    "timezone": "Africa/Addis_Ababa",
    "year": 2017
}
```

You can access the same kind of result from an AJAX query. The jQuery ajax function can be used; it requires a JavaScript map of parameters to specify different parameters, notably the success and error callback functions. In the following code section, those callbacks, written in ClojureScript, are inlined in the map.

```
; first the time API endpoint we will be using
(def api-base
"https://script.google.com/macros/s/
AKfycbyd5AcbAnWi2YnOxhFRbyzS4qMq1VucMVgVvhul5XqS9HkAyJY/exec?tz=")

(defn get-date[tz]                                    ;
    (println "Fetching time for timezone:" tz)
    (.html (js/$ "#banner-message") "")

    (.ajax js/$ (clj->js {                            ; .ajax is a jQuery fn
    :dataType "json"                                  ; expected data is JSON
    :url (str api-base tz)                            ; url + timezone
    :success                                          ; success callback
        (fn[evt]
         (.html                                                  ; set banner
                                                                    html to
         (js/$ "#banner-message")                     ; fulldate element
         (get (js->clj evt) "fulldate")))
    :error                                            ; error callback
        (fn[evt]                                            ; just print error
      (println "error"))}))))
```

After adding the preceding code to the frontend.app namespace and saving the file, the first thing to do is to check that the function is working as expected with a few timezones. From a ClojureScript REPL, or by writing directly in the file, you can check the results of the following calls:

```
frontend.app=> (get-date "Europe/Paris")
frontend.app=> (get-date "Asia/Tokyo")
```

Observe how the content of the browser page is being updated, as usual in-place targeting the DOM and so without a page refresh, as shown in Figure 3-5.

Figure 3-5. *Successive DOM inserts*

Event Handling

Finally, we just link a click on the button with id get-date using a jQuery event and then write a ClojureScript function that does the call to the preceding get-date function with the value of the autocomplete input field.

```
(defn on-btn-click[evt]
  (let [tz (.val (js/$ "#foo"))]
    (if (not (empty? tz))
      (get-date tz)
      (.html (js/$ "#banner-message") "Please type in a timezone"))))
```

That callback is then used for the jQuery event handler, for the "click" event on the btn-date button:

```
(.on (js/$ "#btn-date") "click" on-btn-click)
```

To summarize the flow of the jQuery example, please refer to Figure 3-6.

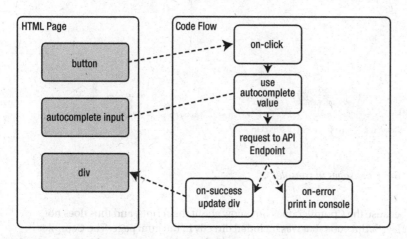

Figure 3-6. *Sequence flow when using jQuery*

Advanced Compilation Mode Problems

We have just seen how to integrate an external JavaScript library and how the ClojureScript Compiler nicely fits pieces of the JavaScript world together.

Now, unfortunately, this setup actually breaks when using ClojureScript advanced compilation mode.

To check that, let's compile the code in advance mode and start a server:

```
# compile cljs in advanced mode and put the result in the target folder
boot cljs -sO advanced - target
# start a server on the target folder
boot serve -d target wait
```

Even through the compilation seems to be going fine, you'll notice the messages in the browser console pretty quickly (Figure 3-7).

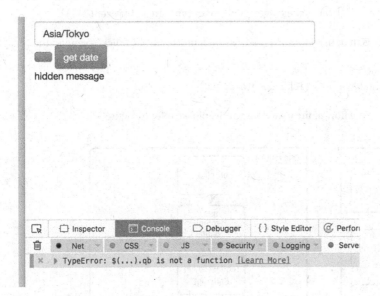

Figure 3-7. *Error messages in console*

That's because the Compiler does not know about the scripts, and thus does not know about JavaScript code that was included directly in the html page. The Compiler does not know about the jQuery and jQuery-ui symbols; thus, those have been **optimized** by being excluded on the ClojureScript side, and symbols are not found.

To understand a bit more about what is happening in the background, let's have a look at the diagram in Figure 3-8.

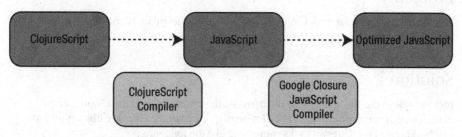

Figure 3-8. *Compilation flow*

The ClojureScript code is compiled to JavaScript using the ClojureScript Compiler in a first step.

In a second step, the Google Closure Compiler is used to optimize the JavaScript code. Yes, this is an S here not a J, so Closure.

The Google Closure Compiler is used to minify the code and also to optimize code by removing dead parts of code, for example.

When the Google Closure Compiler is minifying the code, it replaces symbols with a shorter named version. So, say you have a function in ClojureScript named my-cljs-function; in advanced compilation mode, the Closure, with an S, Compiler will convert its name to something like a0.

The Google Closure Compiler thus needs to know this mapping ahead of time to avoid mangling function name where it should not.

The idea is to add a definition file, called an extern file, that includes all the function names of the library so that optimization of function names can be done accordingly. So, the compilation flow becomes as shown in Figure 3-9.

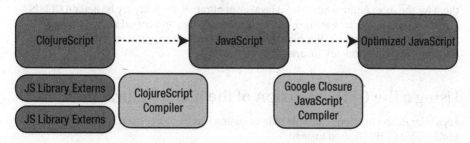

Figure 3-9. *Extended compilation flow*

This is where the CLJSJS project comes into action.

3-2. Working with CLJSJS Libraries

Problem

You want to easily make us of ClojureScript advanced compilation and external JavaScript libraries.

Solution

Include a deps.cljs file, a mapping file between the JavaScript and the ClojureScript namespace. If you are curious, it is a Clojure map, containing a foreign-libs key and an externs key, and for jQuery it looks something like the following:

```
{:foreign-libs
      [{:file "cljsjs/development/jquery.inc.js",
         :provides ["cljsjs.jquery"],
         :file-min "cljsjs/production/jquery.min.inc.js"}],
  :externs ["cljsjs/common/jquery.ext.js"]
}
```

We will review the structure later on again when looking at how to create a cljsjs-compatible library, but for now, it more important to just make sure the external JavaScript libraries can be included and used properly in your final projects.

How It Works

Building on the previous exercise, we would like to easily add the jQuery namespace and JavaScript file. This process consists of two major tasks: using the CLJSJS version of the jQuery library and creating a new CLJSJS library.

So, CLJSJS is a community effort made to create those deps.cljs files and maintain them for the most famous and useful JavaScript libraries. Each library hosted on CLJSJS is presented as a Java Jar file, most of the time as a zip file, and contains the JavaScript file itself, plus the mapping file, plus the externs definition required for the module to be understood by the Google Closure Compiler.

Using a the CLJSJS Version of the jQuery Library

Let's migrate the previous example that was using jQuery to a version where the jQuery library from CLJSJS is used instead.

The first thing to do is to tell the HTML page to use the JavaScript file from a local file.

Step1: Change the jQuery JavaScript Script Location

In the HTML page, let's change the script tags in the head section to **public/jquery.min.js**:

```
<head>
...
  <script type="text/javascript" src="public/jquery.min.inc.js"></script>
  <script src="https://code.jquery.com/ui/1.12.1/jquery-ui.js"></script>
  <script src="https://maxcdn.bootstrapcdn.com/bootstrap/3.3.7/js/bootstrap.
  min.js"></script>
...
</head>
```

Step2: Add CLJSJS jQuery to Dependency Section

In the Boot build file, let's add the cljsjs's jQuery dependency. Usually you can find the dependency on the CLJSJS web site, as well as copy paste the text for the dependency:

```
http://cljsjs.github.io/
```

Now add the jQuery 2.2.4 to the build.boot file:

```
(set-env!
...
:dependencies     '[[adzerk/boot-cljs        "1.7.228-2"]
                    [adzerk/boot-reload       "0.4.13"]
                    ...

               [cljsjs/jquery "2.2.4-0"]
               ])
```

Step3: The from-jars Boot Task

Surprisingly, a required Boot task is not packaged in a jar file already, so let's add it here by ourselves in the build.boot file.

The from-jars task will take an array of tuples, where each tuple is

- a dependency symbol
- a path inside the jar file
- a path in the Boot in-memory fileset (eventually on the filesystem)

Let's copy the following task in the Boot file:

```
(deftask from-jars
  "Import files from jars (e.g. CLJSJS) and move them to the desired
  location in the fileset."
  [i imports IMPORT #{[sym str str]} "Tuples describing imports"]
  (let [add-jar-args
  (into {} (for [[j p]   imports] [j (re-pattern (str "^" p "$"))]))
    move-args
  (into {} (for [[_ p t] imports] [(re-pattern (str "^" p "$")) t]))]

    (sift :add-jar add-jar-args :move move-args)))
```

See how the from-jars task makes use of the sift task?

Step4: Copy the jQuery JavaScript File from the Jar File

In the build.boot file still, let's set up the different options for the different tasks.

- The cljs task should compile in advance mode, using the Google Closure Compiler.

- The fresh from-jars task should copy the minimized jQuery JavaScript file.

- The Garden task for our own set of styles stays the same as before.

```
(task-options!
  cljs {:optimizations :advanced}
  from-jars {:imports #{['cljsjs/jquery
                         "cljsjs/production/jquery.min.inc.js"
                         "public/jquery.min.js"]}}
  garden {:styles-var 'styles/base
                      :output-to     "styles.css"
:pretty-print true})
```

Step5: The Build Task

Everything is in place; now let's write a Boot task that builds as required. The task will

- compile our css from Clojure code
- compile our cljs code in advanced mode
- extract the JavaScript file
- copy files to the target folder

```
(deftask build[]
  (comp
  (garden)
  (cljs)
  (from-jars)
  (target)))
```

Now, let's use this new task!

```
boot build
```

Starting an http server to see the result can be done with the usual serve task.

```
boot serve -d target wait
```

And the good old time application is showing up as shown in Figure 3-10.

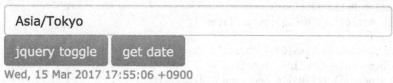

Figure 3-10. *jQuery with advanced compilation mode*

Note that this is completely stand-alone, so only copying the target folder creates a fully working application!

Creating a CLJSJS Library

While I am sure you already rushed and looked through the different libraries hosted on the CLJSJS site, and you cannot wait to use quite a few of them (just like the author!), let's see how to create a wrapper around an existing (or not!) JavaScript library and package it for CLJSJS.

We will write a supersmall JavaScript library named MyLib that will present a dialog when calling a method hello.

Then we will package the library as a jar file, according to cljsjs guidelines.

Finally, we will create a small template project to use the JavaScript library from ClojureScript.

It's harder than it sounds, but you will succeed if you follow the coming lines.

Writing a Dumb Library That Can Display Annoying Dialogs

To create or package an existing library, you need a minimal file setup.

```
.
├── build.boot
└── resources
    └── cljsjs
        └── mylib
            └── common
                ├── mylib.ext.js
                └── mylib.inc.js
```

The build.boot file is now our favorite way to deal with anything surrounding building stuff. Then there is one mylib.inc.js, which is the original JavaScript for the library; finally there is the mylib.ext.js file, which is the externs file used to load modules.

Let's first draft a JS library with a function firing up dialog quickly.

```javascript
(function () {
    // Constructor
    function MyLib () {
        console.log("MyLib instanciated");
    }
    MyLib.prototype.VERSION = "0.0.1";
    MyLib.prototype.hello = function () {
        window.alert("Hello Annoying Dialog !");
    };

    // exports
    if (typeof exports !== 'undefined') {
        if (typeof module !== 'undefined' && module.exports) {
            exports = module.exports = MyLib;
        }
        exports.MyLib = MyLib;
    }

    if (typeof window === "object" && typeof window.document === "object")
    {
        window.MyLib = MyLib;
        window.mylib = new MyLib();
    }
}) ();
```

The first part is for functional code, and the second half is for standard JavaScript module exports. The library exposes a hello function that displays the famous annoying dialog.

To get the Google Compiler to load the module, (thus also to use this library with ClojureScript), we need to create an extern file for this file. You can think about the extern file as an API file defining the public API of the library.

You can write it by hand, but there is also a nice web site that can do that for you now (or at least until a Boot task comes to hand).

```
http://jmmk.github.io/javascript-externs-generator/
```

Your file needs to be hosted on http somewhere for the service to access it, but once this is done, the rest is done in seconds, as can be seen in Figure 3-11.

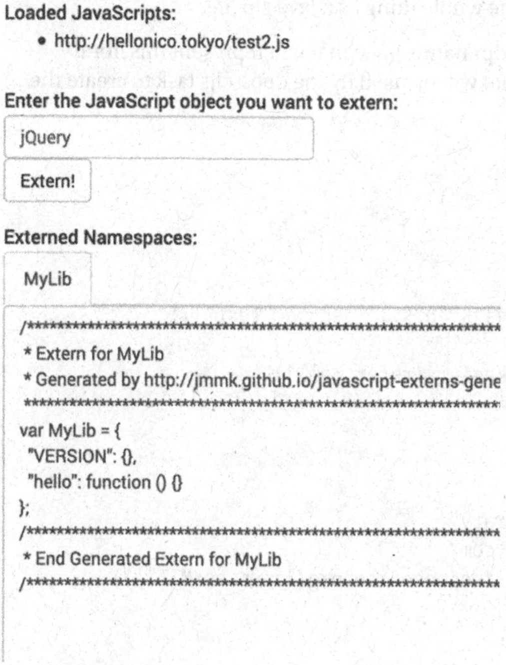

Loaded JavaScripts:
- http://hellonico.tokyo/test2.js

Enter the JavaScript object you want to extern:

jQuery

Extern!

Externed Namespaces:

MyLib

```
/********************************************************
 * Extern for MyLib
 * Generated by http://jmmk.github.io/javascript-externs-gene
 ********************************************************
var MyLib = {
 "VERSION": {},
 "hello": function () {}
};
/********************************************************
 * End Generated Extern for MyLib
 /********************************************************
```

Figure 3-11. *Easy externs*

And as you can see, the necessary code for the extern file has been generated as in the preceding and as follows:

```
var MyLib = {
  "VERSION": {},
  "hello": function () {}
};
```

The full build.boot file is also included in the following, and it mostly is a usage of

- sift, to copy only given files
- deps-cljs, to create the deps.cljs file require to load this library as a module
- pom, to create a descriptor so the library can be included as a Boot dependency in other projects
- and a jar task, to package the whole thing as a Java zip file.

Also, as you can see, the ClojureScript namespace that will represent this library has been set to cljs.mylib, and this is what will be used by the deps-cljs task to create the module named cljs.mylib.

```
(def +lib-version+ "0.0.1")
(def +version+ (str +lib-version+ "-1"))

(set-env!
  :resource-paths #{"resources"}
  :dependencies '[[cljsjs/boot-cljsjs "0.5.2" :scope "test"]])

(require '[cljsjs.boot-cljsjs.packaging :refer :all])

(task-options!
 pom {:project     'cljsjs/mylib
      :version     +version+
      :description "A mylib library"
      :url         http://mylib.com/
      :license     {"MIT" "http://opensource.org/licenses/MIT"}})

(deftask package []
  (comp
    (sift :include #{#"^cljsjs"})
    (deps-cljs :name "cljsjs.mylib")
    (pom)
    (jar)))
```

Now, let's package and install the jar file on your local machine. This is actually the name of the two Boot tasks, one to create the jar the other one to install it.

```
boot package install
```

After the following output, the jar will be installed.

```
Sifting output files...
Writing deps.cljs
Writing pom.xml and pom.properties...
Writing mylib-0.0.1-1.jar...
Installing mylib-0.0.1-1.jar...
```

And the contents of the jar file can be checked; as expected, it includes a deps.cljs file and the file written in the preceding.

```
jar tvf ~/.m2/repository/cljsjs/mylib/0.0.1-1/mylib-0.0.1-1.jar
     0 Wed Mar 15 23:21:27 JST 2017 META-INF/
     0 Wed Mar 15 23:21:27 JST 2017 META-INF/maven/
     0 Wed Mar 15 23:21:27 JST 2017 META-INF/maven/cljsjs/
     0 Wed Mar 15 23:21:27 JST 2017 META-INF/maven/cljsjs/mylib/
   879 Wed Mar 15 23:21:27 JST 2017 META-INF/maven/cljsjs/mylib/pom.xml
   114 Wed Mar 15 23:21:27 JST 2017 META-INF/maven/cljsjs/mylib/pom.
   properties
   135 Wed Mar 15 23:21:27 JST 2017 deps.cljs
     0 Wed Mar 15 23:21:28 JST 2017 cljsjs/
     0 Wed Mar 15 23:21:28 JST 2017 cljsjs/mylib/
     0 Wed Mar 15 23:21:28 JST 2017 cljsjs/mylib/common/
   605 Wed Mar 15 22:36:18 JST 2017 cljsjs/mylib/common/mylib.inc.js
   470 Wed Mar 15 22:26:18 JST 2017 cljsjs/mylib/common/mylib.ext.js
    25 Wed Mar 15 23:21:28 JST 2017 META-INF/MANIFEST.MF
```

Good news: the files are now ready for consumption and we can use them for a different project! Whoo-hoo! Let's try it at once.

Using the MyLib Library in a New Project

We will mostly reuse the usual project template that has served so well so far, shown for convenience again in Figure 3-12.

Figure 3-12. *ClojureScript project template*

The only thing of importance in the build.boot is the new dependency on the cljsjs/mylib library in the dependencies section.

```
[cljsjs/mylib "0.0.1-1"]
```

The html file will contain a reference only on the main output cljs file:

```
<!doctype html>
<html>
<head>
  <meta charset="utf-8">
  <title></title>
  <link href="styles.css" rel="stylesheet">
</head>
<body>
  <h1>Today is a wonderful day!</h1>
  <script src="main.js"></script>
</body>
</html>
```

And the interesting part is all in the simple ClojureScript file itself:

```
(ns frontend.app
  (:require [cljsjs.mylib]))

(enable-console-print!)

(defn init []
  (.hello (js/MyLib.)))
```

The cljsjs.mylib library is imported in the ClojureScript namespace via the modules of the Google Closure Compiler; as the MyLib object of the library is now linked to the Window object.

It can therefore be used: the access is as usual, prefixed with js/. And a small library victory is shown in Figure 3-13.

Figure 3-13. *Your own CLJJS library in action*

Some More CLJJS Tips

You can get inspired by reading the Boot file of different cljsjs project. For example, the build.boot file for the ajv library is downloading the two files from the cdn before moving them in the correct place in the Boot in-memory fs, using the swift :move task.

```
(defn cdn-ver [file]
  (str "https://cdnjs.cloudflare.com/ajax/libs/ajv/" +lib-version+ "/" file))

(deftask package []
  (comp
    (download :url (cdn-ver "ajv.bundle.js")
              :checksum "F453B6BC9BAB6BDD07968CD767F6EDF1")
```

```
      (download :url (cdn-ver "ajv.min.js")
                :checksum "C4E86C8C3CCE66F24E2CA04256D26B8A")
      (sift :move {#"ajv.bundle.js"  "cljsjs/ajv/development/ajv.inc.js"
                   #"ajv.min.js"     "cljsjs/ajv/production/ajv.min.inc.js"})
      (sift :include #{#"^cljsjs"})
      (deps-cljs :name "cljsjs.ajv")
      (pom)
(jar)))
```

You may ask: What does the correct place mean? Well, most of the time, JavaScript libraries have a minified version and a standard version, the same way ClojureScript Compiler has different outputs, depending on the compilation mode (:node, :advance ...)

So instead of having only a **common** directory in your library file structure, you can also have development and production, where development is the human-readable version and **production** is the minified version.

If you place files in those places, the ClojureScript Compiler will make use of them depending on the chosen compilation mode.

But enough tips; let's explore and enjoy using those CLJSJS libraries now.

3-3. Having Fun with JavaScriptProblem

Sometimes it is not very obvious how the ClojureScript interop works, due to the way the JavaScript libraries are written. You would like to master ClojureScript interop and be able to work with just about any JavaScript library.

Solution

We'll use a few examples made from JavaScript libraries taken directly from ClojureScript environment, and see how things fit together.

How It Works

As usual, the base project is the Boot project template that has been introduced early on in the book; then, add a library via the CLJSJS packages and finally write ClojureScript interop code that works.

ECharts for charting, TweenJS for animation, PixiJS for a complete 2D rendering engine for beautiful animation, matter for cool physics feats, phaser for games, and MQTT for a distributed websocket queue system will be presented through simple example. This is a fairly lengthy set of tasks, so let's get to them.

Retrieving a JSON File Asynchronously with oboe

Retrieving a JSON file is a preparation step for the charting example coming right after. Retrieving a JSON file from the same project or remotely can be done using the oboe.js library.

Include it in the build.boot file:

```
[cljsjs/oboe "2.1.2-1"]
```

Then, let's fetch a beautiful configuration file.

As per the documentation, the original oboe JavaScript version of an AJAX call to retrieve a json document is as follows:

```
oboe('/myapp/things.json')
   .done(function(things) {
       // we got it
   })
   .fail(function() {
       // we don't got it
   });
```

This can be turned to ClojureScript, requiring the cljsjs.oboe namespace and then converting using basic ClojureScript interop.

```
(ns frontend.app
    (:require [cljsjs.oboe]))

(enable-console-print!)

(defn init [])

(-> (js/oboe "/sample.json")
    (.done #(.log js/console %))
    (.fail #(println %)))
```

Note that the function associated with .done is handling a JavaScript object. If you need a Clojure form you would need to use js->clj and write something like

```
(-> (js/oboe "/hello.json")
    (.done #(.log js/console (js->clj %))) )
```

oboe also has a nice function to handle nodes as they are read via the Json streaming.

```
(-> (js/oboe "/hello.json")
    (.node (clj->js { "hello" #(println "hello")})))
```

The JavaScript map inside the .node part defines key pairs of {node function}, defining action to take when nodes are encountered while parsing.

It is also possible to not read/stream the full JSON file using abort on the **this** object. Since **this** does not exist in ClojureScript, you can use the **this-as** macro instead.

```
(-> (js/oboe "/hello.json")
    (.node (clj->js {
            "hello" #( this-as h (.abort h))
            "hello2" #( println "2")}))))
```

OK, now that we can retrieve the json file easily, let's create charts.

Writing Beautiful Charts with ECharts

ECharts is a full open source charting solution that has extensive documentation and samples and presents easy ways to create appealing charts in no time. If you want to get excited, head out to the following URL.

```
https://ecomfe.github.io/echarts-examples/public/index.html
```

This section is focused on the ClojureScript integration with JavaScript, so we will not go through all the possibilities of ECharts itself, since that could almost be a book on its own.

Instead, we will focus on a few examples having charts configured using simple JSON first then moving on to ClojureScript-focused examples.

ECharts with JSON-Based Configuration

Most of the examples and the different configurations that can be found for ECharts are based on JavaScript maps.

Using oboe, we know we can load a nice JSON object that will be used for the chart config.

Let's start with a pie chart. A sample configuration for a pie chart is shown in the following:

```
{"title": {"text": "ECharts pie example"},
 "series" : [
        {
            "name": "pie",
            "type": "pie",
            "data" :[
                {"value":400, "name":"Searching Engine"},
                {"value":335, "name":"Direct"},
                {"value":310, "name":"Email"},
                {"value":274, "name":"Alliance Advertisement"},
                {"value":235, "name":"Video Advertisement"}
            ]
        }
    ]
}
```

This will be saved in a **pie.json** file in the resource folder, so it can be found from this application.

Now, let's add the cljsjs EChart dependency and write some ClojureScript code to create the pie chart.

First, add the cljsjs dependency to the build.boot file as usual. You can copy and paste the version from the cljsjs web site, and as it goes, this is the current version:

```
[cljsjs/echarts "2.2.7-0"]
```

This will make sure the files for the EChart JavaScript library are included. After restarting boot dev again, we can type in the ClojureScript code to create the chart.

Restart the Boot process and head to the app.cljs file. You'll recognize the following code from the last recipe; this is pretty much the same way of loading the json content, except that in the done callback we can now create the EChart chart with the init method. The init method takes a config JavaScript, and the config for the pie chart is the one contained in the bar.json file.

```
(-> (js/oboe "/pie.json")
    (.done #(.setOption  (.init js/echarts (by-id "pie")) %))
    (.fail #(println %)))
```

Notice how the config object passed to the setOption method is kept as a pure JavaScript object and does not need any kind of conversion. Inside the .done callback, this is just regular JavaScript.

For the chart to show up, you need require directives at the top of the namespace, for ECharts and oboe, as well as the old by-id function that was written before.

```
(ns frontend.app
    (:require
        [cljsjs.echarts]
        [cljsjs.oboe]
        [frontend.utils :refer [by-id]]))
```

Your echart-based chart should show up, just as in Figure 3-14.

Today is a wonderful day. What to do ?

ECharts pie example

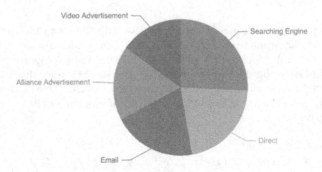

Figure 3-14. *ECharts pie example*

Providing that a div tag with id "bar" is present in the html page, things should go rather smoothly.

You can also quickly create a load-chart function to make things a bit more generic.

```
(defn load-chart[config div-id]
    (-> (js/oboe config)
    (.done #(.setOption (.init js/echarts (by-id div-id)) %))
    (.fail (fn[] (println "config problem: " config)))))
```

The standard ECharts example, the bar sales chart, can be created with the following configuration:

```
{
    "title": {"text": "ECharts sales example"},
    "tooltip": {},
    "legend": {"data" :["Sales"]},
    "xAxis": {
 "data": ["shirt","cardign","chiffon shirt","pants","heels","socks"]},
    "yAxis": {},
    "series": [{
    "name": "Sales",
    "type": "bar",
    "data": [5, 20, 36, 10, 10, 20]}]
}
```

The bar chart then shows up (Figure 3-15).

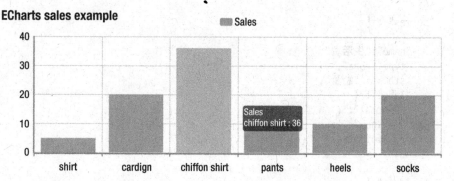

Figure 3-15. *ECharts bar chart*

A slightly more complicated (and slightly more Chinese) chart, also present in the ECharts sample page, can be loaded almost as is. Prepare a bar.json file in the same html folder with the following content:

```
{
  "title": {
    "text": "Staggered positive and negative axis labels",
    "sublink": "http://e.weibo.com/1341556070/AjwF2AgQm"
  },
  "tooltip" : {
    "trigger": "axis",
    "axisPointer" : {
      "type" : "shadow"
    }
  },
  "grid": {
    "top": 80,
    "bottom": 30
  },
  "xAxis": {
    "type" : "value",
    "position": "top",
    "splitLine": {"lineStyle":{"type":"dashed"}}
  },
  "yAxis": {
    "type" : "category",
    "axisLine": {"show": false},
    "axisLabel": {"show": false},
    "axisTick": {"show": false},
    "splitLine": {"show": false},
```

```
      "data" : ["ten", "nine", "eight", "seven", "six", "five", "four",
      "three", "two", "one"]
  },
  "series" : [
    {
      "name":"生活费",
      "type":"bar",
      "stack": "总量",
      "label": {
        "normal": {
          "show": true,
          "formatter": "{b}"
        }
      },
      "data":[
        {"value": -0.07, "label": {"normal": {"position": "right"}}},
        {"value": -0.09, "label": {"normal": {"position": "right"}}},
        0.2,
        0.44,
        {"value": -0.23, "label": {"normal": {"position": "right"}}},
        0.08,
        {"value": -0.17, "label": {"normal": {"position": "right"}}},
        0.47,
        {"value": -0.36, "label": {"normal": {"position": "right"}}},
        0.18
      ]
    }
  ]
}
```

And load it with the ClojureScript method:

```
(load-chart "/bar.json" "bar")
```

If the json loading goes well, the chart up shows just like in Figure 3-16.

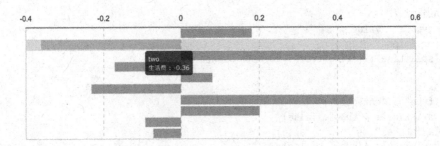

Figure 3-16. *More bar charting with ECharts*

Note how the label can be added inside the data section of the series.

But while a JavaScript config is surely easy to port the samples, to create your own chart, it is usually slightly easier to write the config in pure ClojureScript.

ECharts with ClojureScript-Based Configuration

So, let's try to rewrite the pie chart example in ClojureScript. To make it more native, we will use keywords for keys. The overall feeling is still a simple hashmap.

```
(def config-pie
    {:title {:text "ECharts pie example"}
     :series [
        {
            :name "pie"
            :type "pie"
            :radius "55%"
            :data [
                {:value 400 :name "Search Engine"}
                {:value 335 :name "Direct"}
                {:value 310 :name "Email"}
                {:value 274 :name "Advertisement"}
                {:value 235 :name "Video"}
            ]
        }
    ]
})
```

The map is now in ClojureScript, so to make it compatible with the JavaScript library, there is a need to convert the object to JavaScript. So when creating the chart, we will use the function clj->js:

```
(def myChart
    (.init js/echarts (by-id "main")))
(.setOption myChart (clj->js config-pie))
```

147

Et voila! Figure 3-17 shows the ClojureScript-written EChart.

ECharts pie in ClojureScript example

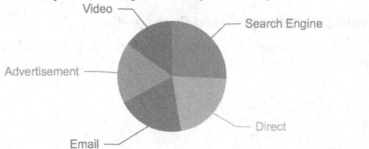

Figure 3-17. *ClojureScript ECharts pie*

Now obviously, you can also have a nice time updating data in real time using ClojureScript watchers.

Reactive ECharts Using ClojureScript Atoms and Watchers

This is an example of mixing a nice JavaScript library with standard ClojureScript features. Here we have an atom named mydata, which will hold the live data. On any change to that atom, the watcher :watcher will refresh the pie data in real time, using the update mode of EChart. In the following, the data will be randomly generated every three seconds.

```
(def myChart
  (.init js/echarts (by-id "main")))

(def mydata (atom [
  {:value 100 :name "Search Engine"}
  {:value 25 :name "Direct"}
  {:value 200 :name "Email"}]))

(add-watch mydata :watcher
  (fn [key atom old-state new-state]
    (.setOption myChart
      (clj->js {:title {:text "ECharts pie in ClojureScript example"}
      :series [
      {
      :name "pie"
      :type "pie"
      :radius "55%"
      :data @mydata
      }]}))))
```

```
(js/setInterval
  #(reset! mydata   [
    {:value (rand-int 300) :name "Search Engine"}
    {:value (rand-int 300) :name "Direct"}
    {:value (rand-int 100) :name "Email"}
    ]) 3000)
```

Figure 3-18 shows a real-time chart update.

ECharts pie in ClojureScript example

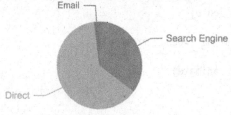

ECharts pie in ClojureScript example

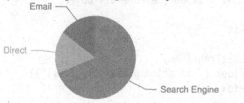

Figure 3-18. *Real-time updated chart*

That's it for charting. Do experiment with the additional graph types. ECharts also support user events, so try to add your own handlers there as well.

Animation with TweenJS

Playing with TweenJS is really refreshing once you get the hang of it. TweenJS allows you to animate different simple div elements on the screen from a simple pattern.

Again, in this example, we will focus on the library usage through ClojureScript, not all the possibilities of the library itself.

In the following example, we will animate and move a small cube randomly across the screen. Let's walk through the ClojureScript code:

```
; the target of the animation is the cube
(def cube
    (by-id "main"))

; the map containing the values that will be part of the animation.
; we convert this to a standard javascript map
(def position
    (clj->js
        {:x 100 :y 100 :rotation 0}))

; the animate function starts the tweenjs framework
(defn animate []
    (js/requestAnimationFrame animate);
    (.update js/TWEEN))
(animate)

; this links the math based animation which is on the position map
; to the graphic animation which is on the cube div object
(defn update-fn[]
    ; set rotation for webkit
    (set!
     (-> cube .-style .-webkitTransform)
     (str "rotate(" (Math/floor (.-rotation position)) "deg)"))
    ; set rotation for firefox
    (set!
     (-> cube .-style .-moz-transform-origin)
     (str "rotate(" (Math/floor (.-rotation position)) "deg)"))

    ; set x position
    (set!
     (-> cube .-style .-left)
     (str  (.-x position) "px"))
    ; set y position
    (set!
     (-> cube .-style .-top)
     (str  (.-y position) "px")))
```

Now that we have the update-fn function, we can prepare the animation itself, and since the animation will be called many times to move the cube, let's wrap this in a ClojureScript function named tween.

This is hardcore ClojureScript chained code from JavaScript, so do follow along line by line.

```
(defn tween [_x _y _rot]
    (->
    ; the tween object takes a before animation object
    ; the TWEEN module contains a Tween class and this
    ; done in clojurescript using the dot . notation
    ; new create a new object
     (new js/TWEEN.Tween position)
     ; the final position. Again a Javascript map with the same
     ; keys as the before animation object
     ; 2000 is the amount of time for the animation
     (.to
        (clj->js {:x _x :y _y :rotation _rot}) 2000)
     ; the delay before the animation is started
     (.delay 100)
     ; what kind of animation to apply
     (.easing js/TWEEN.Easing.Elastic.InOut)
     ; the function to use on frame update
     (.onUpdate update-fn)
     ; start the animation
     (.start)))
```

Finally, let's call the animation every 3 seconds with a random target position on the screen.

```
(js/setInterval
    #(tween (rand-int 300) (rand-int 300) (rand-int 360) 3000)
```

In the index.html file, you obviously need the required div before animating it. Let's make it as rainbow as possible and choose a nice gradient for the square:

```
<style>
    .main {
    background: red; /* not working, let's see some red */
    background: -moz-linear-gradient( top ,
        rgba(255, 0, 0, 1) 0%,
        rgba(255, 255, 0, 1) 15%,
        rgba(0, 255, 0, 1) 30%,
        rgba(0, 255, 255, 1) 50%,
        rgba(0, 0, 255, 1) 65%,
        rgba(255, 0, 255, 1) 80%,
        rgba(255, 0, 0, 1) 100%);
    background: -webkit-gradient(linear, left top, left bottom,
        color-stop(0%, rgba(255, 0, 0, 1)),
        color-stop(15%, rgba(255, 255, 0, 1)),
        color-stop(30%, rgba(0, 255, 0, 1)),
```

```
        color-stop(50%, rgba(0, 255, 255, 1)),
        color-stop(65%, rgba(0, 0, 255, 1)),
        color-stop(80%, rgba(255, 0, 255, 1)),
        color-stop(100%, rgba(255, 0, 0, 1)));
        position:absolute;
        top: 100px;
        left: 100px;
        width: 100px;
        height: 100px;
        padding: 1em;
    }
    </style>
```

Then in the body of the html page, use the .main style:

```
<div id="main" style=".main"></div>
```

And enjoy the square shape moving around... as in Figures 3-19 and 3-20.

oday is a wonderful day. What to do ?

Figure 3-19. *Moving square shape, shot 1*

Today is a wonderful day. W

Figure 3-20. *Moving square shape, shot 2*

In case you want to try it out, you can also chain animation in the TweenJS framework using the chain function. With the following, the shape will be moving back and forth.

```
(def tween
    (-> (new js/TWEEN.Tween position)
    (.to (clj->js {:x 700 :y 200 :rotation 359}) 2000)
    (.delay 1000)
    (.easing js/TWEEN.Easing.Elastic.InOut)
    (.onUpdate update-fn)))

(def tween-back
    (-> (new js/TWEEN.Tween position)
    (.to (clj->js {:x 100 :y 100 :rotation 0}) 3000)
    (.easing js/TWEEN.Easing.Elastic.InOut)
    (.onUpdate update-fn)))

(.chain tween tween-back)
(.chain tween-back tween)
(.start tween)
```

Try it out!

Also, any TweenJS animation can also be used on an image, or on a text or any html element. In the html page, it is possible to replace the simple square shape of the div element, with, say, an img tag.

See an example of a cat, using a simple png image.

```
<img
style="position:absolute;top:100px;left:100px;height:100px;
width:80px;"  src="http://www.freeiconspng.com/uploads/black-cat-png-7.png"
id="main">
</img>
```

And the resulting animation, as in Figure 3-21.

Today is a wonderful day

Figure 3-21. *Rotating cat*

The style="position:absolute;" is a required attribute for TweenJS to calculate the position properly, it seems, so let's not forget to add it to the style of the element.

Animation can be composed as well. So if an animation is changing the opacity of an element, and another one is moving the element around, those two can be done at the same time as well.

The small piece of code changes the opacity of the target element by gradually changing the opacity value defined in the style.

```
(def target {:opacity 0})
(defn update-fn2 []
   (set!
    (-> cube .-style .-opacity)
    (.-opacity target)))

(->
   (new js/TWEEN.Tween target)
   (.to (clj->js {:opacity 0.5}) 10000)
   (.onUpdate update-fn2)
   (.start))
```

Running this animation makes the image slowly fade in. The animation will start on page load/refresh, and so a combination of the shape's movement and fade-in is composed, and the cat will be lying down on its right-hand side, as shown in Figure 3-22.

Figure 3-22. *Composition of move and fade in image*

Your turn to make the cat stand up clear and up again!

For convenience, Table 3-1 provides the most used tweening animation styles. In each case, the In or Out postfix is used to indicate if the animation should be done more from the start-point view or more from the end-point view, and InOut means it should be applied to the beginning and the end of the animation.

Table 3-1. *Most Used Easing Functions*

Easing Method	Move
Cubic.In	
Cubic.Out	
Cubic.InOut	
Bounce.Out	
Bounce.In	
Bounce.InOut	
Back.In	

(continued)

155

Table 3-1. (*continued*)

Easing Method	Move
Back.Out	
Back.InOut	
Elastic.In	
Elastic.Out	
Elastic.InOut	

And more examples have their JavaScript source on the tween github web site:

```
https://github.com/tweenjs/tween.js
```

Tame the HTML5 Creation Engine: Pixi

Animations with TweenJS can be done easily and are pretty powerful already on simple HTML elements. But when you want to use the full power of an animation engine, you can easily migrate to the PixiJS engine.

Now in version 4, the Pixi Engine offers engine-specific feature like Spritesheet animation, tiling, graphics, texture, filters, layers, and so on.

Its usage feels like a full-blown extension to the TweenJS framework.

Setup with Boot feels very similar, and is simply done through gain adding the cljsjs prepackaged library.

Our very first example in ClojureScript will get a rotating cat on the canvas, and we will build up on it to get other Sprites and user interactions set up.

Setting Up the Stage: Init the Pixi Engine

To get started, the build.boot file needs the cljsjs library to be added to the dependencies:

```
[cljsjs/pixi "3.0.7-0"]
```

The required files are in the project, so restarting "build dev" will get you ready for the coding part.

Where TweenJS could work on any HTML element, the Pixi Engine works on a canvas element. The rendering canvas element is added through a renderer. The render has a type, size, and some JavaScript properties.

A minimum WebGL setup is presented in the following:

```
(ns frontend.app
    (:require  [cljsjs.pixi]))

(defn init [])

(def renderer
    (new js/PIXI.WebGLRenderer
        500
        400
        (clj->js {:backgroundColor "0x1099bb"})))

(.appendChild
    (.-body js/document)
    (.-view renderer))
```

Just like other JavaScript interops, the Pixi library is added through require, the renderer is a PIXI.WebGLRenderer, and it is added to the body of the html page. Since the element is added dynamically, the HTML page itself does not have any additional setup this time.

Additionally, the engine has one or many stage object(s) that represent a scene of the animation and are defined as PIXI containers.

```
(def stage
    (new js/PIXI.Container))
```

That's it for the base Pixi setup; now let's welcome the rotating cat.

157

Rotating Cat: Load and Add to the Stage

To first load the cat Sprite, we use the Pixi loader to prefetch its image, and use a callback for when the loading has been finished and the resource has been fetched. The fetch is done via the engine using an AJAX call.

Here, the black-cat.png image is fetched from the html folder of the project. The loaded image is assigned a unique ID, here Neko, and the callback is fired when loading has finished.

```
(defn cat-loaded[loader resources]
    (.alert js/window "cat loaded"))

(.load
    (.add (.-loader js/PIXI) "neko" "black-cat.png")
cat-loaded)
```

Once the loading is finished, the event fires and the dialog shows up, as in Figure 3-23.

Figure 3-23. *Resource loading events*

Obviously we haven't gone all this way just to display an alert message. Let's define a few properties of the cute black cat. Since we will access it through various places, let's make an atom out of it too.

```
(def neko (atom nil))

(defn cat-loaded[loader resources]
    (reset! neko (new js/PIXI.Sprite (.-texture (.-neko resources)) ))
        (set! (.-x (.-position @neko)) 200)
        (set! (.-y (.-position @neko)) 200)
        (set! (.-x (.-scale @neko)) 0.05)
        (set! (.-y (.-scale @neko)) 0.05)

        (.addChild stage @neko))
```

Position and scale are properties of the Sprite object, and those are being set using ClojureScript interop, via the set! Function and the property being referenced using the dot-dash notation (.-).

Finally, the cat is added to the stage, through the addChild method of the stage object.

158

This is all worked and compiled fine, but if you look at the rendered scene, you would find it very, very black, as in, while things were running behind the scene, nothing really happened visually.

The scene needs to be rendered, and for a first try, we'll set the stage to render when the cat has finished loading, so from the cat-loaded callback.

```
(defn cat-loaded[loader resources]
    (reset! neko (new js/PIXI.Sprite (.-texture (.-neko resources)) ))
        ...
        (.addChild stage @neko)
        (.render renderer stage))
```

Look who's in Figure 3-24.

Figure 3-24. *PIXI-based cat*

Rotating Cat: Animate Loop

So the cat is finally showing and all, but it's not being very active. Maybe a Monday morning thing, but let's try to make him be slightly crazier.

We will use three blocks of code for this:

- move-neko: a function updating the math position of the cat

- animate: does the stage rendering using the cat's new position

- JavaScript timer: asks for rendering every x milliseconds

```
; this updates the neko sprite properties, notably, its rotation
(defn move-neko[]
    (when (some? @neko)
        (set! (.-rotation @neko) (- (.-rotation @neko) 0.05))))
```

```
; this updates the sprite, and renders the stage
(defn animate[]
    (move-neko)
    (.render renderer stage))
```

```
; this calls animate every 500milliseconds.
(js/setInterval
    #(js/requestAnimationFrame animate)
    500)
```

Note the (.render renderer stage) call in the cat-loaded callback is not needed anymore, since the stage is already asked to be rendered every 500ms.

And the cat should now be rotating on the screen, as in Figure 3-25.

Figure 3-25. *Rotating cat*

The animation does not have to be looping forever, of course. Here the cat is doing one full rotation by slowly moving its position every 10ms.

```
(dotimes [i 130]
    (js/setTimeout #(js/requestAnimationFrame animate) (* 10 i)))
```

Another way of orchestrating things is to move the cat, and ask for the rendering at different times. In the following updated code, the animate function does not update the cat rotation anymore. The rotation is done in a different timer, where there is no need to ask for the animation frame since it is only updating properties of the cat Sprite.

```
(defn animate[]
    ; (move-neko)
    (.render renderer stage))
```

```
(js/setInterval
    #(js/requestAnimationFrame animate)
    500)

(dotimes [i 130]
    (js/setTimeout move-neko  (* 10 i)))
```

You'll see the updates are notably out of sync, but this is pretty much what was expected.

Except for only a few Sprites, having all the udpate code in the animate function works quite well. Also, to avoid the use of a timer, asking for a new rendering frame at the end of the animate function is the smoothest choice you can make. So the animate function is calling itself via requestAnimationFrame.

Since no timer is calling animate anymore, make sure you are calling it once, to kick-start the animation loop as shown in the following:

```
(defn animate[]
    (move-neko)
    (.render renderer stage)
    (js/requestAnimationFrame animate))

(animate)
```

Rotating Cat: Event Listener

Listeners can be added to Sprite using familiar event handlers. The following short piece of code will double the size of the Sprite, when the Sprite itself is clicked or tapped.

First we create the double-size callback.

```
(defn double-size[sprite]
  (let [scale (-> sprite .-scale)]
    (set! (.-x scale) (* 1.25 (.-x scale)))
    (set! (.-y scale) (* 1.25 (.-y scale)))))
```

The Sprite needs to be told it will be interactive and will receive events with the .-interactive properties.

Then a simple "click" handler is added with the previously defined double-size function as callback parameter. Nicely enough, this is a genuine ClojureScript function.

```
(defn cat-loaded[loader resources]
    (reset! neko (new js/PIXI.Sprite (.-texture (.-neko resources)) ))
          (set! (.-interactive @neko) true)
          ...
          (.addChild stage @neko)
          (.on @neko "click" #(double-size @neko)))
```

And now is the time to give your click addiction some fulfillment. Observe the result in Figure 3-26.

Figure 3-26. *Double-sized cat*

Rotating Cat and Sliding Frog: Two Sprites on Stage

To conclude this short Pixi section, let's review how to add and animate two sprites onscreen.

The following longer code listing takes from the previous code and refactors some methods to be able to add a new Sprite more easily.

The frog is also defined as an atom and has its own loaded and move functions. Finally, clicking the frog does not change the frog size or moves, but changes the cat size itself by making it smaller.

```
(def renderer
    (new js/PIXI.WebGLRenderer
        500
        400
        (clj->js {:backgroundColor "0x1099bb"})))

(.appendChild
    (.-body js/document)
    (.-view renderer))

(def stage
    (new js/PIXI.Container))

(def neko (atom nil))
(defn move-neko[]
    (when (some? @neko)
        (set! (.-rotation @neko) (- (.-rotation @neko) 0.05))))
```

```
(def frog (atom nil))
(defn move-frog[]
    (if (some? @frog)
        (let [pos  (.-x (.-position @frog))]
         (if (> 400 pos)
            (set! (.-x (.-position @frog)) (inc pos))
            (set! (.-x (.-position @frog)) 0)))))

(defn scale-me[sprite factor]
 (let [scale (.-scale sprite)]
    (set! (.-x scale) (* factor (.-x scale)))
    (set! (.-y scale) (* factor (.-y scale)))))

(defn sprite-size[sprite px py sx sy i]
        (set! (.-interactive sprite) i)
        (set! (.-x (.-position sprite)) px)
        (set! (.-y (.-position sprite)) py)
        (set! (.-x (.-scale sprite)) sx)
        (set! (.-y (.-scale sprite)) sy))

(defn cat-loaded[loader resources]
    (reset! neko (new js/PIXI.Sprite (.-texture (.-neko resources)) ))
    (sprite-size @neko 200 200 0.05 0.05 true)
    (.addChild stage @neko)
    (.on @neko "click" #(scale-me @neko 1.25)))

(.load
  (.add (.-loader js/PIXI) "neko" "black-cat.png") cat-loaded)

(defn frog-loaded[loader resources]
    (reset! frog (new js/PIXI.Sprite (.-texture (.-frog resources)) ))
    (sprite-size @frog 20 20 0.5 0.5 true)
    (.addChild stage @frog)
    (.on @frog "click" #(scale-me @neko 0.75)))

(.load
  (.add (.-loader js/PIXI) "frog" "froggu.png") frog-loaded)

(defn animate[]
    (move-neko)
    (move-frog)
    (.render renderer stage)
    (js/requestAnimationFrame animate))

(animate)
```

And here you go! Frog and cat, as shown in Figure 3-27.

Figure 3-27. *Frog and cat Sprite*

Now, this small introduction has probably sparked some inspiration in your mind, so time to go ahead and practice moving the frog, adding many more frogs, and counting points. Who's going to win: the cat or the frog? Your turn to say!

What Really Matters: Physics Engine

On the road to animation and fun screen interaction, you probably remember flying birds and their fantastic usage of a physics engine to get them fly through bricks, walls, barrels, and pretty much everything a bird would wish to be flying through.

In this section introducing the matter engine through ClojureScript, we will review such an engine through different "worlds," each with different shapes, movements, and interaction with other shapes.

Setting Up the Physics Engine

There is also a cljsjs-packaged version of matter, and you can use it by adding the following dependency to your build.boot file:

```
[cljsjs/matter "0.9.1-0"]
```

And the related import in the frontend.app namespace:

```
(ns frontend.app
    (:require [cljsjs.matter]))
```

To get started with the engine, we will add a few sugar-coated shortcuts to the main parts of the engine:

- world

- engine

- Bodies

- composites

- common

Those are all defined under the Matter module, so we will make shortcuts to use from ClojureScript.

```
(def World
    js/Matter.World)
(def Engine
    js/Matter.Engine)
(def Bodies
    js/Matter.Bodies)
(def Composites
    js/Matter.Composites)
(def Common
    js/Matter.Common)

(def engine
    (.create Engine
        (.-body js/document)))
(def options
    (-> engine .-render .-options))
```

We will see slowly how each component does matter. For now, let's remember that

- Bodies are shapes,

- world contains all the Bodies, and

- the engine animates the shapes in the world.

Now let's head to a first example to drop shapes on a ground.

World 1: Free-Falling Wire-Framed Boxes

World-1 will define three boxes and a ground body, all using the Bodies module to define the shapes.

The JavaScript Bodies.rectangle function takes four parameters: x, y, width, height.

Additionally, the function takes in a map to specify its interaction mode with the other Bodies.

165

Here boxA, boxB, and boxC have the same shape in different locations in the world, and ground is set to be static, thus not moved by the gravity.

Finally, shapes are added to the world via the World module, on the engine's world as an array of Bodies.

Finally, the wireframes options specify we are only interested in the contours of the shapes.

```
(defn world-1 []

  (let[ boxA
       (.rectangle Bodies 400 200 80 80)
         boxB
       (.rectangle Bodies 450 50 80 80)
         boxC
       (.rectangle Bodies 450 150 80 80)
         ground
       (.rectangle Bodies 400 610 810 60
           (clj->js {:isStatic true}))]

  (.add World
       (.-world engine)
       (clj->js [boxA boxB boxC ground]))

  (set! (.-wireframes options) true)))
```

The first world is ready, so let's run it! This is done through the nicely named run function on the engine.

```
(world-1)
(.run Engine engine)
```

Observe the shapes falling from their original position, and bouncing on each other, as if really dropped under Earth gravity, as shown in Figure 3-28.

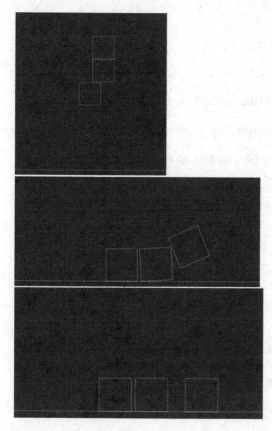

Figure 3-28. *Gravity effect*

After playing around with more shapes, and maybe different grounds laid out in the world, time to put a bit more color and user interaction in a second example.

World 2: So Many Clicks, So Many Shapes

In this second example, we will make composite shapes appear in the world when performing a mouse click on it.

We will need a few more of the Google namespaces we have already seen to manipulate dom and React to events, so let's add those to the current namespace:

```
(ns frontend.app
    (:require
        [goog.dom :as dom]
        [goog.events :as events]
        [cljsjs.matter]))
```

In this example, we'll use stack of Bodies that will be created using the stack function of the Composites module.

Composites are made of multiple simple shapes, and in this example we'll use polygons with random sizes and shapes.

Defining a new group of shapes will be done through the stack function and the shape creating callback.

First comes the composites-fn function that will create a random shape. The first random number is the number of sides, and the second random number is the size of the shape.

```
(defn composites-fn [x y]
    (.polygon Bodies
        x
        y
        (.random Common 1 50)
        (.random Common 1 50)))
```

Then comes the function that makes use of the preceding function for an array of 3×3 with no space in between the shapes (hence the 0 0 as number parameters). The function adds the **stack** of elements to the world using the same module/method that was seen in world-1.

```
(defn add-composites [x y]
    (let [stack (.stack Composites x y 3 3 0 0 composites-fn)]
    (.add World
        (.-world engine) stack)))
```

To add the ground, we reuse again the same Bodies.rectangle function, but add the isStatic properties to the shape.

```
(defn add-ground []
    (let [ground (.rectangle Bodies 400 610 810 60
            (clj->js {:isStatic true}))]
    (.add World
        (.-world engine) ground)))
```

The rest of the code for the world-2 is quite easy to read, linearly adding the ground, a first batch of composite shapes, and a simple click handler using the dom.events library.

```
(defn world-2 []
    (add-ground)
    (add-composites 150 20)
    (set! (.-wireframes options) false)

    (let [body (dom/getElement "mybody")]

  (events/listen
    body
    "click"
    #(add-composites (.-clientX %) (.-clientY %) ))))
```

Then to run world-2!

```
(world-2)
(.run Engine engine)
```

After a few mouse clicks, it should be a nice colored mess as in Figure 3-29.

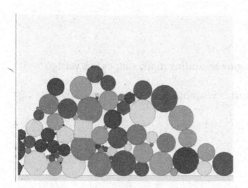

Figure 3-29. *Colored circles*

Now you do not have to be stuck with polygons, and you can use textures on shapes using the render.sprite.texture property of each body. If you replace the composites-fn with the following, that sets a texture on the Sprite creating function.

```
(defn composites-fn [x y]
    (.polygon Bodies x y (.random Common 1 50) (.random Common 1 50)
        (clj->js {:render {:sprite {:texture "landgiraffe.png"}}})))
```

You should end up with something similar to the giraffes from Figure 3-30.

Figure 3-30. A pile of giraffes

World 3: Equilibrum

World-3 plays on the limits of the physics engine by adding many shapes in a vertigo equilibrium.

The sample is very short, and reuses most of what has been seen in a slightly expanded way.

```
(defn composites-fn-2[x y]
    (.circle Bodies x y 20))

(defn world-3[]
    (add-ground)
    (set! (.-wireframes options) false)
    (let[ stack (.stack Composites 100 185 10 10 20 0 composites-fn-2)]
    (.add World (.-world engine) stack)))

(world-3)
(.run Engine engine)
```

Wow. How is this physically possible? Figure 3-31 is loosing its balance already.

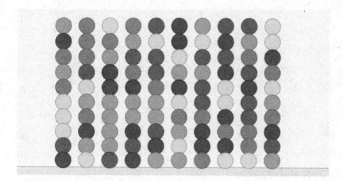

Figure 3-31. *Equilibrium*

World 4: Same Shape, Different Forces

This last matter example plays with the same shape falling at different speeds given their frictionAir property value. The higher the value, the "heavier" the shape looks, and its associated interaction will look like it is slow compared to the other one.

```
(defn world-4[]
    (add-ground)
    (set! (.-wireframes options) false)
    (.add World (.-world engine)
        (clj->js
            [
            (.rectangle Bodies 200 100 60 60 (clj->js {:frictionAir 0.001}))
            (.rectangle Bodies 400 100 60 60 (clj->js {:frictionAir 0.05}))
            (.rectangle Bodies 600 100 60 60 (clj->js {:frictionAir 0.1}))
            ])))

(world-4)
(.run Engine engine)
```

Different friction settings on the shapes give a slower gravity movement, as shown in Figure 3-32.

Figure 3-32. *FrictionAir settings and movement*

For the remaining of the Matter library API, do have a look at the API doc at the following location:

```
http://brm.io/matter-js/docs/index.html
```

Now, you might enjoy physics like never before!

Distributed MQTT Messaging with Paho and Mosquitto

Let's take a small break from animation and graphical interface; this example of communicating with an MQTT server takes more time to set up than to code.

MQTT servers are lightweight messaging servers targeting with a very small footprint; they mostly target IoT devices but can be used in other situations.

Here we want to send distributed messages to a topic defined on an MQTT server using the MQTT server named Mosquitto, and no, it does not bite as much as it sounds.

A ClojureScript client will communicate directly to the websocket-based Mosquitto server and display messages directly in your client application.

Setup

We will introduce the Paho library, which can communicate with Mosquitto, and will add it to your build.boot dependency section. We will also reuse the dommy library to display the new MQTT messages as they are coming along.

```
[cljsjs/paho "1.0.1-0"]
[prismatic/dommy "1.1.0"]
```

Next, get a copy of the Mosquitto server from the download page:

```
https://mosquitto.org/download/
```

The server can be started as is, using the command line. In this example, we go one extra step by adding a configuration file to set up the websocket mode of Mosquitto, so it can be accessed from the JavaScript client directly.

The configuration file will be put in a file surprisingly named mosquitto.conf. containing the following two lines:

```
listener 8000
protocol websockets
```

This configuration tells Mosquitto to start on port 8000 and set up the websocket protocol. Now, the Mosquitto server can then be started using this configuration:

```
NikoMacBook% mosquitto -c mosquitto.conf

1490010758: mosquitto version 1.4.10 (build date 2016-08-31 20:09:41+0100)
starting
1490010758: Config loaded from mosquitto.conf.
1490010758: Opening websockets listen socket on port 8000.
```

Finally, we'll use an external MQTT client to make it transparent this is a can be used from IoT device to JavaScript frontend. We will use mqtt-spy, which can be downloaded from

```
https://github.com/eclipse/paho.mqtt-spy/wiki/Downloads
```

The downloaded client is a executable jar file, that can be started using the following command:

```
java -jar mqtt-spy-0.6.0-beta-b56-jar-with-dependencies.jar
```

A new connection will be set up using settings as shown in Figure 3-33.

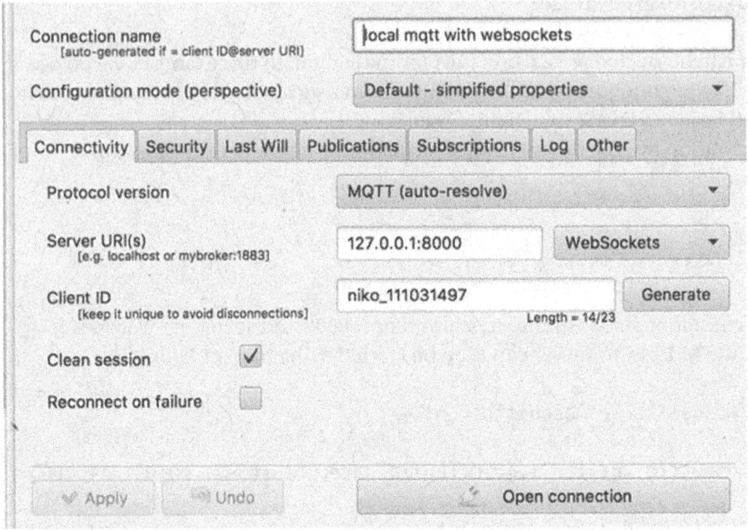

Figure 3-33. *Connection settings*

The connection will be done over websockets, and port is set up to 8000 as defined in the server properties. This could obviously be connecting to a remote server.

MQTT ClojureScript Showcase

In the following code sample, we connect to the MQTT server using the paho client. The client is prepared with one callback each for connectionLost, messageArrived, success, and failure.

On a successful connect, the client will subscribe to the /cljs/paho topic and send/ receive messages to that topic.

Incoming messages will be shown onscreen, by using the dommy library and adding new elements to the html body.

The coming ClojureScript code example comes with two new things:

The {:qos 0} is defined as a JavaScript map directly. This does the same job as the clj->js macro that was used many times before.

```
(.subscribe client topic #js {:qos 0})
```

The second line is the Clojure declare usage:

```
(declare client send-message)
```

The on-connect function makes use of the send-message function before it is actually defined, so we do an ahead declaration so the Compiler does not complain about a missing symbol.

The rest of the code is now rather easy-going, so here comes the frontend.app namespace in full:

```clojure
(ns frontend.app
    (:require
      [cljsjs.paho]
      [frontend.utils :as utils]))

(declare client send-message)

(def topic "/cljsjs/paho")

(defn on-connect []
  (println "Connected")
  (.subscribe client topic #js {:qos 0})
  (println "Subscribed")
  (send-message "Hello MQTT!" topic 0)
  (println "Sent message."))

(defn send-message [payload destination qos]
  (let [msg (Paho.MQTT.Message. payload)]
    (set! (.-destinationName msg) destination)
    (set! (.-qos msg) qos)
    (.send client msg)))

(defn connect []
  (let [mqtt (Paho.MQTT.Client. "127.0.0.1" 8000       "")
        connectOptions (js/Object.)]

       (set! (.-onConnectionLost mqtt)
           (fn [reasonCode reasonMessage]
             (println reasonCode reasonMessage)))

       (set! (.-onMessageArrived mqtt) (fn [msg]
         (utils/append-node "body" "div"
           (str "Topic: " (.-destinationName msg)
           " : "
           " Payload: " (.-payloadString msg)))))

       (set! (.-onSuccess connectOptions) (fn [] (on-connect)))

       (set! (.-onFailure connectOptions ) (fn [_ _ msg]
           (println "Failure Connect: " msg)))

       (.connect mqtt connectOptions )
       mqtt))

(def client (connect))
```

In Figure 3-34, messages sent from MQTT Spy (on the right) are shown in the ClojureScript application (on the left).

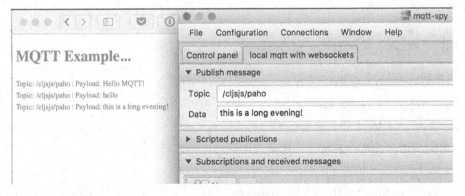

Figure 3-34. MQTT messages in MQTT Spy and ClojureScript application

It would not be too hard to add an input field to get some text from the user, and reuse the send-message function to send messages to the MQTT topic and conversely get them to show up in the MQTT-spy user interface.

It's now up to you!

Upping Your Game with PhaserJS

Talent wins games, but teamwork and intelligence win championships.

Michael Jordan

If you have never heard of this wonderful JavaScript gaming library, then it is indeed a stroke of luck that you got this book, because it will give you a gentle introduction that will set your imagination on fire.

PhaseJS is a gaming library that pretty much sums up all the previous libraries we have seen.

In the same concept you have been following for the other libraries, the idea is to get a solid ClojureScript base for you to make your own adventure. The in and outs of the PhaserJS library will be left out of this book.

This game engine can be used to build your own games, of course, but can also be used in animations with some user interaction, without the need to be a full-blown game.

If you simply need to put sounds asynchronously and change display depending on remote IoT devices, this is also a great way to create a pleasant user interface.

Lay Out the Game

For the most part, PhaserJS will feel comfortable with its asset loader, update, and render functions doing the same tasks as shown in the Pixi Engine examples.

The four functions to create a PhaserJS game are as follows:

- preload: to asynchronously load all the assets

- create: to prepare the stage and put the Sprite in place

- update: to update the positions of the different Sprites, perform collision checks, and so on

- render: to do specific routines needed when performing visual rendering.

This first example puts the different PhaseJS objects and functions in place. We define the four functions, with preload-fn and create-fn preloading and playing music.

The function create-fn also adds some text to the game scene and sets up the background color.

```
(ns frontend.app00
  (:require [cljsjs.phaser]))

(defn init [])

(declare game)

(def music
  (atom nil))

(defn preload-fn []
  (let [loader (.-load game)]
    (.audio loader "boden"  "assets/goaman.mp3")))

(defn create-fn[]
  (let [adder (.-add game)]
    ; add text using adder, and style
    (.text
      adder
      (- (-> game .-world .-centerX) 10)
      (- (-> game .-world .-centerY) 0)
      "Welcome to a \n new world of \n adventures!"
      #js { :font "24px Verdana" :fill "white" :align "center"})

    ; set the stage background color
    (set! (-> game .-stage .-backgroundColor) "#182d3b")

    ; play music
    (reset! music (.audio adder "boden"))
    (.add (.-onDecoded @music) #(.fadeIn @music 4000))))
```

```
(defn update-fn[])

(defn render-fn[])

(def game
  (new Phaser.Game
    800 600
    Phaser.AUTO
    "phaser-example"
    #js
    {:preload preload-fn
     :create create-fn
     :update update-fn
     :render render-fn} ))
```

The html page needs a div element with the same id as the phaser game, here:

```
<div id="phaser-example"/>
```

Everything should be in place, and if compilation works fine, you should now have some peaceful nature sound music playing in the background and the welcoming text showing up on the scene as in Figure 3-35.

Figure 3-35. *Welcome to a new world of adventures*

Adding a Sprite: Where Is the Bee?

Say you now want to add a new Sprite in the game. The Sprite will be a simple bee image that will be animated in the game scene.

First the Sprite is preloaded using the loader as was done for the music. As before, the Sprite is defined as an atom, so it can be easily accessed from different places in the code.

```
(def sprite-bee  (atom nil))
(defn preload-fn []
  (let [loader (.-load game)]
    (.image loader "bee"    "bumblybee.png")
    (.audio loader "boden"  "assets/goaman.mp3")))
```

The create-fn then adds the Sprite at a given location, x=200 and y=400, using the loader reference "bee." For the bee to be able to interact with controls, we also enable the arcade mode on it.

```
(defn create-fn[]
  (let [adder (.-add game)]
    ; start physics engine
    (.startSystem (.-physics game) js/Phaser.Physics.ARCADE)

    ; bee
    (reset! sprite-bee
      (.sprite adder 200 400 "bee"))
    (.set (.-anchor @sprite-bee) 0.5 0.5)
    (.enable (.-arcade (.-physics game)) @sprite-bee)

    ; set the stage background color
    (set! (-> game .-stage .-backgroundColor) "#0db7cf")
```

The bee is flying in Figure 3-36.

Figure 3-36. A bee enters the scene!

Now let's make the bee move around the screen to get closer to the mouse pointer, and at the same time, let's make it fly around in circles, like bees always do.

The update-fn function gets some upgrades. The distance from the bee Sprite to the pointer onscreen is computed through the game.physics.arcade object. The Sprite is moved accordingly to get closer to the pointer, or its velocity is set down to 0 if it is already within 10 pixels.

In the last line, you would remember the same rotation that was applied to the rotating cat a few pages ago.

```
(defn update-fn[]
  (let [arcade (-> game .-physics .-arcade) ]

    (if (> (.distanceToPointer arcade @sprite-bee
         (-> game .-input .-activePointer)) 10)
      (.moveToPointer arcade @sprite-bee 300)
      (.set (-> @sprite-bee .-body .-velocity) 0))

    (set! (.-rotation @sprite-bee) (+ 0.01 (.-rotation @sprite-bee)))))))
```

Figure 3-37 shows the bee rotating.

Figure 3-37. *Rotating bee*

Cat Walk and Moon Walk: The PhaserJS Animation Manager

We know you have been used to cute Sprites moving around the screen, animated, and responding to click events as well, and we know you cannot wait to do the same using code from PhaseJS.

The next example shows how to load a Spritesheet using PhaseJS and then animate the Sprite using the Animation Manager attached to each Sprite.

A Spritesheet loads all the graphic assets of a Sprite in one single file; then, by using offsets or a specific index of elements, you can cleverly access any subsection and display the Sprite or the animation you really want.

The preloading is done using the Spritesheet function on the game assets loader.

The Spritesheet in Figure 3-38 contains four frames.

Figure 3-38. *Cat Spritesheet*

We will load the Spritesheet and use it to make the cat walk on the screen using all the frames.

The preload function has been reduced to only load the given Spritesheet, and the create-fn only loads the sheet, defines the walk animation, and then starts the animation itself.

The parameters for the Spritesheet function are as follows:

1. sheetname, here "Neko"

2. filename, "assets/cats.jpeg", loaded from the html folder

3. width, here 60 (total width 240 divided by nb frames)

4. height here 86

5. total number of frames in the sheet, here 4

```
(def neko (atom nil))

(defn preload-fn []
  (let [loader (.-load game)]
    (.spritesheet loader "neko" "assets/cats.jpeg" 60 86 4)))

(defn create-fn[]
  (let [adder (.-add game)]

  (set! (-> game .-stage .-backgroundColor) "#ffffff")

  (reset! neko (.sprite adder 350 350 "neko"))
  (.set (.-anchor @neko) 0.5)
  (.set (.-scale @neko) 3)

  ; 5 stands for the framerate
  ; true for looping the animation
  (.add (.-animations @neko) "walk" 5 true)
  (.play (.-animations @neko) "walk") ))
```

The (.-animations @neko) refers to the animations module bounded to the loaded Spritesheet.

The .add function defines an animation from the Spritesheet, and .play starts playing it. The result gives an animation of a running cat, as can almost be seen in Figure 3-39.

Figure 3-39. Animated running cat

Now, PhaserJS animations are very flexible, and you can easily customize them by choosing the frames you want to use for any given animation. See this second "cat walk" animation in the following, which uses frames in a specific order, as well as reusing the same frame multiple times in the same animation.

```
(.add (.-animations @neko)"walk2" #js [1 2 3 4 3 2] 10 true)
(.play (.-animations @neko) "walk2")
```

In the preceding code, the .add function takes a new JavaScript array selecting the frames of the animation one by one. The framerate was also updated to 10 frames per second, which resulted in a smoother animation.

Now, it's time to create a few more animations on your own!

Reacting to User Events

Sprites can React to events via the animations module. Each Sprite has one instance attached to it, and the module can be accessed to the animations property of the Sprite.

The running cat could be stopped by clicking it. For this, we would need to

1. enable input on the Sprite

2. register a new event handler for inputdown

3. in the event callback, stop the currently showing animation

The following small snippet can be added to the create-fn function, after the animation definitions.

```
(set! (.-inputEnabled @neko) true)

(.add (-> @neko .-events .-onInputDown)
    (.stop (.-currentAnim (.-animations @neko))))
```

When the cat is clicked, the event handler checks the currentAnim property of the mounted animations module on @neko, and the current animation is stopped.

```
And ... the ... cat ... it stopped...
```

It would be nice to get the cat running on another click. At the same time, it would be nice to see it moving around the screen as well. The create-fn and update-fn function can now be easily adapted:

```
(defn create-fn[]
  (let [adder (.-add game)]
    (.startSystem (.-physics game) js/Phaser.Physics.ARCADE)
    (set! (-> game .-stage .-backgroundColor) "#ffffff")

    (reset! neko (.sprite adder 350 350 "neko"))
    (.set (.-anchor @neko) 0.5)
    (.set (.-scale @neko) 3)
    (.add (.-animations @neko)"walk2" #js [0 1 2 3 2 2] 10 true)
    (.play (.-animations @neko) "walk2")
    (set! (.-inputEnabled @neko) true)
    (.add (-> @neko .-events .-onInputDown)
      #(if
        (.-isPlaying  (.-currentAnim (.-animations @neko)))
        (.stop (.-currentAnim (.-animations @neko)))
        (.play (.-currentAnim (.-animations @neko)))))
  ))

(defn move-cat[]
  (let[ x (.-x @neko)]
    (if (.-isPlaying  (.-currentAnim (.-animations @neko)))
      (set! (.-x @neko)
      (if (< x 10) 800 (- (.-x @neko) 5))))))

(defn update-fn[]
  (move-cat))
```

And the cat Sprite walks from left to right, its position being reset when it approaches the border of the game area, as shown in Figure 3-40.

Figure 3-40. Running cat Sprite and game borders

On user click, the animation is stopped or restarted depending on whether it was in a playing state or not. Sweet.

phzr: PhaserJS Uses Pure ClojureScript

It would not be fair to talk about PhaseJS for ClojureScript without giving an introduction to the phzr project. It is not sure why the phzr project exists in the first place, but basically, every single PhaseJS function has been automatically ported to ClojureScript via a code generator.

The library is still somewhat experimental but works fantastically well. Include it with

```
[phzr "0.1.0-SNAPSHOT"]
```

Provided you use the phzr library in your build.boot file, code will look **way** more native ClojureScript than using the usual JS interop. The hardest part is to remember the numerous namespaces, but the code will look very, very familiar and easier to use:

```
(ns phzr.demo
  (:require [phzr.core :as p :refer [pset!]]
            [phzr.animation-manager :as pam]
            [phzr.game :as pg]
            [phzr.game-object-factory :as pgof]
            [phzr.loader :as pl]
            [phzr.point :as ppo]
            [phzr.signal :as psg]
            [phzr.sprite :as ps]))

(defn preload
  [game]
  (let [loader (:load game)]
    (doto loader
      (pl/spritesheet "zelda2" "images/zelda2.png" 39 39 80))))
```

```
(defn change-sprite
  [pointer event sprite]
  (if (= "walkr" (:name (:current-anim (:animations sprite))))
    (pam/play (:animations sprite) "walkl" 10 true)
    (pam/play (:animations sprite) "walkr" 10 true)))

(defn create
  [game]
  (let [gof    (:add game)
        sprite (pgof/sprite gof 200 200 "zelda2")]
    (pam/add (:animations sprite) "walkr" (range 4 7))
    (pam/add (:animations sprite) "walkl" [3 2 1 0])

    (pam/play (:animations sprite) "walkr" 10 true)
    (ppo/set (:scale sprite) 3)
    (pset! sprite :smoothed false)
    (pset! (:stage game) :background-color "#ffffff")

    (psg/add (get-in game [:input :on-down])
             change-sprite nil 0
             sprite)))

(defn start []
  (pg/->Game 600 400 (p/phaser-constants :auto) "phzr-demo"
             {"preload" preload
"create"  create}))
```

Running the example and clicking the animated sprite will reverse the animation, and make the Sprite look left or right as shown in Figure 3-41.

Figure 3-41. *Left or right?*

Grand Finale: Websockets and Sprites

This last PhaseJS example would like to combine websocket message with some reactive programming parts, tied directly to the screen visuals. Messages coming from the websocket will alter ClojureScript atoms, and those watchable atoms will change the direction the Sprite is moving on the screen.

This decoupled version of the previous example works quite well in an IoT environment as well. A sensor would send a message to MQTT, telling the onscreen Sprite its direction. Conversely, you could change the direction on the screen and send a message to MQTT to update the direction of, say, a surveillance camera. The user interface would be made in PhaseJS and interact directly with the real world.

The sample code assembles code from both the previous example and the MQTT example to have both phzr and MQTT in action in the same project.

The new topic introduced here is that the atom is the point of contact between the two as opposed to having the callback directly bounded to the MQTT message handler. The message handler updates the watchable atom, and the state change of the atom triggers the update of the onscreen animation. This decoupled version allows for less breakage when developing and moving code around. This also allows you to set up an application state on start, to have the application exactly where you want it to be instead of replaying events to reach the wanted game position.

Here we go for the code part:

```
(ns phzr.demo
  (:require [phzr.core :as p :refer [pset!]]
            [phzr.animation-manager :as pam]
            [phzr.game :as pg]
            [phzr.game-object-factory :as pgof]
            [phzr.loader :as pl]
            [phzr.point :as ppo]
            [phzr.signal :as psg]
            [phzr.sprite :as ps]
            [cljsjs.paho]))

(declare change-sprite client)

(def topic "/cljsjs/phaser")
(def asprite (atom nil))

(defn on-connect []
  (println "connected!")
  (.subscribe client topic #js {:qos 0}))

(def go (atom :right))
(add-watch go key
#(change-sprite))

(defn connect []
  (let [mqtt (Paho.MQTT.Client. "127.0.0.1" 8000   "")
        connectOptions (js/Object.)]
      (set! (.-onConnectionLost mqtt)
        #(println "connection lost"))
      (set! (.-onMessageArrived mqtt)
        (fn [msg] (reset! go (keyword (.-payloadString msg)))))
      (set! (.-onSuccess connectOptions) on-connect)
```

```
        (set! (.-onFailure connectOptions ) #(println "failure"))
        (.connect mqtt connectOptions )
         mqtt))

(def client (connect))

(defn preload
  [game]
  (let [loader (:load game)]
    (doto loader
      (pl/spritesheet "zelda2" "images/zelda2.png" 39 39 80))))

(defn change-sprite
 []
  (when (some? @asprite)
    (case @go
      :right (pam/play (:animations @asprite) "walkr" 10 true)
      :left (pam/play (:animations @asprite) "walkl" 10 true)
(str "not a valid direction:" @go))))

(defn create
  [game]
  (let [gof    (:add game) sprite (pgof/sprite gof 200 200 "zelda2")]
    (reset! asprite sprite)
    (pset! (:stage game) :background-color "#ffffff")
    (pam/add (:animations sprite) "walkr" (range 4 7))
    (pam/add (:animations sprite) "walkl" [3 2 1 0])

    (pam/play (:animations sprite) "walkr" 10 true)
    (ppo/set (:scale sprite) 3)
    (pset! sprite :smoothed false)

    (psg/add (get-in game [:input :on-down])
      #(reset! go
        (if (= @go :right) :left :right)))))

(defn start  []
  (pg/->Game 600 400 (p/phaser-constants :auto) "phzr-demo"
             {"preload" preload
              "create"  create}))
```

Before starting the MQTT server, let's bind it to a proper IP, so it can receive requests from remote machines. The mosquitto.conf becomes

```
listener 8000
protocol websockets
bind_address 0.0.0.0
```

Once you have the Mosquitto server up and running, connect a remote MQTT-spy to it. As in the settings shown in Figure 3-42, the Mosquitto server is running on 172.16.2.31; you would have to change this to your own machine IP settings.

Figure 3-42. *MQTT settings*

Then, sending message left or right to the MQTT topic will update the direction of the animation of the Sprite, by reacting to the atom change of value (Figure 3-43).

Figure 3-43. *MQTT-driven animation*

Sweet! Your imagination should be running wild by now. No limits ...

3-4. ClojureScript on Node.js

Problem

You would like to write code in ClojureScript that can also be compiled and run on the server side.

Solution

Make the ClojureScript Compiler target the Node.js runtime instead of the browser, and use your ClojureScript code on the server side.

How It Works

As you know, the JavaScript is not targeting just the browser anymore, and now the Node.js runtime is getting quite its share of hype for command-line and server-side programming as well.

This section looks at compiling and running ClojureScript for the Node.js runtime, first compiling the code manually, then using Boot tasks, and finally setting up an interactive express with ClojureScript on Node.js workflow.

Compiling ClojureScript for Node.js

ClojureScript code can be compiled using the ClojureScript distribution cljs.jar file using the included build API.

Compiling ClojureScript code for Node.js manually requires a Java runtime to use the jar file and a Clojure (not Script) file to use and execute the build API.

The file to be compiled will be in a src folder, as was done for all projects up to now:

src/hello_world/core.cljs

We'll use this file to execute as the entry point of a script and print out a welcoming, if not charming, message.

A new namespace is introduced, cljs.nodejs, which is then used to set up the print's output target.

```
(ns hello-world.core
  (:require [cljs.nodejs :as nodejs]))

(nodejs/enable-util-print!)

(defn -main [& args]
  (println "Hello world!"))

(set! *main-cli-fn* -main)
```

Also, *main-cli-fn* is bounded to the main function to execute when running the script.

To compile, this time without Boot to actually see how it is done, we will write an executable Clojure file. It is very Boot looking and uses a build function with a folder and some Compiler options. Notice how the :target entry is set to :nodejs; this is different from before.

```
(require 'cljs.build.api)

(cljs.build.api/build "src"
  {:main 'hello-world.core
   :output-to "main.js"
   :target :nodejs})
```

Compiling the code is now done by giving the node.clj file as input to clojure.main on the Java runtime. The classpath, cp, is set to the ClojureScript jar file and the src folder containing the code that is to be compiled.

```
java -cp cljs.jar:src clojure.main node.clj
```

The artifact created by the compilation is a single file named main.js. This file can be run using the Node.js runtime.

```
node main.js
```

And the output is nicely

```
Hello world!
```

You can pass in arguments as well to the script so that if the main method of core.cljs is updated to

```
(defn -main [& args]
  (println "Hello" (first args)))
```

Then the output of "node main.js Mario" would be

```
Hello mario
```

Sweet. But what happened to the ClojureScript REPL?

ClojureScript REPL on Node.js

To get the ClojureScript REPL, we will use another executable Clojure (not script) file.

```
(require 'cljs.repl)
(require 'cljs.repl.node)

(cljs.repl/repl (cljs.repl.node/repl-env)
  :watch "src"
   :output-dir "out")
```

To start the REPL, you can execute this Clojure script; beware of the pun, as for the preceding compilation.

```
java -cp cljs.jar:src clojure.main node_repl.clj
```

If you can install rlwrap, this is highly recommended, so you can get command history by using the up and down keys:

```
rlwrap java -cp cljs.jar:src clojure.main node_repl.clj
```

You can type in ClojureScript code at the REPL, and you can also load any file located in the src folder using require:

```
(require '[hello-world.core])
(ns hello-world.core)
(-main "hello")
```

This will use the –main method from the hello-world.core namespace and will output:

```
Hello  hello
```

Compile to Node.js: Back to Boot

You obviously do not want to do too much of this gymnastic playing with Clojure files, so eventually it will be time to go back to boot and use a regular development workflow.

The following build.boot will do just that, and define two tasks: either compile for dev, by watching the source paths, or a one-off compilation step using advanced compilation mode.

```
(set-env!
 :source-paths    #{"src"}
 :dependencies '[[adzerk/boot-cljs   "1.7.228-2"    :scope "test"]
                 [org.clojure/clojurescript "1.9.456"]])
```

```
(require '[adzerk.boot-cljs        :refer [cljs]])

(deftask dev []
  (comp
    (watch)
    (cljs :optimizations :none
          :compiler-options {:target :nodejs})
    (target)))

(deftask prod []
  (comp
    (cljs :optimizations :advanced
          :compiler-options {:target :nodejs})
    (target)))
```

With the namespace and source file set up just the same as previously, boot dev will compile the ClojureScript code and put the resulting files in the target folder.

To use the generated file with optimizations set to :none, you need to change the directory to the top of the target folder before running the node command.

So:

```
cd target && node main.js
; Hello world!
```

Updating code in the src folder will trigger compilation via the boot dev task, and the generated files in the target folder will be updated accordingly. While the first compilation cycle takes a bit of time, any incremental build is significantly less time-consuming and almost instantaneous on most modern and not-so-modern machines.

Using nodejs-Specific Namespaces: fs

The next example in the Node.js series shows how to use a nodejs-specific object. In particular, we are going to have a quick look at the famous Node.js filesystem object, fs.

While keeping the same project template as the previous Boot for Node.js project, let's update the hello-world.core namespace to use a bit more of node.

See how the Node.js "fs" module is loaded using js/require and then accessed using standard JavaScript/ClojureScript interop code.

```
(ns hello-world.core
  (:require
    [cljs.pprint :as pprint]
    [cljs.nodejs :as nodejs]))

(nodejs/enable-util-print!)
```

```
(def fs (js/require "fs"))
(defn -main [& args]
  (if (empty? args)
    (println "Usage: node main.js <dir>")
    (pprint/pprint
      (js->clj
        (.readdirSync fs (first args))))))

(set! *main-cli-fn* -main)
```

The rest of the file is quite standard ClojureScript code, using cljs.pprint to output pretty formatted data structures.

With "boot dev" running in a command prompt or in a terminal, you would have a new main.js file in the target folder. Executing the file gives

```
% node main.js ..
; ["build.boot" "src" "target"]
```

HTTP Requests with a Third-Party Module

Third-party modules installed via node's package manager npm are behaving the same way and can be used in a similar fashion from ClojureScript code.

To install the dependency itself, place the node_modules in the target folder. To do that, run the install command from the target folder itself, like so:

```
npm install request
```

Once installed, your target folder should contain the following files and folder:

```
main.js
main.out
node_modules
```

As a reminder, the JavaScript code sample to use request on the Google home page is shown in the following:

```
var request = require('request');
request('http://www.google.com', function (error, response, body) {
  console.log('error:', error);
  console.log('statusCode:', response && response.statusCode);
  console.log('body:', body);
});
```

Here, we want to reuse the time example that was used to play earlier on with jQuery, and target the same time API hosted on Google.

The third-party Node.js module is accessed using the same js/require used to import the other core Node.js namespaces.

The request function takes an endpoint and one callback for error and success alike.

```
(ns hello-world.core
  (:require
    [cljs.pprint :as pprint]
    [cljs.nodejs :as nodejs]))

(nodejs/enable-util-print!)

(def request
  (js/require "request"))

(def api
  (str "https://script.google.com/macros/s/"
  "AKfycbyd5AcbAnWi2YnOxhFRbyzS4qMq1VucMVgVvhul5XqS9HkAyJY/"
  "exec?tz="))

(defn -main [& args]
  (request
    (str api (first args))
    (fn[error response body]
      (pprint/pprint body))))

(set! *main-cli-fn* -main)
```

Then you'll be able to run this new node script with

```
node main.js Asia/Tokyo
```

And find out it is the middle of the night in Tokyo again.

A Few Express Notes

Since we are in Node.js and talking about third-party libraries, it would be hard not to talk about express, the uber-famous web framework for node.

Express plays great all the same with ClojureScript and our boot-based workflow.

Our first example will have only one route, and always return the same message.

The main cljs file uses express through js/require and creates a new express app using regular introp code: (express.).

```
(ns hello-world.core
  (:require [cljs.nodejs :as nodejs]))

(nodejs/enable-util-print!)

(def express (js/require "express"))
```

```
(defn -main [& args]
  (doto (express.)
    (.get "/"
      (fn [req res]
        (.send res (str "Hello World"))))
    (.listen 3000))
  (println "nodecljs started on port 3000"))

(set! *main-cli-fn* -main)
```

You'll need to install the third-party library in the target folder:

```
npm install express
```

And then you can start the server from the target folder using

```
node main.js
; nodecljs started on port 3000
```

Accessing localhost:3000 gives the hopeful and optimistic message shown in Figure 3-44.

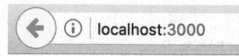

Hello World

Figure 3-44. Hello ClojureScript on Node.js

Because it would not be so fun without a simplistic API and a bit of curl, let's have a look at a slightly more advanced example.

This second express with ClojureScript example introduces a ClojureScript atom, and three routes.

The base route "/" shows some date info based on a JavaScript date object.

The two other routes, get and put on "/counter", display the value of or update the value of an atom named counter in the ClojureScript/express application:

```
(ns hello-world.core
  (:require [cljs.nodejs :as nodejs]))

(nodejs/enable-util-print!)

(def express (nodejs/require "express"))
(def app (express.))
```

```
(def counter (atom 0))
(defn -main [& args]
  (doto app
    (.get "/"
      (fn [req res]
        (.send res
          (str "Hello World<br/>Time is:" (.toISOString (js/Date.))))))
    (.put "/counter"
      (fn [req res] (swap! counter inc) (.send res (str @counter))))
    (.get "/counter"
      (fn [req res] (.send res (str @counter))))
    (.listen 3000))
  (println "nodecljs started on port 3000"))

(set! *main-cli-fn* -main)
```

Starting the app using *node main.js* in the target folder starts the express application, and with the server setup, the following curl commands will update or show the value of the atom.

```
curl localhost:3000/counter
; shows the current value of atom
; returned value is 0
curl -X PUT localhost:3000/counter
; update the counter. In the ClojureScript code, this uses inc
; so the value of the counter is incremented by 1.
; returned value is 1
```

Typing this example, you may have come across a few compilation errors, and you would probably get the server to restart automatically at the same time. Let's see how to do this.

Auto Reload Express App on Code Change

With the same Boot setup as in the preceding, we will be using a Node.js third-party module named nodemon to detect changes in source folders just like Boot watch, and reload the Node.js/express server on code refresh.

The install is straightforward:

```
npm install -g nodemon
```

And if not already done, you should install express in the target folder again.

Then, from the root of the project, the command to start nodemon is simply

```
cd target && nodemon --config ../nodemon.js main.js
```

To get a visual notification on server restart, we will use osascript on OSX, but snoretoast (`https://github.com/KDE/snoretoast`) on Windows works about the same. That notification is included in the ../nodemon.js pointed at in the preceding.

```
{
  "events": {
    "restart": "osascript -e 'display notification \"app restarted\" with
    title \"nodemon\"'"
  }
}
```

With the config in place, we can start "boot dev" first and then nodemon, daemon listening for changes in the usual suspects' folders:

```
NikoMacBook% ./monitor.sh
[nodemon] 1.11.0
[nodemon] to restart at any time, enter `rs`
[nodemon] watching: *.*
[nodemon] starting `node main.js`
```

Now, any update to the ClojureScript files will trigger a ClojureScript-to-JavaScript compilation, and the nodemon will pick up the JavaScript file update to reload the Node.js application.

Instant programming using ClojureScript on top of Node.js! Try updating the routing of the express application and reloading the page to see the code changes picked up almost in real time.

Summary

This chapter presented ClojureScript setup and interaction with the two main JavaScript runtime, the browser and Node.js.

You have seen how to have a JavaScript workflow using Boot, and the cljsjs way of packaging third-party libraries, as well as using those libraries from ClojureScript.

You then were presented with a few famous JavaScript libraries, and you looked at how to convert JavaScript code to ClojureScript and make use of a blend of JavaScript's strong points with ClojureScript's freedom.

You wrote a few lines of gaming using the PhaseJS framework and a grand finale to bind all the different pieces of the reactive framework together.

Finally, you saw how to write code in ClojureScript that can be compiled and run on the Node.js environment, including external libraries.

The next chapter will take the Functional Reactive Programming approach, using the Reagent framework. We will particularly focus on making the application decoupled for easier maintenance and code upgrades.

But first, maybe time for a late-night coffee?

CHAPTER 4

■ ■ ■

Functional Reactive Programming with Reagent

Linear relationships can be captured with a straight line on a graph. Linear relationships are easy to think about... Linear equations are solvable... Linear systems have an important modular virtue: you can take them apart, and put them together again the pieces add up.

James Gleick (1987) *Chaos: Making a New Science*

We are finally coming to it. Functional reactive programming in the Web using Reagent. In the last chapter, we saw how smooth interaction with the host JavaScript platform was a key feature of ClojureScript. Reagent, a ClojureScript wrapper for Facebook React, brings another key feature in the ClojureScript ecosystem. Reagent also abstracts difficult concepts from React and brings its own version of reactive programming to you.

You may recall that ReactJS presents the concept of building web applications using small, modular, reusable components. That's every programmer's dream isn't it? Modular, reusable. This chapter will present several recipes addressing how Reagent makes creating those small and bigger ReactJS components easy.

In a first section, we will go over the core concepts of the framework, with a few simple Reagent examples. We will also see the life cycle of those components and the why, when, and how of their visual updates.

In a second section, we will see some small applications, like audio players and video players, and Reagent interaction with some libraries, such as your favorite async library core.async; in addition, we'll see how to deal with web workers. We will also go over server-side rendering of Reagent's components by using the library on Node.js.

Level 1 Recipes: Reagent Basics

You may remember the temperature converter example presented in the first chapter. There is a top temperature component, with two subcomponents, one for Fahrenheit display, and another one for Celsius.

© Nicolas Modrzyk 2017
N. Modrzyk, *Reactive with ClojureScript Recipes*, DOI 10.1007/978-1-4842-3009-1_4

Each of the component outputs HTML nodes via a hiccup-like DSL.

```
(defn fahrenheit []
 [:div
 [:label "fahrenheit"]
 [:input {
   :on-change  #(...)
   :value (c-to-f @celsius-v)}]])

(defn celsius []
 [:div
 [:label "celsius"]
 [:input {
   :value @celsius-v
   :on-change  #(...)}]])

(defn temperature []
 [:div
 [:h3 "Temperature Converter"]
 [celsius]
 [fahrenheit]])

(defn init []
 (reagent/render-component [temperature]
   (.getElementById js/document "container")))
```

When you look at the resulting DOM tree in Figure 4-1, the temperature component is rendered following the generative rules of the Hiccup DSL.

```
▼ <div id="container">
  ▼ <div data-reactroot> == $0
      <h3>Temperature Converter</h3>
    ▼ <div>
        <label>celsius</label>
        <input value="32">
      </div>
    ▼ <div>
        <label>fahrenheit</label>
        <input value="89.6">
      </div>
    </div>
  </div>
```

Figure 4-1. DOM tree resulting generated by Hiccup

Let's see how to create those components with Reagent in more detail.

4-1. Creating Reagent Components
Problem

You would like to parameterize Reagent components to make it easy to customize and reuse them in various applications.

Solution

Easy! Reagent components can be parametrized using regular Clojure function parameters.

How It Works

If you remember the temperature component from the previous example, to make it possible to switch the order of the Fahrenheit and Celsius div nodes, you could add a celsius-above? parameter to the function defining the temperature component.

That celsius-above? parameter can then be checked in the body of the function using an if-statement, generating a different inner div node depending on the if condition.

See how this is done in the following snippet:

```
(defn temperature [celsius-above?]
  [:div
   [:h3 "Temperature Converter"]
   (if celsius-above?
   [:div [celsius] [fahrenheit]]
   [:div [fahrenheit][celsius]])])
```

In this case, where celsius-above? is set to true, the Celsius component will be added first, and in the case where celsius-above? is false, the same Celsius component will come last. Both Celsius and Fahrenheit components are untouched.

Mounting the component can be done using the parameter directly when rendering the component. In the following, the temperature component is mounted using celsius-above to true.

```
(defn init []
  (reagent/render-component [temperature true]
    (.getElementById js/document "container")))
```

Now, try setting the celsius-above? parameter to false, and see the visual difference in Figure 4-2.

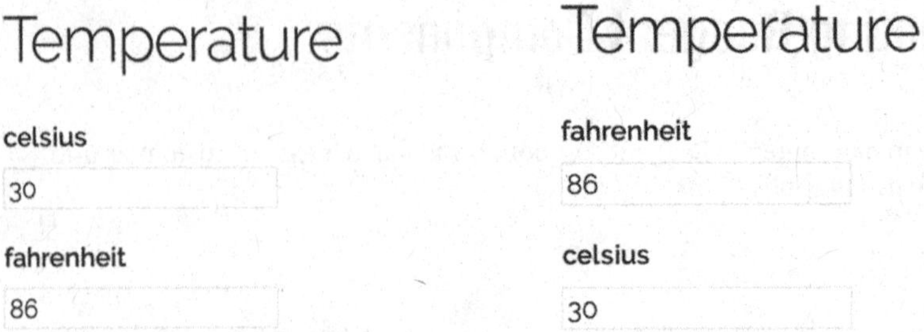

Temperature

celsius

```
30
```

fahrenheit

```
86
```

Temperature

fahrenheit

```
86
```

celsius

```
30
```

Figure 4-2. *Switching visual order of input fields*

A component renders to HTML nodes; this seems to be static so far, but a rendering function is actually being used.

So in its most simple version, you could simply mount an embedded function in the reagent/render-component top-level function.

```
(defn init []
  (reagent/render-component [
    (fn[]
      [:div {:style {:color "white" :background "blue"}}
        (str "The time is:" (js/Date.))])]
    (.getElementById js/document "container")))
```

The embedded component does not depend on any external data, is stand-alone, and always renders to the same set of nodes, as seen in Figure 4-3.

The time is:Wed Mar 29 2017 16:34:19 GMT+0900 (JST)

Figure 4-3. *Rendered Reagent component*

Note that the same set of nodes does not mean the same rendering in the browser. So mounting the same component twice in the DOM tree results in two different sets of nodes, as you can see in the following:

```
(defn show-time[]
    [:div {:style {:color "white" :background "blue"}}
    (str "The time is:" (.getTime (js/Date.)))])

(defn init []
  (reagent/render-component show-time
    (.getElementById js/document "container"))
  (reagent/render-component show-time
    (.getElementById js/document "container2")))
```

Figure 4-4 shows how the rendering in the browser is different for each mounted React root.

Figure 4-4. *Multiple mounted components, visual*

Figure 4-5 details how the DOM rendering of each data-reactroot is also different, pointing at two independent and separate component instances.

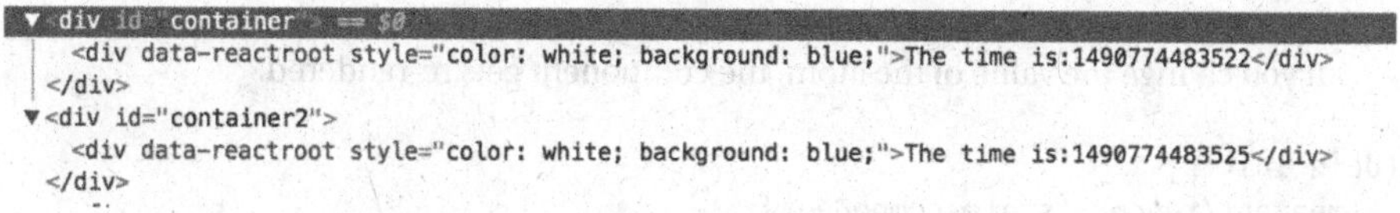

```
▼ <div id="container"> == $0
    <div data-reactroot style="color: white; background: blue;">The time is:1490774483522</div>
  </div>
▼ <div id="container2">
    <div data-reactroot style="color: white; background: blue;">The time is:1490774483525</div>
  </div>
```

Figure 4-5. *Multiple mounted components, DOM*

Now, if you have a simple binding that is not a function to define your component, while it works, some part of the component will be initialized at the wrong time, and not being rendered as expected.

```
(def show-time
    [:div {:style {:color "white" :background "blue"}}
    (str "The time is:" (.getTime (js/Date.)))])

(defn init []
  (reagent/render-component show-time
    (.getElementById js/document "container"))
  (reagent/render-component show-time
    (.getElementById js/document "container2")))
```

The preceding mounts the same set of static nodes twice, with the JavaScript time string being done when show-time is bound.

So, the rendering will be as seen in Figure 4-6.

Figure 4-6. *Statically mounted nodes are identical*

If you think a bit about it, that was expected.

Components Using a Function

A Reagent/Reactjs component can also be created using a function or a map of functions.

So let's say we go back to a simple component, with an external state. Here, a simple Reagent atom is used to hold some data outside of the component.

```
(def astate (reagent/atom "hello"))

(defn state-component []
     [:div "State: " @astate])

(defn init []
   (reagent/render [state-component]
     (.getElementById js/document "container")))
```

If you change the value of the atom, the component gets re-rendered.

```
(defn init []
   (reagent/render [state-component]
     (.getElementById js/document "container"))
   (js/setTimeout #(reset! astate "hello world") 1000))
```

Figure 4-7 shows the atom value and the component's text being updated after 1 second.

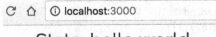

State: hello world

Figure 4-7. *Updating the state of a component*

But it is a bit annoying to have the state, and the delayed change of state, outside of the component itself. So, you can put all of this in the same Reagent component using a function inside the component definition.

```
(defn state-component []
  (let [local-state (reagent/atom "hello")]
  (js/setTimeout #(reset! local-state "hello world") 1000)
  (fn []
     [:div
       "State: " @local-state])))

(defn init []
  (reagent/render [state-component]
    (.getElementById js/document "container")))
```

The Reagent component returns a function used for rendering, but also holds the local state of the component, that state itself being used for rendering when the function is called.

Just as a JavaScript timeout works, the component can React to its own click events too. This next component owns a local state of the number of times its own button has been clicked.

```
(defn counter-component []
  (let [local-state (reagent/atom 0)]
  (fn[]
   [:div
    [:button { :style {:color :white :background-color :blue}
               :on-click #(swap! local-state inc)}
     "Click here"]
    [:div "Blue has been clicked " @local-state " times"]])))

(defn init []
  (reagent/render [counter-component]
    (.getElementById js/document "container")))
```

Figure 4-8 shows the resulting mounted component.

Blue has been clicked 7 times

Figure 4-8. *Component reacting to click events*

It is of course still possible to have parameters even when returning a render function in a component. A local state is used per instance of the component, not of the class, and so the rendering is done independently. In the following, see how the JavaScript timeout is different for each instance, and how the rendering is done separately:

```
(defn timer-component [lap]
  (let [seconds-elapsed (reagent/atom 0)]
    (fn []
      (js/setTimeout #(swap! seconds-elapsed inc) lap)
      [:div
       "Lap Elapsed: " @seconds-elapsed])))

(defn init []
  (reagent/render [timer-component 500]
    (.getElementById js/document "container"))
  (reagent/render [timer-component 300]
    (.getElementById js/document "container2")))
```

Figure 4-9 shows two components rendering differently but using the same parameterized rendering function.

Figure 4-9. *Same definition, different rendering*

Components Using a Map of Functions

You will rarely need to use this way of creating Reagent components, but it is highly informative to see all the different life-cycle states of a component, as well as the different callbacks.

The last way to create a Reagent component is through reagent/createclass and a map of functions, one for each component state transition and for rendering.

:components-will-update and :components-did-update are probably some of the most useful callbacks.

Here is an example showing a few things:

- It uses create-class to define a new component

- It has a local state

- It has parameters used at creation and for rendering

- It uses its internal state to keep track of how many times it has been rendered

See how this goes:

```
(defn my-component [x y z]
  (let [local-state (atom 0) ]

    (reagent/create-class
      {:component-will-update
       (fn [this new-argv]
         (swap! local-state inc)
         (println "will-update"))

       :display-name  "my-sweet-component"

       :reagent-render
       (fn [a b c]
        [:div
         [:div (str "Parameters:" a " " b " " c)]
         [:div (str "Rendered Count:" @local-state)]
         [:div (str @astate)]])})))
```

That component made with create-class can be mounted just like all the components you have defined until now.

```
(defn init []
  (reagent/render [my-component 1 2 5]
    (.getElementById js/document "container"))
```

It is also rather nice to see that further updates to the external state are updating the internal states:

```
(defn init []
  (reagent/render [my-component 1 2 5]
    (.getElementById js/document "container"))

(js/setTimeout #(reset! astate "hello world") 3000)
(js/setTimeout #(reset! astate "hello world...") 5000)
(js/setTimeout #(reset! astate "hello world...") 5000)
; the last timeout does not trigger a re-render
```

Figure 4-10 shows a time-lapse of the rendering of the component.

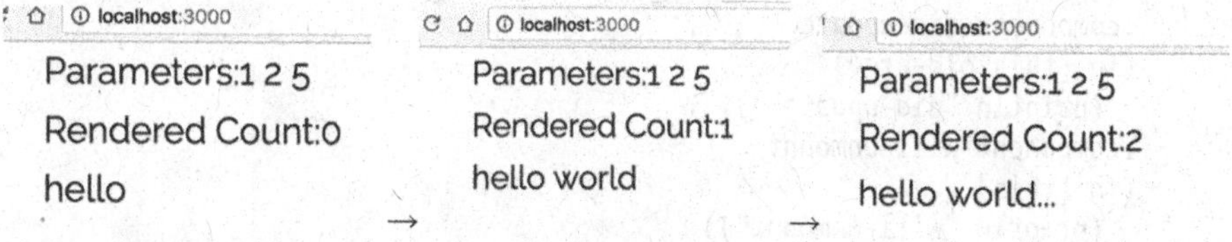

Parameters:1 2 5

Rendered Count:0

hello

→

Parameters:1 2 5

Rendered Count:1

hello world

→

Parameters:1 2 5

Rendered Count:2

hello world...

Figure 4-10. *Same component, different rendering*

Also, you may be surprised to see the last timeout did not trigger an update of the component. Could you get why? Try to come up with a reason before reading further.

```
(js/setTimeout #(reset! astate "hello world...") 5000)
```

Well actually, to know if a component needs to be visually updated or not, ReactJS (and so Reagent) uses something called a Virtual DOM, a set of virtual nodes, along a diff-ing algorithm. More on that in a few pages. In short, Reagent really only updates DOM nodes if the result of a diff function call between the old nodes and the new nodes is nonempty.

Here, while setting the state to "hello world..." a second time, while the data input has been touched, the rendering of the node to a DOM subtree remains the same; thus, React does not perform an update. And so the third time the atom is updated, no visual update is required; thus, the updated trigger is not fired, and the rendered count stays at 2.

Finally, for your reference, the full set of callback functions that can be used when creating a component is shown in the following.

Rendering, global state, and local state are all in!

```
(defn my-component [x y z]
  (let [local-state (atom 0) ]
    (reagent/create-class
      {:component-did-mount
       (fn[this]
         (println "component-did-mount"))
       :component-will-mount
       (fn[this]
         (println "component-will-mount"))
       :get-initial-state
       (fn [this]
         (println "initial-state"))
       :component-will-receive-props
       (fn [this new-argv]
         (println "will-receive-props"))
       :should-component-update
       (fn [this old-argv new-argv]
         (println "should-update"))
       :component-will-update
       (fn [this new-argv]
         (swap! astate inc)
         (println "will-update"))
       :component-did-update
       (fn [this old-argv]
         (println "did-update"))
       :component-will-unmount
       (fn [this]
         (println "will-unmount"))
      :display-name  "my-sweet-component"
      :reagent-render
      (let [seconds-elapsed (reagent/atom 0)]
      (js/setInterval #(swap! seconds-elapsed inc) 1000)
      (fn [a b c]
      [:div
      [:div (str "Parameters:" a " " b " " c)]
      [:div (str "Rendered Count:" @local-state)]
       [:div (str "Seconds:" @seconds-elapsed)]
      [:div (str @astate)]])
       )}))))
```

If you mount the component in the DOM, the console will print the different used states, notably initial, will-mount, and did-mount, as well as a series of "will-update", "did-update" messages.

Figure 4-11 highlights the life-cycle messages printing at the console.

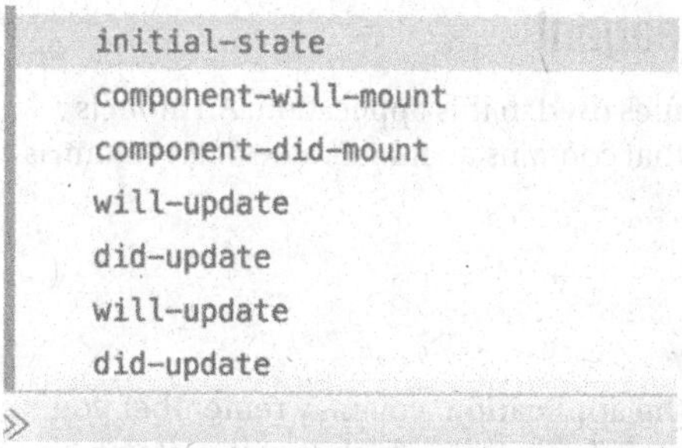

```
initial-state
component-will-mount
component-did-mount
will-update
did-update
will-update
did-update
```

Figure 4-11. *React component life-cycle events*

You can add your own custom logic in each callback, but you should obviously limit processing as much as possible, and rather act on Reagent atoms to update the rendering after the component has been mounted.

4-2. Working with Reagent Atoms

> *The beauty of a living thing is not the atoms that go into it, but the way those atoms are put together.*
>
> Carl Sagan, *Cosmos*

Problem

You may like to use atoms to make your application Reactive and act smoothly with user interactions.

Solution

Reagent atoms are at the core of the reactive part of the Reagent framework. You may remember that Clojure pushes forward immutable data, and that Clojure atoms make immutable data effectively mutable by using safe transactions for every update of the atom's value.

How It Works

You have seen how to work with atoms before, but let's review them a bit more closely again.

Let's work on an updated version of our temperature-setting application. The application will have two buttons—hotter and cooler—to set the temperature up or down, current Celsius and Fahrenheit settings, and an image to show a graphical indication of the current settings.

HTML, ClojureScript Atoms, No Reagent

We are going to use a set of atoms to define values used in this application. An atom is defined with the ClojureScript atom function that contains an initial value of this atom as seen in the following.

```
(def celsius-v
  (atom 30))
```

If you connect a ClojureScript REPL to the application, you may remember you can get the current value of that atom use deref, or @ mark, which is just syntaxic sugar for deref.

```
@celsius-v
; 30
```

We will define two more atoms, color and temp-step, to define an application state with them:

```
; color of the thermometer
(def color
  (atom "black"))

; increment counter when using buttons
(def temp-step
  (atom 1))
```

Let's work quickly on the HTML part of the setup. to lay out the different components: two select boxes for colors and increment/decrement step, two buttons for hotter and cooler actions, two input fields to show the current temperature, and one image.

```
<div class="row">
    <div class="one-half column" style="margin-top: 5%">
      <h4>Thermostat</h1>
        <select id="color">
          <option value="black" selected>black</option>
          <option value="red">red</option>
          <option value="blue">blue</option>
        </select>
        <select id="step">
          <option value="1" selected>1°C</option>
          <option value="3">3°C</option>
          <option value="5">5°C</option>
        </select>
        <br/>
        <button id="cool">Cool</button>
        <button id="hot">Hot</button>
```

```
    <label for="container">Celsius</label>
    <input type="text" id="container" placeholder="celsius">
    </input>
    <label for="container2">Fahrenheit</label>
    <input type="text" id="container2" placeholder="fahrenheit">
    </input>
 </div>
 <div class="one-half column" style="margin-top: 5%">
    <img id="thermo" src="/img/blue/Thermometer-25.svg"/>
       <br/>
 </div>
</div>
```

Back to the ClojureScript code: what would you start to write first? Let's try by putting together the helper functions.

We need the usual function to convert from Celsius to Fahrenheit.

```
(defn c-to-f [myc]
  (pprint/cl-format nil  "~,1f" (+ (* myc 1.8) 32)))
```

We add a basic helper function to set the value of an html element easily:

```
(defn set-value[dom html]
  (set! (.-value (.getElementById js/document dom) ) html))
```

The following three functions, somewhat extraneous here, are used to convert from Celsius temperature to a range between –20 and 50 Celsius degrees. Here we first convert the range from –20~50 to 0~100 and then use this scale to pick up an image (or a value here) for the thermometer.

```
(defn make-project-range-fn
  [source-start source-end target-start target-end]
  (fn[input]
    (+ target-start
        (* (/ (- target-end target-start )
        (- source-end source-start)) (- input source-start)))))
(defn map-range[c]
  ( (make-project-range-fn -20 50 0 100) c))

(defn c-to-img [c]
  (let [y (map-range c)]
  (condp > y
    20 0
    40 25
    60 50
    80 75
    100) ))
```

Next, we add the method that updates the image of the thermometer from the new Celsius value, and use the color atom to choose the color:

```
(defn update-img [newv]
  (let[imgi (c-to-img newv)]
  (set!
    (.-src (.getElementById js/document "thermo") )
    (str "/img/" @color "/Thermometer-" imgi ".svg"))))
```

The next step here is to add watchers to those ClojureScript atoms, notably to the celsius-v atom and the color atom.

For example, when changing the value of the color atom, we need to redraw the image with the proper color set. You can achieve this by using a watcher on the color atom:

```
(add-watch color
  :color
  (fn [k r os ns]
    (update-img @celsius-v )))
```

The function passed to the watcher has four parameters (k, r, os, ns):

- k for key, here the keyword :color, to make the difference between different watchers

- r, the atom itself, here color

- os, old state, or the value before the change is applied to the atom

- ns, new state, or the value after the change is applied to the atom.

A watcher is also added to the celsius-v atom. It is slightly more complicated but is implemented in a similar way. The callback on atom update will

- update the value of the Celsius field

- update the value of the Fahrenheit field

- update the image, since the color has not changed; this is for the level of the thermometer.

Finally, the full logic of the application. Assuming here you are getting familiar with most of the JavaScript syntax so let's focus mostly on the interaction with the atoms.

The button handlers are using the function swap! to change the value of the celsius-v atom. The value of the atom is either increased or decreased using a partial function, and the current value of the temp-step atom.

The partial function is applied to the current value of the atom, and the atom value is updated transactionally.

So the value of the atom is changed, but the interesting part is that when the value of the atom updates, watcher functions are being called.

So if you press the cool button, the callback for the event handler on the cool button is to change the value of the celsius-v atom, and also indirectly to update the value of the fields in the Celsius and Fahrenheit input boxes. No tight coupling between the button and the input fields! This makes the application more resistant to changes, and also indicates quite directly what is acting, or react-ing, pun intended, to what.

In a similar way, the select boxes use the reset! function on the atoms to force a new value on the atom, whatever the previous value was. In the case of color, the color atom is updated to one of black, red, or blue. In the case of the step select box, the value of the step atom is updated to 1, 3, or 5.

```
(defn init[]
  ; update image on load
  (update-img @celsius-v)

  ; add handler for the cool button
  (set! (.-onclick (.getElementById js/document "cool"))
    #(swap! celsius-v (partial + (* -1 @temp-step))))

  ; add handler for the cool button
  (set! (.-onclick (.getElementById js/document "hot"))
    #(swap! celsius-v (partial + @temp-step)))

  ; add listener to the color selector
  (let[select-box (.getElementById js/document "color") ]
    (set! (.-onchange select-box)
      #(reset! color (.-value select-box) ) ))

  ; add listener to the step selector
  (let[select-box (.getElementById js/document "step") ]
  (set! (.-onchange select-box)
    #(reset! temp-step (js/parseInt (.-value select-box)) ))))
```

Let's go! Loading and accessing the application give you a cute little frontend for your thermostat needs.

Thermostat

black ♦ 1°C ♦

COOL   HOT

Celsius

38

Fahrenheit

100.4

As described, Cool and Hot buttons increase or lower the temperature by acting on the atom celsius-v, and the select boxes affect the other atoms.

Thermostat

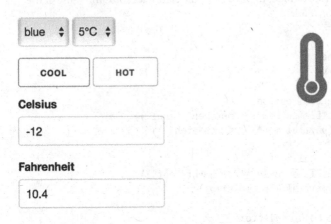

HTML, Reagent Atoms, Reagent Cursor

Now, you probably already have a complaint about the preceding application. Yes, it is okay to say it.

The state is somewhat scattered across different atoms.

The atom watchers feel inconvenient and disconnected from the view.

And as a poor side effect it also makes it slightly hard to restore the application view in a known state.

Wouldn't that be nicer if

- The state was grouped in the same atom?

- The view was directly in sync with the atom?

Yes. Very correct, so let's see how to get this in a slightly better state (here it goes again; that pun was intended too).

First, there is a bit of good news: ClojureScript atoms can be interchanged with Reagent atoms and in fact are extended by them.

So providing the namespace requires Reagent properly:

```
(ns chapter01.app
  (:require
    [reagent.core :as reagent]))
```

Then, all the atoms in the example can be replaced by their Reagent counterparts.

```
(def celsius-v
  (reagent/atom 30))
(def color
  (reagent/atom "black"))
(def temp-step
  (reagent/atom 1))
```

Yes, the change was easy, and yes, the application still works, but... no, it seems we did not get much closer to our goal of a single atom. That was a transition.

Let's define a Reagent atom that is a map and contains all the different parameters of the application, namely, :color, :temperature, :step:

```
(def state
  (reagent/atom {:color "black" :temperature 30 :step 1}))
```

This single application state builds on a Reagent atom, and provides a way to use Reagent cursors, each cursor being focused on one part of the state. Let's redefine the atoms using cursors.

Reagent/cursor takes an atom and a Clojure path inside the atom. See the following:

```
(def color
  (reagent/cursor state [:color]))

(def celsius-v
  (reagent/cursor state [:temperature]))

(def temp-step
  (reagent/cursor state [:step]))
```

The application works again, but the state is held in a single place. It makes it very easy to load or reload the state of the application, or easy to test transitions from one step to another.

You could add a size key in the map, and update the size of the thermometer picture based on that key. Try it out!

Reagent Atoms, Reagent Components

But, and this tackles the second of the preceding pain points, the most interesting part of Reagent atoms is that they hold the key to what component needs to be redrawn by tracking atom references.

The Reagent framework tracks calls to deref, or its shorter version @, in the Bodies of the different Reagent components and can then decide what components should be redrawn after the change of an atom.

So, let's rewrite this little application using the Reagent way.

You'll be pleased to know that the div element in the html page is down to a one-liner:

```
<div id="top" class="row">
```

That's correct: the full html code will be generated by a Reagent component.

Before getting started coding the component itself, you'll need to add one more dependency to build.boot. reagent-forms helps us in doing binding between html form elements and Reagent atoms in a simple way. Reagent-forms and Reagent go hand in hand, so the version number would usually be similar. Here's what to add to the build:

```
[reagent-forms "0.6.1"]
[reagent "0.6.1"]
```

We will create a top thermostat component with the different subcomponents. Note the four to-be-defined components in the following code; we will get to them in a few seconds:

```
(defn thermostat[]
  [:div {:id "top" :class "row"}
   [:div {:class "one-half column" :style {:margin-top "5%"}}
    [:h4 "Thermostat"]

    [selectors] ; to be defined
    [buttons] ; to be defined
    [:br]
    [inputs] ; to be defined
    ]

   [:div {:class "one-half column" :style {:margin-top "5%"}}
    [thermo-img] ; to be defined
    [:br]]])
```

The top component is defined using the now-familiar hiccup-style DSL, with quite many square brackets and parentheses, but the structure of the component can be grasped straightaway.

Let's skip the selectors for now, which are slightly more difficult; instead, let's implement components starting from the easiest one, the thermo-img.

thermo-img is simply an image whose source, src attribute, is computed from the color and the celsius-v atoms.

```
(defn thermo-img[]
  [:img
   {:id "thermo"
    :height 256
    :width 256
    :src (str "/img/" @color "/Thermometer-" (c-to-img @celsius-v) ".svg")
    }])
```

The inputs component returns a div with two labels and two inputs, one set of label/input displaying Celsius, so the value of the celsius-v atom as is, the other set label/input displaying something computed from the value of the atom.

Also note that the inputs' value cannot be updated by typing in the fields; this is on purpose.

```
(defn inputs[]
  [:div
     [:label {:for "container"} "Celsius"]
     [:input {:type "text" :id "container"
              :placeholder "celsius" :value @celsius-v}]

     [:label {:for "container2"} "Fahrenheit"]
     [:input {:type "text" :id "container2"
              :placeholder "fahrenheit" :value (c-to-f @celsius-v)}]])
```

Next come the buttons component, each button coming with an on-click handler, updating the value of the celsius-v atom by increasing or decreasing by a given amount.

```
(defn buttons[]
  [:div
     [:button {:id "cool"
      :on-click
      #(swap! celsius-v
        (fn[x] (+ x (* -1 (js/parseInt @temp-step)))))} "Cool"]

     [:button {:id "hot"
      :on-click
      #(swap! celsius-v
        (fn[x]  (+ x (js/parseInt @temp-step))))} "Hot"]])
```

Finally, we'll consider the selectors component, with two select fields. Select html elements work a bit in a strange way in general, so the binding is done through a special form from the reagent-forms library. bind-fields picks up the id of the component and binds its value to a key in the atom.

bind-fields works like [bind-fields *forms-elements atom*] bind-fields can be used with the following form. In the example below, bind-fields is used once per each select box.

```
(defn selectors[]
  [:div
    [bind-fields
     [:select {:id :color}
       (for [opt ["black" "red" "blue"]] [:option {:key opt} opt])]
     state]

     [bind-fields
     [:select {:id :step}
       (for [opt [1 3 5] ] [:option {:key opt} (str opt "°C")])]
     state] ])
```

Note that this may not be very obvious at first read, but those bindings will also update the state atom at key :step and key :color.

That's it: our main component is ready to be mounted to the div element with id #top.

```
(defn init[]
  (reagent/render [thermostat]
    (.getElementById js/document "top")))
```

You'll surprised to see that the application looks exactly the same, and you may wonder what's with all the rewriting!

But already you can see how each component is related to the others, and how all the quirks from the previous version have been fixed, like the initial loading of the application state, or the removal of any discrepancy between atoms and their visual impact on the UI.

Basics in hand, now is the time to put all this into action. Congratulations, you have just reached level 2!

Level 2 Recipes: Reagent Exercises

This section will go through a substantial set of exercises, from simple HTML table, to animation, navigation, html5 location, SVG via Reagent, all the way to web workers and server-side rendering.

Those short examples are all based on the same project template that we have used so far, so you could mostly just keep on coding and see immediate visual UIs. Sometime, a library will be added to the Boot file.

The examples are in no specific order, each approaching a different way of using Reagent and ClojureScript, so go ahead and enjoy them in any order you like (but be sure to complete them all to validate your graduation to the next level).

4-3. Creating a Sortable Table
Problem

You would like to create a table of sortable elements. The sort key and the sort order, ascending or descending, can be decided.

Solution

To achieve this, the sort-by key and the sort order will be kept in ClojureScript atoms, and the sorted table Reagent component will then be recomputed and will render the sorted element as needed.

How It Works

First, a Reagent atom can be used, holding the key used for sorting and the order.

You may then define the content of the table in a simple array of maps.

On clicking the table header, the sort key defined in the app-state atom will be updated. Clicking the same header twice will reverse the sort order.

When the atom for sorting changes, the sorted content is updated, and thus the loop used to create the HTML rows of the table will be updated.

Finally, a Reagent component will be created, mostly an HTML table. The component loops over the data in the currently defined sort order and sort key. Headers of the table have :on-click handlers to simply update the app-state atom with the proper sort key.

Code

```
(ns chapter01.app
  (:require [reagent.core :as reagent]))

(def app-state
  (reagent/atom
    {:sort-val :first-name :ascending true}))

(def table-contents
  [{:id 1 :first-name "Bram"    :last-name "Moolenaar"  :known-for "Vim"}
   {:id 2 :first-name "Richard" :last-name "Stallman"   :known-for "GNU"}
   {:id 3 :first-name "Dennis"  :last-name "Ritchie"    :known-for "C"}
   {:id 4 :first-name "Rich"    :last-name "Hickey"     :known-for "Clojure"}
   {:id 5 :first-name "Guido"   :last-name "Van Rossum" :known-for "Python"}
   {:id 6 :first-name "Linus"   :last-name "Torvalds"   :known-for "Linux"}
   {:id 7 :first-name "Yehuda"  :last-name "Katz"       :known-for "Ember"}])

(defn update-sort-value [new-val]
  (if (= new-val (:sort-val @app-state))
    (swap! app-state update-in [:ascending] not)
    (swap! app-state assoc :ascending true))
  (swap! app-state assoc :sort-val new-val))

(defn sorted-contents []
  (let [sorted-contents (sort-by (:sort-val @app-state) table-contents)]
    (if (:ascending @app-state)
      sorted-contents
      (rseq sorted-contents))))

(defn table []
  [:table
   [:thead
    [:tr
     [:th {:width "200" :on-click #(update-sort-value :first-name)} "First Name"]
     [:th {:width "200" :on-click #(update-sort-value :last-name) } "Last Name"]
     [:th {:width "200" :on-click #(update-sort-value :known-for) } "Known For"]]]
```

```clojure
    [:tbody
    (for [person (sorted-contents)]
      ^{:key (:id person)}
      [:tr [:td (:first-name person)]
      [:td (:last-name person)]
      [:td (:known-for person)]])])])

(defn home []
  [:div {:style {:margin "auto"
    :padding-top "30px"
    :width "600px"}}
    [table]])

(defn ^:export init []
  (reagent/render [home]
    (.getElementById js/document "container")))
```

The sorted table is shown in Figure 4-12.

Result

First Name	Last Name	Known For
Bram	Moolenaar	Vim
Dennis	Ritchie	C
Guido	Van Rossum	Python
Linus	Torvalds	Linux
Rich	Hickey	Clojure
Richard	Stallman	GNU
Yehuda	Katz	Ember

Figure 4-12. *Table with sorted elements*

Comments

In the for loop, pay attention how a key property is added to the row element so it is made unique. This is to please the underlying framework of Reagent: React.

React needs a single id for each element generated from a loop, so it does not get confused by similar DOM elements.

If keys are missing, you may see a message, as in Figure 4-13, in the browser error console:

```
✕  ▶  "Warning: Each child in an array or iterator should have a
       unique "key" prop. Check the render method of
       `chapter01.app.table`. See https://fb.me/react-warning-keys
       for more information.
           in tr (created by chapter01.app.table)
           in chapter01.app.table (created by chapter01.app.home)
           in div (created by chapter01.app.home)
           in chapter01.app.home"
```

Figure 4-13. Missing unique key error message

4-4. Using Local Storage
Problem

You may like the state of the application, or parts of it, to be stored in the browser so that even if the browser is closed, or the user navigates away from your page, the value can be reread when loading the page again.

Solution

Using HTML5 local storage to store data in the browser is of course the way to go. There is a ClojureScript wrapper named alandipert.storage-atom that can be used to make the integration with ClojureScript even more transparent.

How It Works

An app-state atom will be created using storage-atom, which looks like a wrapper around a regular Reagent atom.

Accessing the enhanced app-state is done as usual.

Code

The library required is shown in the following:

```
[alandipert/storage-atom "1.2.4"]
```

The ClojureScript code is rather short:

```
(ns localstorage.core
  (:require [reagent.core :as reagent]
    [alandipert.storage-atom :refer [local-storage]]))

(def app-state
  (local-storage
    (reagent/atom {:counter 0})
    :app-state))
```

```
(defn home []
  [:div
  [:div "Current Counter count: " (@app-state :counter)]
  [:button {:on-click #(swap! app-state update-in [:counter] inc)} "+"]
  [:button {:on-click #(swap! app-state update-in [:counter] dec)} "-"]])

(defn ^:export main []
  (reagent/render [home]
    (.getElementById js/document "app")))
```

Result

If you access the page for the first time, the counter will be 0. If you play with the buttons and reload the browser page, you will find the counter is not 0, as would be the case normally, but the value it was when last accessed, as shown in Figure 4-14.

Figure 4-14. *Local storage-based atoms*

Comments

The recipe's key point is the wrapper around the standard Reagent atom; everything else is standard Reagent coding.

Note that this way of storing data is a great way to keep local settings, helping users customize your application in a way that is more personal to each user.

4-5. Single Page Application and Multiple Pages
Problem

You would like the user of your application to be able to navigate to different pages without leaving your Single Page Application.

The SPA would prevent loading pages from the server, and handle all the navigation directly in the browser.

Solution

A first approach is to use a ClojureScript library that can handle anchor link clicks before they submit a request to the server. This will be hooked inside the browser navigation, so forward and back buttons works as expected even though the pages are not reloaded from the server.

How It Works

The current page will be held in a Reagent atom so that the top Reagent component can be refreshed as expected when clicking to change page.

Code

The library we want to use here is named secretary and we can add it to our project with the following:

```
[secretary "1.2.3"]
```

Then the full ClojureScript code:

```
(ns hello.core
    (:import goog.History)
    (:require [secretary.core :as secretary :refer-macros [defroute]])
            [goog.events :as events]
            [goog.history.EventType :as EventType]
            [reagent.core :as reagent])

; the current page is held in a reagent atom
(def app-state
  (reagent/atom {:page :about}))

; secretary hooks into the browser history object. On page move secretary ;
dispatches an internal event
(defn hook-browser-navigation! []
  (doto (History.)
    (events/listen EventType/NAVIGATE #(secretary/dispatch! (.-token %)))
      (.setEnabled true)))

; here we define the application navigation
ww(defn setup-navigation []
    ; first the library settings, using a special prefix
    ; to identify routes computed on the client
    ; here #
    (secretary/set-config! :prefix "#")
    ; setup the hook to the browser navigation
    (hook-browser-navigation!)

    ; define simple routes here
    (defroute "/" []
      (swap! app-state assoc :page :home))
    (defroute "/about" []
      (swap! app-state assoc :page :about)))
```

```clojure
; this is the page home, a reagent component
(defn home []
  [:div
  [:img {:src "/home-icon.png" :height 90 :width 90}]
  [:h1 "Home Page"]
   [:a {:href "#/about"} "about page"]])

; this is the page about, another reagent component
(defn about []
  [:div
  [:img {:src "/about-icon.svg" :height 90 :width 90}]
  [:h1 "About Page"]
   [:a {:href "#/"} "home page"]])

; a reagent component is a function.
; here we use Clojure's defmulti to simulate
; a parameterized function, or a function
; whose body is dependent on a parameter
; computed when the function is called
;
; so, a call to:
; (current-page)
;
; results in a dispatch to one of the
; defmethod body defined after
; each time depending on the result of
; #(@app-state :page)
;
(defmulti current-page #(@app-state :page))
(defmethod current-page :home [] [home])
(defmethod current-page :about [] [about])
(defmethod current-page :default [] [:div ])

; this is a standard reagent application
; the setup of the navigation is done before the rendering.
(defn ^:export main []
  (setup-navigation)
  (reagent/render [current-page]
    (.getElementById js/document "app")))
```

Result

The application loads and the root(!) route / goes directly to the home Reagent component via the call to [current-page], with the current page atom value being :home, as in Figure 4-15.

Home Page

about page

Figure 4-15. *Client-only navigation, home page*

When the about page is clicked, no request is sent to the server, since the browser navigation hook has been set.

The new route is dispatched, and the atom value is now :about. This tells Reagent to rerender the current-page component, and so the DOM is updated and the view in the browser is also updated with the rendering of the about Reagent component, as can be seen in Figure 4-16.

About Page

home page

Figure 4-16. *Client navigation, About Page*

Comments

First, right after trying this example, you can play with the back and forward buttons of the browser and enjoy a navigation without making any calls to the server.

You can also enjoy the fact that you could also have multiple paging components in a single HTML page. Why not try it?

Instead of secretary, which has been proven in production, some other developers have also reported great results with the combination of the bidi and accountant libraries.

Those can be added with the following dependencies:

```
[bidi "2.0.0"]
[venantius/accountant "0.1.7"]
```

An example has been placed in the chapter04-reagent/12-reagent-bidi-accountant folder for this chapter, but it would take a bit too long to talk about the same thing again, and so is left to the curiosity of the reader. Yes, that's you!

4-6. Using HTML5 Location
Problem

You want to propose localized content to your user. You know it is possible to use the HTML5 navigation capability, so you might like to have a Reagent way of making use of it.

Solution

The geolocation feature of your browser will be accessed through interop, and the result will be stored in an atom for a Reagent component to access and render.

How It Works

The code will make use of the browser geolocation feature, with the use of core async to simulate/handle the JavaScript callback in a sensible manner, but no other extra external libraries will actually be needed.

Code

```
; start with namespaces definition
(ns hello.core
    (:require
      [reagent.core :as reagent]
      [cljs.core.async :as async :refer [put! <! >! chan]])
    (:require-macros [cljs.core.async.macros :as m :refer [go]]))


; the get position function which uses the geolocation module
; from the navigator object
; the getCurrentPosition function has a callback
; here the callback is piped on the core.async channel
(defn get-position []
    (let [out (chan)
      geo (.-geolocation js/navigator)]
      (.getCurrentPosition geo (fn [pos] (put! out pos)))
      out))
```

```clojure
; the location is stored in a map atom
; with latitude and longitude values
(def loc
     (reagent/atom {:lat nil :long nil}))


; this is our main reagent component here
; the visual depends on whether the location has been set or not
; 1. If the location is not set yet, we display a compass via a gif image
; 2. If the location is set, we display the location using the atom value
(defn current-page []
     [:div
     (if (nil? (@loc :lat))
             [:div
                 [:img {:src "/compass.gif" :height 256 :width 350}]
                 [:p "Locating ..."]]
             [:div
                 [:img {:src "/green.png" :height 256 :width 256}]
                 [:h2 "Lat"]
                 [:div (@loc :lat)]
                 [:br]
                 [:h2 "Lon"]
                 [:div (@loc :long)]])])

(defn- main[& args]
   ; the reagent mounting part

   (reagent/render [current-page]
         (.getElementById js/document "app"))

   ; the async call to fetch the location
   (go
     (let [coords     (.-coords (<! (get-position)))
           latitude   (.-latitude coords)
           longitude  (.-longitude coords)]
          (reset! loc  {:lat latitude :long longitude}))))
```

Result

The page first impression in Figure 4-17 is that of a moving compass.

Locating ...

Figure 4-17. Animation while retrieving the geolocation

Meanwhile, the browser should also ask to check for your position. (You usually need to tell them somehow that they can track you before they actually do. Unless of course ....)

Once the location has been found, the atom value is updated by the core.async go block. The atom update forces a refresh of the Reagent component, as shown in Figure 4-18.

Lat

35.6830897

Lon

139.7782215

Figure 4-18. Location has been retrieved

Comments

Obviously it would not be a location demo without some sort of map showing up on the screen. So let's quickly update the Reagent component to display a map with the location found.

In the Reagent component, in the location div, try adding a Google map.

Once you have done it, you can look at the necessary code:

```
[:div
  [:iframe
    { :width 500
      :height 500
      :src
    (str "https://www.google.com/maps/embed/v1/view?"
      "key=AIzaSyA36bY9Hd3nmOIzB5ih668GwQa2kZWXOLc"
      "&center=" (@loc :lat) "," (@loc :long)
        "&zoom=18")}]]
```

And the holiday hint, showing in Figure 4-19, for your next vacation.

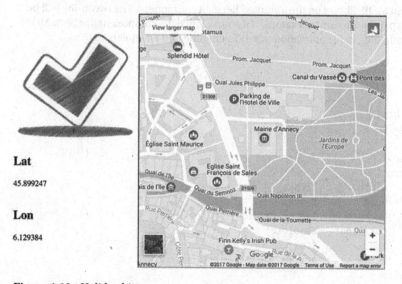

Lat

45.899247

Lon

6.129384

Figure 4-19. Holiday hint

4-7. Animating Components with MOJS

Problem

You have seen many times how to declare Reagent components using Hiccup markup. Now, you would like to animate those components on the screen.

You could use raw CSS, but to smoothly integrate with onscreen interactions, let's try and use the tween library MOJS, the Animation toolbelt.

Solution

You could create a Reagent component using reagent/create-class and enhance the :component-did-mount function to add the MOJS tweening code.

How It Works

The HTML code only contains minimum information, mostly the placeholders for the Reagent components to be mounted.

The ClojureScript code makes use of the :component-did-mount function to plug in the JavaScript MOJS library on the mounted Reagent component. The tween-ing will be done in that part in the coming example. Of course, once the component has been MOJS-ized, you could plug in the animation at a different time of your choice.

HTML

```
<!DOCTYPE html>
<html lang="en">
<head>
    <style>
    .square {
            width:      150px;
            height:     150px;
            background: linear-gradient(white, blue);
            position:   absolute;
            top:        10px;
            left:       40%;}
    </style>
</head>
<body>
    <div id="app"></div>
    <script src="vendor/js/mo.min.js"></script>
    <script src="main.js"></script>
</body>
</html>
```

CLJS

```clojure
(ns hello.core
    (:require [reagent.core :as reagent]))

; the animation, updating the CSS properties of
; the node using CSS transform.
; this set the transform property of the style property of the node
; to a percentage of 200px.
(defn translate-y [node]
  (fn [progress]
    (set! (-> node .-style .-transform)
    (str "translateY(" (* 200 progress) "px)"))))

; the callback in use when the reagent component has been mounted
; here again see the use of reagent/dom-node to
; pass in the dom node to the javascript library
(defn animation-did-mount [this]
  (.run
  (js/mojs.Tween.
  (clj->js
    {:repeat 999
     :delay 2000
     :onUpdate (translate-y (reagent/dom-node this))}))))

; create the reagent component with reagent/create-class
; and pass in the animation-did-mount function
(defn animation []
  (reagent/create-class
    {:render (fn [] [:div.square])
     :component-did-mount animation-did-mount}))

; create and render the component
(defn ^:export main []
  (reagent/render [animation]
      (.getElementById js/document "app")))
```

Result

On animation start, the square shows up at the top of the page, as in Figure 4-20.

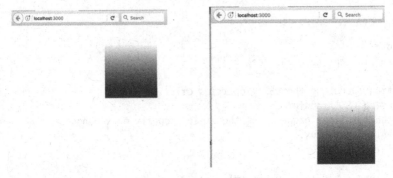

Figure 4-20. *Tweening square with MOJS, top down*

> *You spin my head right round, right round*
> *When you go down, when you go down down*

Flo Rida

Comments

From there on, a few things the reader can do to play a bit more is to have a look at the Single Page API, SPAI, not to be confused with the Single Page Application, SPA!

```
https://github.com/legomushroom/mojs/blob/master/api/tweens/tween.md
```

Also, playing with the other CSS transform is easy, so replacing the translate transform CSS function content with something more exciting is just a matter of replacing the translate-y function. Say:

```
defn translate-y [node]
  (fn [progress]
    (set! (-> node .-style .-transform)
      (str "rotateZ(" (* 360 progress) "deg)"))))
```

The CSS transformation can be applied on the square, and the result is shown in Figure 4-21.

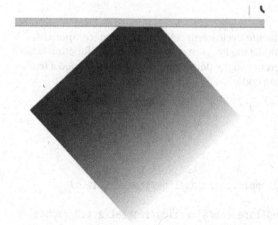

Figure 4-21. CSS transformation plugged in with MOJS

The Mozilla documentation is also quite useful for reviewing all the possible CSS transform functions. For reference, this is added here:

```
https://developer.mozilla.org/en/docs/Web/CSS/transform?v=control
```

4-8. Creating Dynamic Donut-Shaped Charts

Donuts. Is there anything they can't do?

Matt Groening

Problem

This is us getting back in shape with donut charts. This time we have this charting library named Morris, based on the RaphaelJS framework. You might like to create a donut-shaped chart in no time, but eventually you'd also like to have the donut refresh when fresh data is coming.

Solution

Well first, the data will be kept in a Reagent atom; that is a given. Then, it's probably best to have a did-mount callback function added to the reagent/create-class function. But what trick can we do for the refresh?

How It Works

The answer lies around the usage of the life-cycle event callback function :component-will-update; there is a simple trick to make the Reagent component render function know that it has to update with a forced reference to the data atom. Once you have tried a few things, you can read along the following code.

HTML

```
<div id="app"></div>

<script src="https://ajax.googleapis.com/ajax/libs/jquery/1.11.1/
jquery.min.js"></script>
<script src="http://cdnjs.cloudflare.com/ajax/libs/raphael/2.1.0/raphael-
min.js"></script>
<script src="http://cdn.oesmith.co.uk/morris-0.4.1.min.js"></script>

<script src="main.js"></script>
</body>
```

CLJS

```
(ns morris.core
  (:require [reagent.core :as reagent]))

; the reagent atom is defined with a few of your favorite drinks.
; or simply add your own?
(def data (reagent/atom [
    {:label "Wine" :value 12}
    {:label "Beer" :value 30}
    {:label "Whisky" :value 20}]))

; this is the render function. With the added not-empty-data if statement,
; we make the reagent framework knows it needs to refresh the component and
; then trigger the update callback.
(defn home-render []
  [:div
  (if (not (empty? @data))
    [:div#donut-example {:style {
      :height "150px"
      :width "150px"}}])])
```

```clojure
; the function that call on the morris framework to create the donut.
; something more subtle could potentially be done here
; without knowing the library in too much details, let's recreate the
; donut from scratch each time this is called
(defn refresh-donut []
  (.Donut js/Morris
    (clj->js {:element "donut-example" :data @data})))


; the donut shape is created using reagent/create-class
; this allows to define the two needed callback for mount
; and for update.
; if you do not plan on refreshing the data, did-mount is sufficient
(defn alcoholic-donut []
  (let [donut (atom nil)]
    (reagent/create-class {
      :reagent-render           home-render
      :component-will-update    refresh-donut
      :component-did-mount      refresh-donut})))


; the main method of the namespace mounting the donut.
; and a totally free random-donut-data generator
; (use at your own risk) that will refresh the dounut data every
; seconds, here with random values for the already defined drinks.
(defn ^:export main []
  (reagent/render [alcoholic-donut]
    (.getElementById js/document "app"))

  (js/setInterval
    #(reset! data [
      {:label "Wine" :value (rand-int 10)}
      {:label "Beer" :value (rand-int 100)}
      {:label "Whisky" :value (rand-int 50)}]) 1000))
```

Result

The donut is showing on page load, with the different segments of the donut sized according to their corresponding values. Default behavior hovering works, and you can see in Figure 4-22 the different values of each section.

Figure 4-22. Donuts and beer

After a second, the random generator kicks in and updates the data atom's map.

The data atom is referenced from the body of the render function so that it triggers the update callback, which itself calls the Morris library to regenerate the chart, and the donut is visually updated, as in Figure 4-23.

Figure 4-23. Real-time donut updates

Comments

No donut was harmed in this small example! And since there is nothing a donut cannot do, you could turn it into a multiple-line chart.

Update the refresh-donut function code with the following area graph, also not forgetting to remove the data generator timer.

```
(defn refresh-donut []
  (.Area js/Morris
    (clj->js {
      :element "donut-example"
      :behaveLikeLine true
      :data [
          {:x "2011 Q1" :y 3, :z 3}
          {:x "2011 Q2" :y 2, :z 1}
          {:x "2011 Q3" :y 2, :z 4}
          {:x "2011 Q4" :y 3, :z 3}
      ]
      :xkey "x"
      :ykeys ["y", "z"]
      :labels ["Y" "Z"]})))
```

Figure 4-24 shows a rendering of one of the many other types of Morris chart.

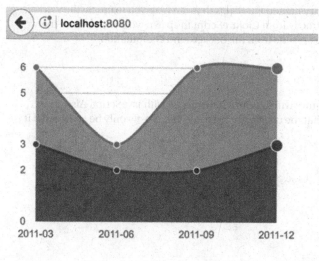

Figure 4-24. *Many Morris charts to choose from*

Other JavaScript examples can be found here, and at this stage, it should not be a problem for the reader to convert quickly to ClojureScript.

4-9. Using Web Workers with Reagent

The secret to success is good leadership, and good leadership is all about making the lives of your workers better.

Tony Dungy

While operating mostly in a single-threaded environment, the browser can actually make use of parallel computing through the use of HTML5 web workers. The technology itself has been around for some time, but most of the time, putting things in place is too complicated and developers tend to scorn those workers altogether.

Problem

Basically, you would like to spawn threads to do CPU-heavy computation in the browser and then display the result in a Reagent component.

Solution

There is this JavaScript library named Parallel.js that can help you to create the workers. You could use the library directly from ClojureScript to spawn web workers and then update Reagent atoms to see results from the background computation.

How It Works

The use of the Parallel.js library will require some interop with JavaScript. Also, a limitation of the library is that the code to be spawned can mostly only be spawned if it is pure JavaScript.

Let's SPAWN.

HTML

```
<!DOCTYPE html>
<html lang="en">
<head>
<title>hello wokers</title>
<!-- The Paralle Javascript Library -->
<script src="js/parallel.js"></script>
</head>
<html lang="en">
  <body>
  <div id="app"></div>
    <!-- clojurescript code -->
    <script src="main.js"></script>
  </body>
</html>
```

ClojureScript

The Annotated ClojureScript code is shown in parallel here.

```clojure
(ns hello.simple
  (:require [reagent.core :as reagent]))

; reagent atoms that will hold results computed by the workers
(def result-1 (reagent/atom nil))
(def result-2 (reagent/atom nil))

; a sample that will contain the description and the
; the to-be-computed result
(defn one-sample[title desc vale]
  [:div
   [:h1 (str title)]
   [:table
    [:tbody
     [:tr [:td.desc (str desc)] [:td.result (str @vale)] ]]]])

; the main reagent component made up of one subcomponent: sample
(defn results[]
  [:div
   (one-sample "sample 1" "simple array do nothing" result-1)
   (one-sample "sample 2" "last element of a reversed array" result-2)
])

; a helper function to generate random javascript arrays
(defn random-array [n-elements]
  (to-array (repeatedly n-elements (partial rand-int 10))))

(defn main[& args]

  ; prepare the parallel context and the initial value
  (let [a (new js/Parallel (clj->js [1 2 3 4 5]))]
    ; do not do anything and just read the result.
    (reset! result-1 (.-data a)))

  ; real example
  (let [
    ; prepare the context with a large second array
    a (new js/Parallel (random-array 1000000))
    ; the spawn function will reverse the array
    ; completely in a worker
    ; not we are using the javascript version of reverse
    ; here using the dot notation.
    sp (.spawn a (fn[x] (.reverse x)))]
    (.then sp
```

```
        ; display the last element of the reversed array
        ; using the reagent atom
     #(reset! result-2 (last %))))

  ; render the
  (reagent/render [results]
    (.getElementById js/document "app"))

)
```

Result

Loading the page sends the workers to work, just like your team of Japanese salarymen at 8am. The results are displayed in Figure 4-25, with a different Reagent component for each section.

sample 1

simple array do nothing   2,2,5,4,4,1,4,6,6,6

sample 2

last element of a reversed array. (same as first above)   2

Figure 4-25. *Parallel workers, and parallel results*

Unfortunately, if you write a bit of ClojureScript code in the worker body, so in the spawn function, you'll see some weird error about not finding namespaces or function names.

As a rule, it is simply easier to just use standard JavaScript to run in the worker. The reason is that while your ClojureScript code is emitted properly, the dependencies (on ClojureScript core itself) are harder to pull in.

Comments

Even though the almost JavaScript-only limitation exists, a few other nice computations can easily be done using this little framework you have put in place, especially the part where you are using Reagent to update the results on the screen one by one.

Following are a few more annotated examples on what can be computed with web workers.

More ClojureScript Examples

```
; an updated reagent component with more samples.
; each of result-* is a reagent atom.
(defn results[]
  [:div
  (one-sample "sample 1" "simple array do nothing" result-1)
  (one-sample "sample 2" "last element of a reversed array." result-2)
  (one-sample "sample 3" "last cubic value up to 100000" result-3)
  (one-sample "sample 4" "slow square of 1000" result-4)
  (one-sample "sample 5" "Fib with JS" result-5)
  (one-sample "sample 6" "Easy Factorial" result-6)
  (one-sample "sample 7" "reverse string" result-7)
  (one-sample "sample 8" "extreme power of Math/pow " result-8)
  (one-sample "sample 9" "biggest prime below ..." result-9)
  (one-sample "sample 10" "find all prime factors ..." result-10)])

(defn spawn [init-value apply-fn result-fn]
  (-> (new js/Parallel init-value)
    (.spawn apply-fn)
    (.then result-fn)))

(defn random-array [n-elements]
  (to-array (repeatedly n-elements (partial rand-int 10))))

(def test-array (random-array 10))

  (let [a (new js/Parallel test-array)]
    (reset! result-1 (.-data a)))
```

Sample 1 result is shown in Figure 4-26.

sample 1

simple array do nothing   9,5,8,4,2,1,2,3,8,0

Figure 4-26. *Do-nothing parallel array computation*

```
(let [
    a (new js/Parallel test-array)
    sp (.spawn a (fn[x] (.reverse x)))]
    (.then sp
      #(reset! result-2 (last %))))
```

Sample 2 result is shown in Figure 4-27.

sample 2

last element of a reversed array. (same as first above)   9

Figure 4-27. Parallel reversed array

```
; perform a "map" on each element of a large list
; then grab the result using .then
(-> (new js/Parallel (clj->js (range 0 100000)) )
  (.map (fn[x] (+ x x x)))
  (.then #(reset! result-3 (last %))))
```

Sample 3 result is shown in Figure 4-28.

sample 3

last cubic value up to 100000   299997

Figure 4-28. Parallel cubic values

```
; compute the square value of each element of the input data
; very very stupidly so it takes a lot of time
; this *should not* be used in production systems, but you may
; be surprised to find it somewhere.
(let[
  a (new js/Parallel (clj->js (range 0 1000) ))
  ]
  (.then
    (.map a
      (fn[n] (loop [i 0]
        (if (< i (* n n)) (recur (inc i)) i ))))
    (fn[x] (reset! result-4 (last x)))))
```

Sample 4 result is shown in Figure 4-29.

sample 4

slow square of 1000   998001

Figure 4-29. Parallel slow square

```
; compute the fibonacci value of each element of the input data
; then display only the last value
; the js/fib method can be found in the pure javascript file
; that was presented above. the js/ prefix refers to it using
; standard ClojureScript notation.
(let[
  a (.require (new js/Parallel (clj->js (range 0 30) )) js/fib)
  ]
  (.then
    (.map a js/fib)
    (fn[x] (reset! result-5 (last x)))))
```

Sample 5 result is shown in Figure 4-30.

sample 5

Fib with JS   832040

Figure 4-30. Parallel Fibonacci sequences

```
; compute the factorial value of each element of the input list
; using .map
(let[
  a (new js/Parallel (clj->js (range 0 30) ))
  ]
  (.then
    (.map a
      (fn[x]
        (loop [i x res 1]
          (if (< i 1) res (recur (dec i) (* res i)) ) )))
    (fn[x] (reset! result-6 (last x)))))
```

Sample 6 result is shown in Figure 4-31.

sample 6

Easy Factorial   8.841761993739701e+30

Figure 4-31. Parallel factorial

```
; this simply reverse a string using pure javascript in clojurescript
; functions
(let [p (new js/Parallel
        "this is a very long string... but eventually it will be a long
reversed string.")
      sp2 (.spawn p (fn[data]
        (.join (.reverse (.split data "")) " ")))]
  (.then sp2 (fn[x] (reset! result-7 x))))
```

Sample 7 result is shown in Figure 4-32.

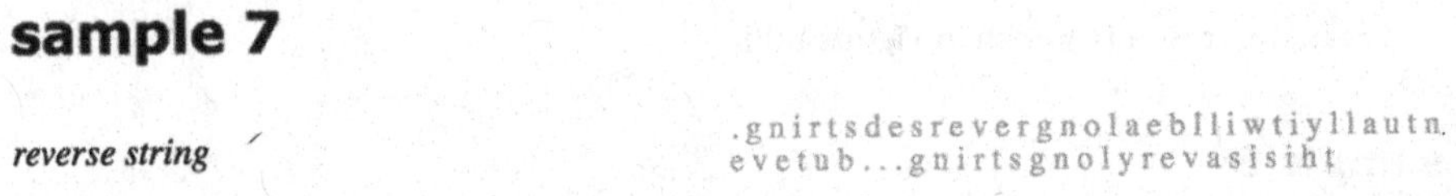

sample 7

reverse string

.gnirtsdesrevergnolaeblliwtiyllautn.
evetub...gnirtsgnolyrevasisiht

Figure 4-32. *Parallel reverse string*

```
; an example of map/reduce that can be perform by the worker.
; the first element of reduce is the .map function of the parallel
; library, the second function is the reducing function. It takes two
; first elements of the map-ped data and apply the function on them
(let [
  p (new js/Parallel (clj->js (range 0 50000)))
  ]
  (.then
    (.reduce
      (.map p (fn[x] (/ (.pow js/Math 10 x) )))
      (fn[d] (+ (aget d 0) (aget d 1))))
    (fn[x] (reset! result-8x) )))
```

Sample 8 result is shown in Figure 4-33.

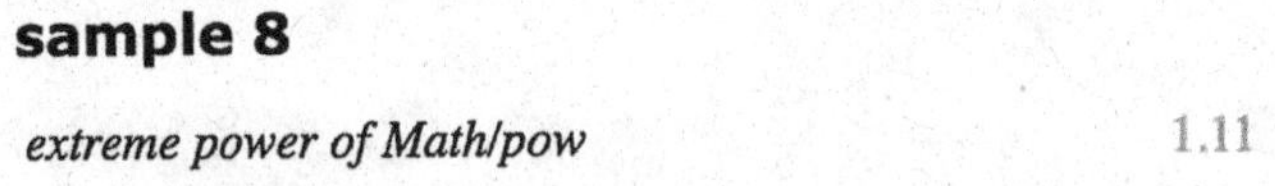

sample 8

extreme power of Math/pow   1.11

Figure 4-33. *Parallel math/pow*

```
; this looks for the biggest prime using a pure javascript function.
(-> (new js/Parallel 10000000)
    (.spawn js/primeSieve)
    (.then #(reset! result-9 (last %))))
```

Sample 9 result is shown in result in Figure 4-34.

sample 9

biggest prime below ...   9999991

Figure 4-34.   The parallel quest for prime numbers

```
; this uses some sweet sugar to make it easier to read and spawn the
; different Parallel functions. Here a wrapper around spawn is
; introduced and all the prime factors for the input are being computed.
(spawn
   600851475143
   js/getAllFactorsFor
   #(reset! result-10 %))
```

Sample 10 result is shown in Figure 4-35.

sample 10

find all prime factors ...   71,839,1471,6857

Figure 4-35.   Parallel finding of prime factors

A nice effect of running the preceding example is that you can see the different results popping up onscreen in the order their computation has completed.

Your turn to compute the next secret value using your army of workers!

4-10. Using the TypeAhead HTML Input Box
Problem

Your next challenge is now to write a Reagent component: an input text box that, as you type, will interactively present you with a list of options drawn from a list.

When typed, the TypeAhead feature of the input box will display a sublist of a full list of people matching the characters being typed in the box.

Solution

The example can make use of the JavaScript library named TypeAhead, presented by Twitter.

```
https://twitter.github.io/typeahead.js/
```

How It Works

The typeahead.js library takes a node, a list of choices, and some simple settings, and does most of the work for you. Let's see how you can make it work with Reagent and ClojureScript.

HTML

The main html page loads jQuery, TypeAhead, and the people's list.

```
<!DOCTYPE html>
<html lang="en">
  <head>
  <meta charset="UTF-8">
  <script src="jquery-3.0.0.min.js"></script>
  <script src="typeahead.js"></script>
  <script src="people.js"></script>
  <link rel="stylesheet" type="text/css" href="style.css">
  </head>
  <body>
    <div id="app"></div>
    <script src="main.js"></script>
  </body>
</html>
```

ClojureScript

```
(ns hello.core
  (:require [reagent.core :as reagent]
            [clojure.string :as s]))


; supposing the list of people has been defined using
; window.people = ["Adele", ...]
; we can retrieve it via ClojureScript as is
(def people
  (.-people js/window))

; the matcher function that will be given to the typeahead
; object constructor
; the ClojureScript matcher function returns a JavaScript
; function that filters element from the original list strs
; depending on the typed "text"
;  the ->> threading macro is used so each statement is passed
; as the last parameter of the next statement.
; (filter #(..) strs) is then passed to clj->js
; then the result of clj-> js is passed to callback.
(defn matcher [strs]
  (fn [text callback]
    (->> strs
        (filter #(s/includes? % text))
        (clj->js)
        (callback))))
```

```
; the mounted function of the reagent component
; here the dom-node function of reagent is used to retrieve
; the dom node.
; .typeahead call requires a jquery object, thus the js/$
(defn typeahead-mounted [this]
  (.typeahead (js/$ (reagent/dom-node this))
              (clj->js {:hint true
                        :highlight true
                        :minLength 1})
              (clj->js {:name "people"
                        :source (matcher people)})))))

; the reagent atom that will hold the selected person
(def typeahead-value
     (reagent/atom nil))

; the render view of the typeahead reagent component
(defn render-typeahead []
  [:input.typeahead
   {:type :text
    :on-select #(reset! typeahead-value (-> % .-target .-value))
    :placeholder "Famous People"}])

; the typeahead input box created using the extended
; reagent/create-class function
(defn typeahead []
  (reagent/create-class
    {:component-did-mount typeahead-mounted
     :reagent-render render-typeahead}))

; the main reagent component, displaying the value of the atom
; and the typeahead component
(defn home []
  [:div.ui-widget
   [:p "Selected Famous Person: " @typeahead-value]
   [typeahead]])

; the mounting part
(defn main[& args]
  (reagent/render [home] (.getElementById js/document "app")))
```

Result

With all this in place, loading the page loads a ready-to-use input box and the selected value, as defined in the home component. This is shown in Figure 4-36.

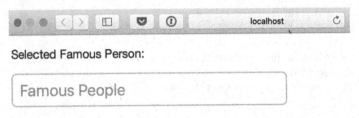

Selected Famous Person:

Famous People

Figure 4-36. TypeAhead input box

Typing in the box shows a sublist created on the spot by the TypeAhead library. The sublist is created from the matching element on the original list.

Typing "John Le" in the box updated the list and the selected person, as in Figure 4-37.

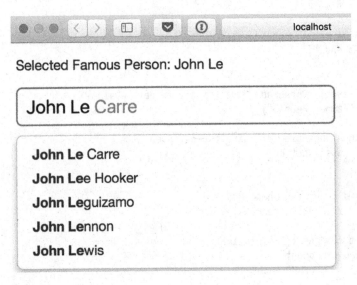

Figure 4-37. TypeAhead value selection

Comments

Sweet: an easy-to-use TypeAhead component! Obviously, the next step is to load the list from the server or remotely, and this will be left as an extra exercise for the reader.

4-11. Using the Mini Audio Player
Problem

It's been quiet for a little while around here, so you will probably agree it's time to crank up the volume and play some tunes.

The next exercise will ask you to play some sound on demand in the browser.

Solution

Use the SoundJS pure JavaScript library to handle the audio, and keep the state of the audio player in an atom, whose value is updated from the audio player events.

How It Works

This is supposed to be a relaxing problem, so let's use CreateJS's SoundJS library to get rid of all the complex sound setup and discovery of what can be used or not in the user's browser. CreateJS will also help you preloading content as you want, send you events on sound start and sound end, and so on...

```
http://www.createjs.com/docs/soundjs/modules/SoundJS.html
```

You're also suggested to use the CLJJS version to put in your build file, using

```
[cljsjs/soundjs "0.6.2-0"]
```

HTML

The HTML code makes use of some Twitter bootstrap styling, and so the scripts and stylesheets are being added. The demo also works great on a cell phone, so let's add the view port definition.

```
<!DOCTYPE html>
<head>
<meta name="viewport" content="width=device-width, initial-scale=1">
<title>Audio Player</title>
<link rel="stylesheet" href="bootstrap.min.css">
</head>
<html lang="en">
  <body>
    <h1>My small little audio player</h1>
    <div id="app"></div>
    <script src="jquery.min.js"></script>
    <script src="bootstrap.min.js"></script>
    <script src="main.js"></script>
  </body>
</html>
```

ClojureScript

```
(ns hello.core
 (:require
  [cljsjs.soundjs]
  [reagent.core :as reagent]))
```

```
; let's make a shortcut to the SOUND object for
; reuse
(def SOUND
  (.-Sound js/createjs) )

; the playing status will be kept in an atom
(def is-playing
  (reagent/atom false))

 ; the sound setup here will pre-load the acdc short sample.
 ; we add an extra callback for when the player has played the
 ; full sound requested.
 (defn setup-sound[]
  (-> SOUND
    (.registerSound (clj->js {"src" "acdc.ogg" "id" "sound"})))
  (.on SOUND "complete" #(reset! is-playing false)))

; the main play button is pretty classic
; the event callback is added through the :on-click handler.
(defn play-button []
  [:div
  [:button {:class "btn btn-default" :style {:width "70px"} :on-
  click      (fn[event]
    (reset! is-playing (not @is-playing))
    (if @is-playing
      (.play SOUND "sound")
      (.stop SOUND "sound")))} (if @is-playing "pause" "play")]])

; finally mounting the
(defn ^:export main []
  (setup-sound)
  (reagent/render [play-button]
    (.getElementById js/document "app")))
```

Result

This works great from your usual browser, as shown in Figure 4-38.

My small little audio player

Figure 4-38. *Your own web audio player*

But also works pretty neat if you type your server IP directly from your cell phone, as in Figure 4-39.

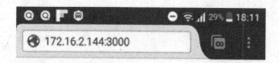

My small little audio player

Figure 4-39. *Audio player running on a smart device*

Comments

With just a bit of added Reagent magic, it is pretty easy to add volume buttons as well.

```
; the atom containing the volume value
(def volume
  (reagent/atom 1))


; the clojurescript function changing the volume
; through the SOUND Api
(defn volume-button[plus]
  (let [curr (aget SOUND "volume")
        p (.toFixed (+ curr 0.1) 1)
        m (.toFixed (- curr 0.1) 1)]
    (if plus
      (if (<= p 1) (do (reset! volume p) (aset SOUND "volume" p) ))
      (if (>= m 0) (do (reset! volume m) (aset SOUND "volume" m) )))))
```

```
; lazy shortcuts
(defn volume-plus[]
 (volume-button true))
(defn volume-minus[]
  (volume-button false))

; the reagent component
(defn volume-control[]
  [:span
  [:h1 "Volume " @volume]
   [:button
     {:style {:margin-right "20px" :width "70px"}
      :class "btn btn-info" :on-click volume-plus} "+"]
   [:button
     {:style {:margin-right "20px" :width "70px"}
      :class "btn btn-info" :on-click volume-minus} "-"]   ])
```

And then you can add the volume control to the main Reagent component.

```
(defn play-button []
  [:div
[volume-control]
...])
```

And enjoy louder or softer sound, as cannot be shown in Figure 4-40.

My small little audio player

Volume 1

Figure 4-40. Louder music

Done! Almost no need for a separate application to play your favorite tracks from your smartphone.

4-12. Using the Mini Video Player

> *South Park started as a little video Christmas card.*
>
> Joel Hodgson

Problem

We've just seen how to create a sound player using a few lines of ClojureScript code and a library, but now you would like to write a video player.

Solution

Writing a video player is actually even easier than an audio player these days. For most cases, there is no need for an external library, and you can just go with a now-widely-supported video tag. Can you figure it out by yourself before reading the code?

How It Works

What about simply creating a Reagent component with a video element? You could also add a did-mount function that preloads the video when the component is mounted.

Code

```
(ns hello.core
      (:require [hello.views :as views] [reagent.core :as reagent]))

(defn video []
      [:div
      [:h1 "video"]
      [:video#player
    {:width "320" :height "240" :controls true
      :poster "http://media.w3.org/2010/05/sintel/poster.png"}
        [:source {:src "https://media.w3.org/2010/05/sintel/trailer.mp4"
            :type "video/mp4"}]
        "Your browser does not support the video tag."]])

(defn simple-player[]
    (reagent/create-class
     {:component-did-mount #(.load (.getElementById js/document "player"))
      :reagent-render video}))

(defn ^:export main []
    (reagent/render [simple-player]
        (.getElementById js/document "app")))
```

Result

Things work quite well, and the video is also preloaded when the component is mounted, as shown in Figure 4-41.

Figure 4-41. Snowy Mountains video

There is no more excuse for not showing your own videos now.

Comment

Taking this to a slightly different level, the w3.org has a page showing behaviors, events, and the API to control a video container.

https://www.w3.org/2010/05/video/mediaevents.html

Converting the page to Reagent is a fun exercise, and worthwhile, since you can learn about the different HTML5 video features.

While the CSS and the events recording have been kept, the core of the page has been ported to ClojureScript, and the resulting code is shown in the following:

```
(ns hello.views)

; the available videos metadata
(def videos [
  {:id "mp4" :url "https://media.w3.org/2010/05/sintel/trailer.mp4" :format
   "video/mp4" :poster  "http://media.w3.org/2010/05/sintel/poster.png" }
  {:id "bunny" :url "http://media.w3.org/2010/05/bunny/trailer.mp4" :format
   "video/mp4" :poster   "http://media.w3.org/2010/05/bunny/poster.png" }
  {:id "bunnymovie" :url "http://media.w3.org/2010/05/bunny/movie.mp4" :format
   "video/mp4" :poster   "http://media.w3.org/2010/05/bunny/poster.png" }
  {:id "video" :url "http://media.w3.org/2010/05/bunny/movie.mp4" :format
   "video/mp4" :poster   "http://media.w3.org/2010/05/video/poster.png" }])
```

```clojure
; util ClojureScript function to change a property value
; depending on its current value
(defn setp[elem prop ufn]
(aset elem prop (ufn (aget elem prop))))
; a shortcut
(defn video-el []
  (.getElementById js/document "video"))

; the switch video function, all in ClojureScript
(defn switch-video[n]
  (let[ vid (get videos n) ]
    (doto (video-el)
      (aset "poster" (vid :poster))
      (aset "src" (vid :url))
      (.load))))

; the video player and the different buttons
; and the list of recorded events below.
(defn video-player[]
  [:div
    [:video#video
      {:controls true :preload "none" :poster ((first videos) :poster)}
      (for [vid videos]
        [(keyword (str "source#" (vid :id)))
         {:key (vid :id) :src (vid :url) :type (vid :format)}])

      [:p "Your user agent does not support the HTML5 Video element." ]]

    [:div#buttons
      [:button {:on-click #(.load (video-el))} "load()"]
      [:button {:on-click #(.play (video-el))} "play()"]
      [:button {:on-click #(.pause (video-el))} "pause()"]
      [:button {:on-click (fn[] (setp (video-el) "currentTime" #(+ % 10)))}
        "currentTime+=10"]
      [:button {:on-click (fn[] (setp (video-el) "playbackRate" dec))}
        "playbackRate--"]
      [:button {:on-click (fn[] (setp (video-el) "playbackRate" inc))}
        "playbackRate++"]
      [:button {:on-click (fn[] (setp (video-el) "volume" #(- % 0.1)))}
        "volume-=0.1"]
      [:button {:on-click (fn[] (setp (video-el) "volume" #(- % 0.1)))}
        "volume-=0.1"]
      [:button {:on-click #(aset (video-el) "muted" true)} "Muted true"]
      [:button {:on-click #(aset (video-el) "muted" false)} "Muted false"]
      [:button {:on-click #(switch-video 0)} "Sintel teaser"]
      [:button {:on-click #(switch-video 1)} "Bunny trailer"]
      [:button {:on-click #(switch-video 2)} "Bunny movie"]
      [:button {:on-click #(switch-video 3)} "Test movie"]]
```

```
[:table
  [:caption "Media Events"]
  [:tbody#events]]
[:table
  [:caption "Media Properties"]
  [:tbody#properties]]
[:table#canPlayType
  [:caption "canPlayType"]
  [:tbody#m_video]]
[:table#tracks
  [:caption "Tracks"]
  [:tbody
[:tr
  [:th "Audio"][:th "Video"][:th "Text"]]
[:tr
  [:td#m_audiotracks {:class false} "?"]
  [:td#m_videotracks {:class false} "?"]
  [:td#m_texttracks {:class false} "?"]]]]
])
```

The Reagent-based video player is shown in Figure 4-42.

Figure 4-42. w3.org player in ClojureScript

Events are shown and recorded on the page, along with metadata of the currently playing video as found by the browser.

4-13. Generating Scalable Vector Graphics

Problem

At this stage you might be wondering if Reagent can be used to generate something other than HTML. What about SVG?

In this problem, we would like to generate vector graphics using the Reagent techniques we have seen so far.

While searching for cute SVG examples in standard JavaScript, an example of a carousel came up:

https://github.com/snabbdom/snabbdom/blob/master/examples/carousel-svg/script.js

Solution

We will get Reagent to generate SVG, and the SVG will be used to create a carousel entirely from ClojureScript.

How It Works

You'll be happy, or surprised, to know that there is No. Extra. Step. Required. to generate SVG graphics from Reagent. The output of the Reagent render function can be used as is to generate XML, and since SVG is an XML-based format, it all works as expected.

```
(ns chapter01.app
  (:require [reagent.core :as reagent]))

(defn svn-circle []
  [:svg {:width 300 :height 300}
   [:circle
     {:cx 80 :cy 80 :r 70
      :stroke "orange" :stroke-width 10 :fill "yellow"}]])

(defn init []
  (reagent/render-component [svn-circle]
    (.getElementById js/document "container")))
```

Mount the preceding Reagent component, and you can see the effective DOM generated in Figure 4-43.

```
▼ <svg data-reactroot width="300" height="300">
    <circle cx="80" cy="80" r="70" stroke="orange" stroke-width="10" fill="yellow"></circle>
  </svg>
```

Figure 4-43. *Generated SVG elements*

And as you have seen up to now, you can update your code, and the component is refreshed in semi-real time in the browser, as in Figure 4-44.

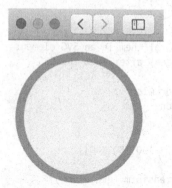

Figure 4-44. *Sweet sunshine*

ClojureScript

The code is pretty much a direct translation of the JavaScript code ported to use Reagent for components. The rotation is kept in a Reagent atom, so rotation directly triggers the rotation of the carousel.

```clojure
(ns chapter01.app
  (:require [reagent.core :as reagent]))

; reagent atom
(def degRotation
  (reagent/atom 30))

(defn gRotation []
  (str "rotate(" @degRotation "deg)"))

; simply increase or degreat the value of the atom
(defn handleRotate [deg]
 (reset! degRotation (+ deg @degRotation)))

; set the rotation to 0
(defn handleReset []
 (reset! degRotation 0))

; draw one triangle of the carousel
; the points as attributes are SVG points
; the rotation is added directly as the transform attribute
```

```clojure
(defn hTriangle[id degRotation]
    [(keyword (str "polygon#" id)) {
        :points "-50,-88 0,-175 50,-88"
        :transform (str "rotate(" degRotation ")")
        :stroke-width 3}])

; the carousel itself is made of 6 triangles, all of them in an SVG element
; each triangle has a color name used for id, access after from the CSS
; and an initial roration in a rotation value.
; remaining part are three buttons to trigger clockwise or
; counter-clockwise roration, and the reset button
(defn carousel []
    [:div.view
     [:svg {:width 380 :height 380 :viewBox [-190 -190 380 380]}
      [:g#carousel
       {:style {:-webkit-transform (gRotation) :transform (gRotation)}}
       [hTriangle "yellow" 0]
       [hTriangle "green" 60]
       [hTriangle "magenta" 120]
       [hTriangle "red" 180]
       [hTriangle "cyan" 240]
       [hTriangle "blue" 300]]]
     [:button {:on-click #(handleRotate 60)} "Rotate Clockwise"]
     [:button {:on-click #(handleRotate -60)} "Rotate Counter Clockwise"]
     [:button {:on-click #(handleReset)} "Reset"]])

; the reagent mounting part.
(defn init []
  (reagent/render-component [carousel]
    (.getElementById js/document "container")))
```

CSS

The extra CSS styling is done here. Only the parts relevant to the nodes inside the SVG element are shown in the following. See how the colors of each triangle are controlled. Also notice how the transitions are slowed down a bit, using a 2-second animation time, applied on each rotation.

```css
svg {
  display: block;
  margin-bottom: 10px;
  border: 1px solid gray;
}
g#carousel {
  -webkit-transition: -webkit-transform 2s ease;
  transition: transform 2s ease;
}
```

```
polygon {
  stroke: #808000;
  transition: fill 0.5s linear;
}
polygon#yellow {
  fill: rgba(255,255,0,0.4);
}
polygon#yellow:hover, polygon#yellow:active {
  fill: yellow;
}
polygon#green {
  fill: rgba(0,128,0,0.4);
}
polygon#green:hover, polygon#green:active {
  fill: green;
}
polygon#magenta {
  fill: rgba(255,0,255,0.4);
}
polygon#magenta:hover, polygon#magenta:active {
  fill: magenta;
}
polygon#red {
  fill: rgba(255,0,0,0.4);
}
polygon#red:hover, polygon#red:active {
  fill: red;
}
polygon#cyan {
  fill: rgba(0,255,255,0.4);
}
polygon#cyan:hover, polygon#cyan:active {
  fill: cyan;
}
polygon#blue {
  fill: rgba(0,0,255,0.4);
}
polygon#blue:hover, polygon#blue:active {
  fill: blue;
}
```

Result

The carousel has taken shape using a simple Reagent component, with SVG. The carousel result in Figure 4-45 is colorful:

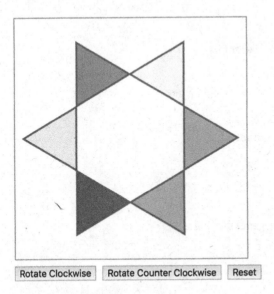

Figure 4-45. *Colorful carousel*

The rotation is triggered using the buttons and simple functions plugged into the on-click handlers (Figure 4-46).

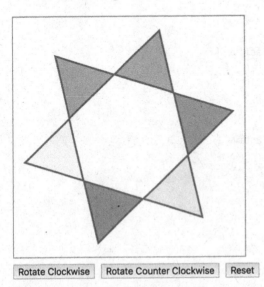

Figure 4-46. *Rotating carousel*

Comments

From there, a few more adventures could lead you to add more triangles or to randomly change their colors based on the rotation of the main SVG element.

> *After all, spinning is its own reward. There wouldn't be carousels if it weren't so.*
>
> Adam Gopnik, *Paris to the Moon*

4-14. Dragging and Dropping Components
Problem

You need to find a way to drag and drop Reagent components around the screen. This is a widely used technique, and while it is not too difficult to put in place, let's see how it can be applied to Reagent components.

Solution

You could make use of the Dragula library, which is an all-in-one shopping place for your in-browser drag-and-drop needs. The library is in pure JavaScript but is packaged and available on the cljsjs web site.

How It Works

The library has a simple API made of only one function, Dragula, so it quite easy to use. The function requires one or more HTML containers to enable for drag and drop, and an optional set of parameters passed as a map.

The library is simply to be added to your project's build.boot file:

```
[cljsjs/dragula "3.6.8-1"]
```

You would then create a Reagent component made of one top div, used as the Dragula container, and a few sub-HTML divs that will be the draggable parts.

The Reagent component will be created using create-class with a simple render view for the div, and a component-did-mount to set up the Dragula JavaScript code.

Code

Apart from some CSS coloring, the real meat of the work is in ClojureScript. Unfortunately for all the meat-lovers, this is only a small amount of meat.

```
(ns chapter01.app
  (:require
    [cljsjs.dragula] ; refer to the dragula library using cljsjs
    [reagent.core :as reagent]))
```

```clojure
; the rendering part of the reagent component
; with the top div to tbe the target of the dragula setup
; and the sub divs.
(defn dragula-view []
  [:div#draggingalong
   [:div#first.box "first"]
   [:div#second.box "second"]
   [:div#third.box "third"]
   [:div#fourth.box "forth"]
   [:div#fifth.box "fifth"]])

; the did-mount function.
; dragula is at the root of the javascript world
; and see how the component is retrieved directly using dom-node
(defn dragula-mount[_this]
    (js/dragula (clj->js [(reagent/dom-node _this)])))

; the reagent component brought to vampire life with
; create-class
(defn dragula-all []
  (reagent/create-class
    {:component-did-mount dragula-mount
     :reagent-render dragula-view}))

; usual reagent mounting
(defn init []
  (reagent/render-component [dragula-all]
    (.getElementById js/document "container")))
```

Result

Mounting the component gives a nice layout and smooth colors (Figure 4-47), but also, each of the divs can now be dragged along according to Dragula parameters.

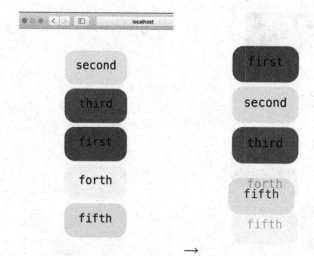

Figure 4-47. *Dragging and dropping Reagent components*

Comments

From there, you could obviously read along the different options that can be passed to Dragula to manage the dragging and dropping parts. You could also load the page from your smartphone and discover that touch events are also supported without changing any lines of code.

Figure 4-48 shows the same page loading from an Android device.

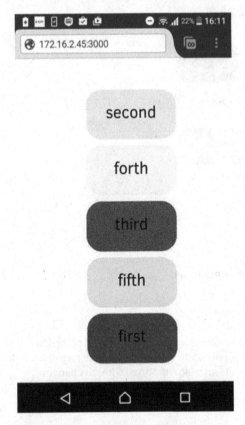

Figure 4-48. Dragging on Android

Time to drag along!

4-15. Generating Code on Server-Side Reagent on Node.js/Express
Problem

Remember when you were playing with ClojureScript on Node.js a few pages ago? Let's get back to it and see how to use Reagent to generate code on the server side!

Solution

Create a server-side counter that will increase on page visits, and see if it is also possible to use embedded components.

The small exercise will have an express application, written in ClojureSript of course, and a Reagent-rendering part, also written in ClojureScript.

How It Works

The small application will be set up as a node application, as was seen in Chapter 3, and the response from the express setup will send a serialized version of a Reagent component to the client.

The serialized Reagent component will be done in its own namespace.

Node Setup. Package.json

The necessary node/express setup, with the added React dependencies, are shown in the following file. This is only for the node part. The ClojureScript dependencies are pulled in via the build.boot setup, which would be the same as usual.

```json
{
  "name": "demo",
  "version": "0.1.0",
  "private": "true",
  "engines": {
    "node": "0.12.x"
  },
  "dependencies": {
    "express": "^4.15.2",
    "serve-static": "^1.12.1"
  },
  "devDependencies": {
    "react": "15.4.2",
    "react-dom": "15.4.2",
    "source-map-support": "0.4.0",
    "ws": "0.8.1"
  }
}
```

ClojureScript: Express Part (core.cljs)

```clojure
(ns hello-world.core
  (:require [cljs.nodejs :as nodejs]
            [hello-world.views :as views]))

; enable nodejs printing
(nodejs/enable-util-print!)

; require the express library
(def express
  (nodejs/require "express"))

; the request handler always sends the same
(defn handle-request [req res]
  (.send res (views/render-page (.-path req))))
```

```
; the main function of the node script
; mount and start the express application
; and plug in the express handler
(defn -main []
  (let [app (express)]
    (.get app "/" handle-request)
    (.listen app 3000 (fn []
      (println "Server started on port 3000 ! [READY]")))))

; set the up the main node function.
(set! *main-cli-fn* -main)
```

ClojureScript: Reagent Part (views.clj)

This is the interesting part. The Reagent component is built just as it would be in the browser .. and ...

```
(ns hello-world.views
  (:require
    [reagent.core :as reagent]
    [reagent.dom.server :as server]))

; the reagent counter
(def counter
  (reagent/atom 0))

; the inside reagent component
(defn my-app[]
  [:div#app
    [:h1 "This is sweet Server Rendering!!!"]
    [:div "Visited••: " @counter " times.."]])

; the outer reagent component
; this renders the whole page for simplicity reasons
(defn template []
  [:html
   [:head
    [:meta {:charset "utf-8"}]
    [:meta {:name    "viewport"
            :content "width=device-width, initial-scale=1.0"}]]
   [:body
    [my-app]]])

; this is using the server namespace of reagent.
(defn ^:export render-page [path]
  (swap! counter inc)
  (server/render-to-static-markup [template]))
```

Result

Compiling and starting the express/node application and loading the page show the counter incremental (Figure 4-49).

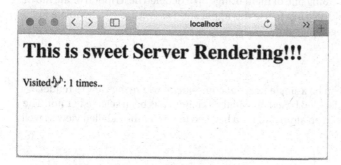

Figure 4-49. Server-side Reagent rendering

Comments

Obviously, the main point of concern with this approach is that the component's reactive part is being turned off completely (as can be seen if you read the code of the server/render-to-static-markup function).

```
https://github.com/reagent-project/reagent/blob/master/src/reagent/dom/
server.cljs
```

But when you are in need of a bit of server-side templating, especially when running off IoT devices, to show the value of different sensors, or network connections, this solution can come in quite handy.

Level 3 Recipes: Writing Reagent Applications

You have now been through a wide range of Reagent exercises, you have built up your skills, and now you want to go one step higher.

This section will show slightly longer Reagent examples involving multiple concepts combined together to create not just stand-alone components anymore, but small applications made of many components.

We will go through three different examples in this section, with each application focusing on a different set of core concepts. Those concepts will be explained throughout the building and the writing of the application code.

The base is still the same as we have seen all along up to now, so we will skip the usual project setup for each application; all of these use the same Boot foundation and very similar build.boot files.

Instead, we will focus on the potential pain points, so if something basic is not clear yet, please go back a few pages in time. All in all, you should be able to follow things easily.

4-16. Using a Movie Catalog as a Template

Problem

You would like to create a movie catalog application, where a front page shows a list of movies, and clicking or tapping one of them brings up a detailed description of the movie.

Eventually, you would also like to use this application as (yet again) a template to build other similar catalog applications.

Solution

The catalog application can be a single Reagent component, where the view to render, list view, or detailed view is decided based on whether an item has been selected or not. The selected item can be kept in an atom and then be used to render the detailed view as well.

How It Works

The movie catalog presents two different screens, one for the list of the top seven movies. When an item of the list is clicked, the application takes you to a different screen, with a full description of the movie clicked.

The layout feels like your usual iPhone application, and in fact, the SPA also loads nicely on your smartphone.

This time as well, the navigation is done through a simple Reagent atom. The selected item will be stored in that atom. When the atom is nil (and it always is when you load the application), the Reagent component shows the list. On clicking an item in the list, the atom is set to the clicked item, and the React component gets rerendered.

The rendering is switched to the detailed view, with another X mark to allow you to close the detail view and go back to the list view.

Let's try to write a ClojureScript skeleton directly from the preceding description. Make sure you try it before reading next.

```clojure
(ns chapter01.app
  (:require [reagent.core :as reagent]))

(def selected
  (reagent/atom nil))

(def movies [...])

(defn detail []
  [:div.page
   [:div.header
    [:div.header-content.detail
     ; detail view header
     ]]
   [:div.page-content
    [:div.desc
     .; detail view content
     ]])
```

```
(defn  overview []
  [:div.page
    [:div.header
      [:div.header-content.overview
      ; list view header
      ]]
    [:div.page-content
      [:div.list
      ; list view, list of movies
      ]]])

(defn my-movies []
  [:div.page-container
    (if (nil? @selected)
    [overview]
    [detail])])

(defn init []
  (reagent/render-component [my-movies]
    (.getElementById js/document "container")))
```

As you can see, the rendering of just the one top component is decided solely on the value of the "selected" atom. The rest flows with the detailed view and the overview, two distinct rendering functions.

Now let's put some content in the application. Supposing the movies list contains elements such as

```
(def movies [
    {:rank 1 :title "Shawshank Redemption" :date 1994 :desc "Two imprisoned
men bond over a number of years, finding solace and eventual redemption
through acts of common decency. "}
; ...
])
```

Then the overview list loops through each of those elements to generate the rendered list. Notice the header and page-content sections. Also notice the added key metadata value to make React happy about subcomponents.

```
(defn  overview []
  [:div.page

    [:div.header
      [:div.header-content.overview
        [:div.header-title (str "Top " (count movies) " movies")]
        [:div.spacer]]]

    [:div.page-content
      [:div.list
      (for [movie movies]  ^{:key (:rank movie)}
        [:div.row {:on-click #(reset! selected movie)}
```

```
      [:div.hero.rank
      [:span.hero {:id (str "rank" (:rank movie)) } (:rank movie)]]
      [:div.hero {:id (:title movie)} (:title movie)]] )]]])
```

On clicking (or tapping), a movie is selected and the detailed view shows. The detailed view has the same header and page-content divs to keep the layout consistent.

```
(defn detail []
  [:div.page
    [:div.header
      [:div.header-content.detail
      [:div.rank
          [:span.header-rank.hero
          {:id (str "rank" (:rank @selected))} (:rank @selected)]
        [:div.rank-circle]]
      [:div.hero.header-title
          {:id (:title @selected)} (:title @selected)]
      [:div.spacer]
      [:div.close {:on-click #(reset! selected nil)} "x"]]]
    [:div.page-content
      [:div.desc
        [:h2 "Description "]
        [:span (:desc @selected)]]]])
```

With the added CSS styling, the component renders in its list mode when the component is loaded (Figure 4-50).

Figure 4-50. Movie catalog application in list view mode

On tapping or clicking one item, the component turns into its detailed view mode (Figure 4-51).

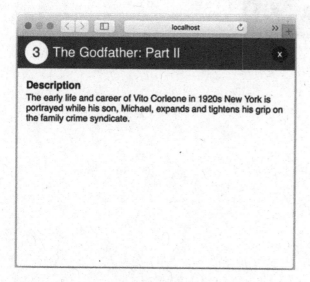

Figure 4-51. Movie catalog application in detailed view mode

From there on, you could add deeper levels of navigation, or you could also expend the layout to cover your favorite restaurants in town. Also note that the page loads on smartphone without a glitch (Figure 4-52).

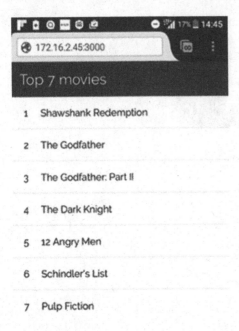

Figure 4-52. *Movie catalog application on a smart device*

The point to remember here is to draft a small scenario in your head about how to go ahead and write the Reagent component, and then the application coding in Reagent should simply flow along.

4-17. Adding Add and Delete Buttons to the Address Book

Problem

The editable address book application takes on some concepts from the previous example. In this one though, we allow editing the content of the list through add and delete buttons.

Solution

The application is made of an internal database that will be stored in a Reagent atom again. That atom will hold the list of friends.

How It Works

A few functions will be written to edit the list by adding or removing contacts from the list. The application itself will be made of three div elements:

- a colorful header, with the title

- a colorful list of people

- an input field to add more people

Here again, let's start by writing a skeleton of the main Reagent component of the application:

```
(defn app[]
  [:div.holder
   [:div.topbar.orange
    [:h1 "My Friends"]]
   [:div.inbar
    [contact-list]]
   [:div.topbar.orange
    [new-contact]]])
```

Obviously, we also need some friends; otherwise life would be very boring and lonely. The initial state adds some of those contacts in the application state. Replace those names with your own friends here.

```
(def app-state
  (r/atom
   {:contacts
    [{:first "Ogier" :last "Eidesheim" }
     {:first "Arnaud" :last "Grandemange" }
     {:first "Cyril" :last "Mayeur" }
     {:first "Benedicte" :last "Rey" }
     {:first "Sylvain" :last "Richard" }
     {:first "Shigenari" :last "Abe" }
     {:first "Joris" :last "Mazille" }]}))
```

The subcomponents follow easily; let's start with the contact-list, looping through the different people of the list. Do not forget to add the :key here again so React does not complain.

Each element of the list is made of a contact subcomponent.

```
(defn contact [c]
  [:li [:span  {:on-click #(remove-contact! c)} "X"]
    [:p (display-name c)]])
```

```
(defn contact-list []
  [:div.orange
   [:ul
    (for [c (:contacts @app-state)]
      ^{:key c} [contact c])]])
```

Removing contacts is just a matter of updating the atom at the proper key. The callback remove-contacts needs to be created.

```
(defn update-contacts! [f & args]
  (apply swap! app-state update-in [:contacts] f args))

(defn remove-contact! [c]
  (update-contacts!
    (fn [cs] (vec (remove #(= % c) cs))) c))
```

The update-contacts is made so it is also possible to update the list using a common block of code.

```
(defn add-contact! [c]
  (update-contacts! conj c))
```

Finally, a simple input field and a button to add new contacts. A helper method is used to properly map the first and last name of the entered person.

```
(defn parse-contact [contact-str]
  (let [[first last :as parts] (string/split contact-str #"\s+")]
    {:first first :last last}))

(defn new-contact []
  (let [val (r/atom "")]
    (fn []
      [:div
       [:input {:type "text"
                :placeholder "Firstname Lastname"
                :value @val
                :on-change #(reset! val (-> % .-target .-value))}]
       [:button
        {:on-click #(when-let [c (parse-contact @val)]
                      (add-contact! c)
                      (reset! val ""))} "Add"]])))
```

See in the preceding how new-contact is returning a function with a local atom to hold the local state of the component. It makes things clean and local to where it is used.

It would also have been possible to add a new-contact key to the app-state, but usually the local version is preferred.

Figure 4-53 shows the resulting application screen.

Figure 4-53. *Contact application*

To further enjoy this little application, you could probably add a sort option up and down to find friends more easily. You would add a sort key to the app-state first.

```
(def app-state
  (r/atom
   {:sort true
    :contacts
    [{:first "Ogier" :last "Eidesheim" }
     ; more friends
    ]}))
```

The toggle-sort function takes the current contact list from the app-state, and the sort order as well; then, it calls swap! on the two keys to update their values.

```
(defn toggle-sort[]
  (let [ord (get @app-state :sort)
        updated-list (sort-by :last (@app-state :contacts))
        to-store (if ord updated-list (reverse updated-list)) ]
    (swap! app-state assoc
      :contacts to-store
      :sort (not ord) )))
```

Finally, we add a place to call that toggle-sort function, say, from the header of the application and ... let's add more friends!

```
(defn app[]
  [:div.holder
   [:div.topbar.orange
    [:h1 {:on-click toggle-sort} "My Friends"]]
   [:div.inbar
    [contact-list]]
   [:div.topbar.orange
    [new-contact]]])
```

The application with the added toggle-sort feature is shown in Figure 4-54.

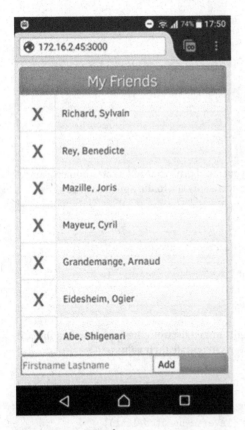

Figure 4-54. *Friends*

4-18. Creating a Customized Painting Application

Painting is just another way of keeping a diary.

Pablo Picasso

Problem

You want to write your own painting application with your favorite web framework.

Solution

The application is this section will create a drawing board using an SVG surface. Mouse events will be relayed using the previously seen core.async and library then matched again to different types. State will obviously be a Reagent atom.

Created paths are inserted directly in the SVG element, as polyline nodes, with their related points and fill colors.

How It Works

Let's start by writing a skeleton of the main component of the application.

How would you do it?

```
(defn hello-world-app[]
  ; the app state contains a drawing color, all the paths, and the
  ; current path
  (let [app-state (atom {:color "black" :paths [] :current-path []})
        event-channel (chan) ; a core-async channel
        proc ;the main core-async event processing loop
        handler-fn ;event handler to go from SVG to core async]
  ; the component returns a render function here
  ; so let's not forget the (fn[] ..)
  (fn[]
    [:div
    ; the SVG drawing board
    ; with all the mouse event redirecting to a common event handler
    [:svg {:height 480 :width 640
           :on-mouse-up handler-fn
           :on-mouse-down handler-fn
           :on-mouse-move handler-fn
           :on-touch-start handler-fn
             :style {:border "thin solid black"}}
    ; we draw directly inside the svg element as we saw in an earlier
    ; recipie
    ; the current path has a different color
```

```
(cons [path-component (@app-state :current-path) "magenta"]
; retrieve all the :paths from the app state
; and append them directly
(map
  #(vector path-component % (@app-state :color))
  (@app-state :paths)))]

; an options bar to change colors and some other commands
 ; will be added towards the end of the section
[option-bar app-state]
])))
```

The path component here is a Reagent component itself. It is made of a list of x and y points, along with a color.

The element is then finally turned into an SVG polyline element.

```
(defn path-component [path fill-color]
  (let [xys (map (fn [{:keys [x y]}] (str x " " y)) path)
        points (apply str (interpose ", " xys))]
    [:polyline {:points points :stroke fill-color :fill "none"}]))
```

Next, let's see how to write the event handler function. You know it will grab the events generated by the SVG element; then, we will put those events in the core.async channel.

```
(let [app-state (atom {:color "black" :paths [] :current-path []})
      event-channel (chan)
      proc (controller event-channel app-state)
      handler-fn (partial event-handler-fn event-channel)]
         ; ...
      )
```

The handler-fn usually only receives the JavaScript event, so here we create a ClojureScript partial function, made of the to-be-used event-handler-fn and a reference to the core.async channel. We then create a map element as a message to pass to the event loop controller.

```
(defn event-handler-fn [event-channel event]
  (let [x (.-pageX event) y (.-pageY event)]
    (put! event-channel {:type (.-type event) :x x :y y})))
```

Almost there, no? Now only the event loop controller needs to be finished.

The controller parameters are

- the channel to receive events, relayed by our event handler

- the main state ref, which is a Reagent atom

The core of the controller is a core-async go-loop. The inside of the loop is a single match function call from the core.match library. The match is then done on the incoming new event and the mouse-state.

```
(defn controller [inchan state-ref]
  (go-loop [cur-x nil cur-y nil mouse-state :up]
      (match [(<! inchan) mouse-state]
              ; the event is mousedown, and the mouse is :up
              ; put the mouse state to :down and wait for next event
          [({:type "mousedown" :x x :y y} :as e) :up]
          (do
            (recur x y :down))

              ; the mouse is in state :down and is moving,
              ; let's update:current-path in the app state, by adding the
              ; coordinates of the new point.
          [({:type "mousemove" :x x :y y} :as e) :down]
          (do
            (swap! state-ref update-in [:current-path] conj {:x x :y y})
            (recur x y :down))

              ; mouse is in state :down, and we get a up event
              ; let's insert the current-path content to an item
              ; in :paths of the app state
              ; and clear :current-path
          [({:type "mouseup" :x x :y y} :as e) :down]
          (do
            (swap! state-ref
                  (fn [{:keys [current-path paths] :as state}]
                    (assoc state
                            :paths (conj paths current-path)
                            :current-path [])))
            (recur x y :up))

              ; ignoré other events for now
          [s e]
            (recur cur-x cur-y mouse-state)))))
```

With all this defined and ready, the painting application in its simplest state is ready and can be mounted (Figure 4-55).

Figure 4-55. *Painting application with a homemade smiley*

It is a bit hard to change the color, and especially to remove the last path onscreen.

Let's brush this up a bit with a menu bar. You'd remember the option-bar component. Here it is.

```
(defn option-bar[state-ref]
  (let [val (reagent/atom "")]
    (fn[]
     [:div
       ; a simple input field to type and choose the color
       ; local state handling is very reagent-like.
       [:input {:type "text"
                :placeholder "Color Code"
                :value @val
                :on-change #(reset! val (-> % .-target .-value))}]
       ; display the color of the color code that was entered in the
       ; input field. Obviously a color selector would be welcomed here.
       [:input {:type "text"
                :style {:width 50 :background-color @val}} ]
       ; set the color in the app-state.
       ; all paths will be drawn using that color
       [:button {:on-click #(swap! state-ref assoc :color @val)}
        "SET COLOR"]
       ; the current color set in the app state
       [:input {:type "text"
                :style {:width 50  :background-color (@state-ref :color)}} ]
       ; undo the last path, by removing the path that was added last
       ; using clojure butlast to keep all elements but last one
       [:button {:on-click #(swap! state-ref
                  (fn [{:keys [paths] :as state}]
                    (assoc state :paths (butlast paths) )) )}
            "UNDO"]
```

```
; remove all paths from the app-state.
[:button {:on-click #(swap! state-ref
              (fn [{:keys [paths] :as state}]
                (assoc state :paths [] )) )} "CLEAR"]
[:h1 {:style {:margin-left "10%"}} "Drawing Board"]
              ])))
```

You might have noticed that the modifications in the app state are done through swap! and assoc. In its simplest form this is actually simply

```
swap! state-ref (update-function state)
```

Where update-function first destructures the state, which is a map, and then uses assoc to update value of particular keys inside the state. In the last swap! Call, see how the update-function clears the paths by setting the :paths key value to an empty array.

```
(fn [{:keys [paths] :as state}]
   (assoc state :paths []))
```

And here we go! The painting app with a (somewhat) useful menu bar (Figure 4-56). Peace.

Figure 4-56. Drawing board with a cat

Executive-Level Recipes: Advanced Reagent

4-19. TODO App Using Reagent/DataScript

The only thing more important than your to-do list is your to-be list. The only thing more important than your to-be list is to be.

Alan Cohen

Problem

This book has not presented me with how to write a TODO application yet; all the JavaScript frameworks do it and I want to write one too.

Solution

Throughout this chapter, you have been using Reagent components and Reagent atoms, and Reagent will still be at the forefront of the architecture. Here, though, we will use an extended version of Reagent's atom, using Posh, which introduces an evolved version of the atoms.

The reactive part will come from a client-side database, where the components are reacting to queries on the database.

So instead of having one value for an atom, or one map of key/values, we will use a full-blown database.

When the database content changes, only components that have a read query related to the database change will be enabled for a rerender.

How It works

DataScript is based on inserting facts and querying them using a query language based on datalog.

Reviewing all of DataScript features is beyond the scope of this section; however, since the database engine used in the browser is based on DataScript, let's review the "just enough for jazz," especially the CRUD operation and queries.

Create Connection and Insert Data

The datascript.core namespace is the main namespace you need. You can create a schema and create a connection to that new database.

In the following example, we will do the following:

- Create a schema, specifying that for one inserted fact, there can be many values for the sports key.

- Create a connection on this schema, creating a database at the same time.

- Finally, insert data, what is called a fact, in the database. The :name and :age keys have only one value, and the :sports key has two values based on the database schema.

Here you go.

```
(require '[datascript.core :as d])

(let [schema {:sports {:db/cardinality :db.cardinality/many}}
      conn   (d/create-conn schema)]
  (d/transact! conn [ { :db/id -1
                        :name  "Nico"
                        :age    38
                        :sports  ["Soccer", "Hockey"] }])
```

Insert or Upsert

Inserts and Upserts can be done by very similar methods, using the :db/add key in the newly inserted fact. The first version in the following suggests the element is new and has no id yet:

```
(d/transact! conn [{
   :db/add -1
   :age 37
   :name "Nico" }])
```

The second version, using the same construct, says we are updating an existing fact by adding a new fact, while the old fact will be discarded.

```
(d/transact! conn [{
   :db/add fact-id
   :age 38
   :name "Nico" }])
```

Here, fact-id is either a lookup reference, like [:name "Nico"] or the id of the fact itself, like 101017.

Queries

Queries are executed via datascript.core/q functions. Calls to q take a quoted vector '[...] containing the query. A query is made of two or three keywords:

- :find, the tuplets that we want to be returned.
- :in, optional query parameters. Think of them as the parameters of a SQL prepared statement.
- :where, the query, which is a set of matching rules as per the datalog query language.

The following query finds all the facts [:name :age] that are such that a corresponding :sports == "Soccer" subfact is matching.

```
(require '[datascript.core :as d])
(d/q '[ :find   ?n ?a
        :where   [?e :sports "Soccer"]
                 [?e :name ?n]
                 [?e :age  ?a] ]
@conn))
```

And if you were asking: yes, in a :find query you need to repeat the values you are searching for, so the following two query elements are needed:

```
[?e :name ?n]
[?e :age  ?a]
```

Rewrite the query so that we can parametrize the query via the use of the :in keyword inside the query. This gives

```
(require '[datascript.core :as d])
(d/q '[ :find   ?n ?a
        :in ?sport
        :where   [?e :sports ?sport]
                 [?e :name ?n]
                 [?e :age  ?a] ]
@conn "Soccer"))
```

"Pull"-ing Data

An extra pull is added to the API when querying data, to make simple queries easier to write. **Pull** takes a database connection and a simplified query made of the tuples we expect and a matching

```
(d/pull [db [:name :age] fact-id])
```

Deleting Data

In DataScript language, deleting data is called retracting data. The fact itself is actually still in the database, but cannot be retrieved through standard database queries anymore.

Deleting the data is actually done through the insert of a :db/retract fact in the database.

```
(d/transact! conn [{ :db/retract entity-id }])
```

Full Tutorial

We have just scratched the surface of DataScript. A complete tutorial on all the different possibilities of DataScript is available online at

https://github.com/kristianmandrup/datascript-tutorial

You can also refer to it if you get stuck writing queries.

Posh

Alright, we have seen all this DataScript stuff, but how is that linked to the TODO Reagent application?

Well, as was discussed, Reagent components are extended in a way that their view rendering depends on the result of crafted database/datascript queries.

Turned into a simple diagram, this would be represented as in Figure 4-57.

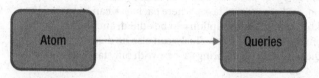

Figure 4-57. From reactive atoms to reactive queries

Where, again, each Reagent component will be redrawn when related data is updated. Related data means that Posh is analyzing the content of the query to create a graph of data dependency for each Reagent component.

So now that we know what Posh is, let's put it in place for this most wonderful reactive TODO application.

Application Overview

The TODO application presented in this section is largely based on, but also largely a refactored version of, the original posh-todo, namely the following:

https://github.com/mpdairy/posh-todo

The code and the look and feel have been changed. Figure 4-58 is a brief overview of what your code will do once you have finished coding.

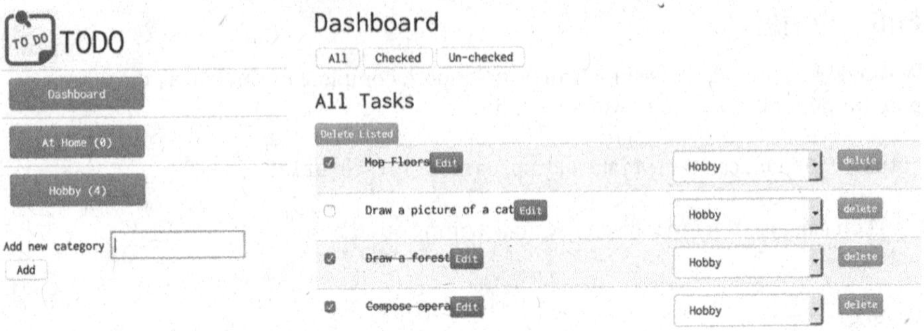

Figure 4-58. A TODO app based on reactive queries

The left-hand side will have a **menu** listing all the different categories available. A new category can also be added in the database, and will be shown graphically in that menu.

If the dashboard button is clicked, all the tasks available will be shown. If a category is clicked, only tasks from that category will be shown in the right-hand section.

In the right-hand section, we have a list of tasks, where each task can be marked as done or not through a checkbox. The task description can be edited, and the assigned category can be updated from the dashboard view. Tasks can also be deleted.

Clicking a category in the left-hand menu brings a view with only tasks related to that category, as shown in Figure 4-59.

Figure 4-59. Category-based filtering of TODO items

Tasks can then be added to that category using the input for this effect.

The relationship between the different namespaces is shown in Figure 4-60.

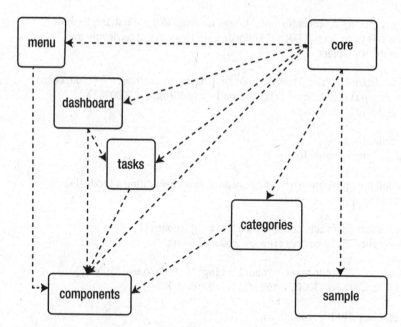

Figure 4-60. Namespaces graph

Reactive Database Queries

Most of the new code comes from the reactive database queries, so understanding the queries is quite important for this demo.

Let's review almost all of the required queries for our coming TODO app through the following listing:

```
(defn db-demo[]
(let [todo-id    (db/new-entity! {:todo/name "TODO" :todo/listing :all})
       hobby      (db/new-entity! {:category/name "Hobby" :category/todo
                      todo-id})]
```

Insert the data as a batch. The preceding new-entity functions simply set an id of –1 to specify that the insertion is part of the same transaction.

```
(d/transact!
db/conn
[{:db/id (db/tempid) :task/name "Buy Soccer Ball" :task/done true :task/
  category hobby}
 {:db/id (db/tempid) :task/name "Prepare T-Shirt" :task/done true :task/
  pinned true :task/category hobby}]))
```

The main application object (or state) is now inserted in the database; its :todo/ name property has been set to "TODO". Following are two ways of retrieving the information of the top object:

```
(let [todo-id (d/q '[:find ?todo . :where [?todo :todo/name _]] @db/conn)
  todo-id-2 @(p/pull db/conn '[:todo/name] [:todo/name "TODO"])]
  (println todo-id)
  ; 1
  (println todo-id-2)
  ; {:db/id 1, :todo/name TODO}
```

Now, we tell the application to show only done tasks, by adding a {:todo/listing :done} object to the application state.

```
(p/transact! db/conn [[:db/add 1 :todo/listing :done]])
(println "--- show main properties of todo element ")
(println
 @(p/pull db/conn '[:todo/name :todo/listing] [:todo/name "TODO"]))
; {:db/id 1, :todo/name TODO, :todo/listing :done}
(println
 @(p/pull db/conn '[*] [:todo/name "TODO"]))
; {:db/id 1, :todo/listing :done, :todo/name TODO}
```

Now, let's play a bit with the category that has id:2. This is the first category inserted.

```
(let[
  c @(p/pull db/conn
      '[:category/name {:task/_category [:db/id]}]
      [:category/name "Hobby"])
  cat-name (:category/name c)
  tasks (:task/_category c)]
  (println "All tasks for category Hobby")
  (println tasks)
  ; [{:db/id 3} {:db/id 4}
```

We find out that the two tasks are associated to the category with :category/name "Hobby". Now let's find out how to add a task.

```
(let [ new-t-id (db/new-entity! { :task/name "Buy long sockes"
  :task/category category-id
  :task/done false})]
(println "new task id: " new-t-id)
; new task id: 5
```

The task has been created, and deleting that task is according to the manual:

```
(p/transact! db/conn [[:db.fn/retractEntity new-t-id]])))
```

Playing with categories, we can perform a before-and-after analysis of the list of categories. We add a new category and then delete it again.

```
(let [ list-categories (fn[] @(p/pull db/conn
  '[{:category/_todo [:db/id :category/name {:task/_category [:db/id]}]}]
  todo-id ))
before (list-categories)
]
(println "Categories")
(println before)
(let [newc (db/new-entity! {:category/name "Hobby2" :category/todo 1})]
  (println (list-categories))
  (p/transact! db/conn [[:db.fn/retractEntity newc]]))
(println (= before (list-categories)))
(println "___"))
```

Now, getting things done is mostly about doing tasks. As we have seen in the DataScript review, we upsert the :task/done to true with :db/add on element with id of 4.

```
(println "All done tasks")
  (let[
      find-done-tasks (fn[done-param]
          @(p/q '[:find [?t ...]
                        :in $ ?done
                        :where
                            [?t :task/category ?c]
                          [?t :task/done ?done]]
                      db/conn true))]
(println (find-done-tasks))
; [3]
(p/transact! db/conn [[:db/add 4 :task/done true]])
(println (find-done-tasks))
; [3 4]
)
```

And yes, we got the two tasks marked as done showing in the list. Whoo-hoo! Figure 4-61 shows the output from the console logs, taken when running the preceding query scripts.

```
1
{:db/id 1, :todo/name TODO}
--- show main properties of todo element
{:db/id 1, :todo/name TODO, :todo/listing :done}
{:db/id 1, :todo/listing :done, :todo/name TODO}
All tasks for category 2
[{:db/id 3} {:db/id 4}]
new task id:  9
Categories
{:db/id 1, :category/_todo [{:db/id 2, :category/name Hobby, :task/_category [{:db/id 3} {:db/id 4}]}]}
{:db/id 1, :category/_todo [{:db/id 2, :category/name Hobby, :task/_category [{:db/id 3} {:db/id 4}]} {:db/id 10, :category/name Hobby2}]}
true

---
{:db/id 1,
 :category/_todo
 [{:db/id 2,
   :category/name "Hobby",
   :task/_category [{:db/id 3} {:db/id 4}]}]}
All done tasks
[3]
[3 4]
```

Figure 4-61. *Output of DataScript queries*

Reactive Queries

If you notice, a few of the queries had a p/ namespace prefix from the posh.Reagent namespace. What that means is that any Reagent component made with one of those queries will be rerendered when the underlying data changes. This is sweet, because that means it is like having turbo-charged Reagent atom-based application state. It's not about specific atoms anymore; it is about complex queries.

The entire code base rests on this simple concept, and with all you have seen so far this should be just a piece of cake.

core.cljs

The main Reagent component is constructed here, with the app component split between a left and a right panel. The require section might be a bit long and could be better organized. Your call, when you write the code yourself.

```
(ns posh-todo.core
  (:require [reagent.core :as r]
            [posh.reagent :as p]
            [posh-todo.tasks :as tasks]
```

```
        [posh-todo.sample :as sample]
        [datascript.core :as d]
        [posh-todo.db :as db :refer [conn]]
        [posh-todo.categories :as cats]
        [posh-todo.menu :as menu]
        [posh-todo.dashboard :as dash]
        [posh-todo.components :as comp]]))

(enable-console-print!)

(defn left-panel [todo todo-id]
    [:div#left
     [:div#left-header
      [:img
       {:style {:float :left } :width 64 :height 64 :src "/reminder.png"}]
      [:h1 {:style {:padding-left 15 :padding-top 15}} (:todo/name todo)]]
     [:div#left-content {:style {:clear :both}}
      [menu/category-menu todo-id]
      [cats/add-new-category todo-id]]])
```

As a reminder, the left panel looks like the following image; see how the code follows along the view of the Reagent component (Figure 4-62).

Figure 4-62. *Categories panel of the TODO list application*

```
(defn right-panel [todo-id]
(let [c @(p/q '[:find ?c . :in $ ?t :where [?t :todo/display-category ?c]]
db/conn todo-id)]
  (if (not c)
    [:div
     [:h2 "Dashboard"]
     [dash/listing-buttons todo-id]
     [dash/task-list todo-id]]
    [:div
     [:h2 [comp/editable-label c :category/name]]
     [cats/delete-category c]
     [tasks/task-panel c]]])))
```

The right panel is in dashboard mode and the sample data is loaded as shown in Figure 4-63.

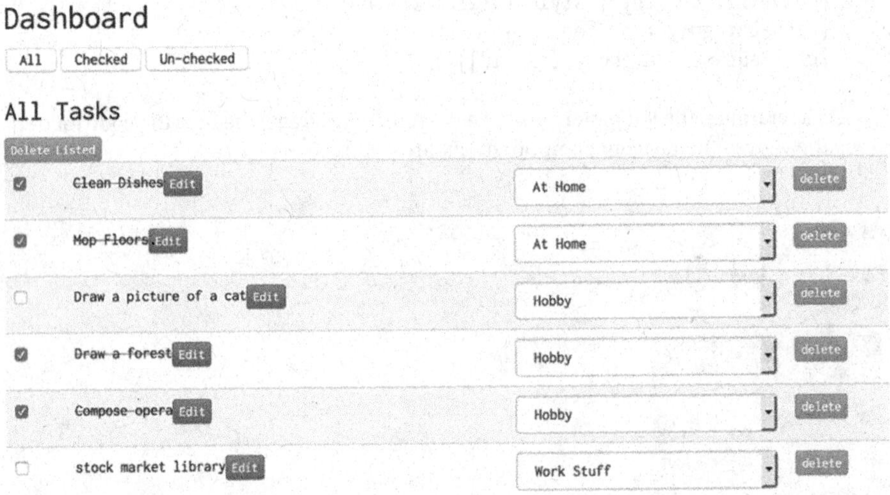

Figure 4-63. *Dashboard view*

menu.cljs

```
(defn app [todo-id]
  (let [todo @(p/pull db/conn '[:todo/name] [:todo/name "TODO"])]
    [:div.row
     [:div.col-md-4
     [left-panel todo todo-id]]
     [:div.col-md-8
     [right-panel todo-id]]]))

; Sets up the tx-report listener for a conn.
(p/posh! db/conn)
```

```
(defn ^:export init
  []
(sample/populate-with-sample-data!)
  (let [todo-id (d/q '[:find ?todo . :where [?todo :todo/name _]] @db/conn)]
    (r/render-component
     [app todo-id]
     (.getElementById js/document "app"))))
```

Finally, see how the menu and the category buttons are done through DataScript. Queries through **p/pull** are built to set UI data and text, while **transact!** updates the DataScript data and Posh triggers rendering of **only** the components which have data related to the updates.

```
(ns posh-todo.menu
  (:require [posh.reagent :as p]
            [posh-todo.components :as comp]
            [posh-todo.db :as db]))

(defn dashboard-button [todo-id]
  (let [current-category
                (-> @(p/pull db/conn [:todo/display-category] todo-id)
                            :todo/display-category :db/id)]
    [:button.menu-button.btn.btn-info
     {:on-click #(p/transact!
                  db/conn
                  (if current-category
        [[:db/retract todo-id :todo/display-category current-category]
         [:db/add todo-id :todo/listing :all]] []))}
     "Dashboard"]))

(defn category-item [todo-id category]
  [:button.menu-button.btn.btn-info
   {:on-click #(p/transact!
                db/conn
                [[:db/add todo-id :todo/display-category (:db/id
                 category)]])}
   (:category/name category)
   " (" (count (:task/_category category)) ")"])

(defn category-menu [todo-id]
  (let [cats (->> @(p/pull db/conn
     '[{:category/_todo [:db/id :category/name {:task/_category [:db/id]}]}]
                      todo-id)
                  :category/_todo
                  (sort-by :category/name))]
    [:table.table
     [:tbody
```

```
[:tr [:td [dashboard-button todo-id]]]
(for [c cats]
  ^{:key (:db/id c)}
  [:tr [:td [category-item todo-id c]]])]]))
```

Opening

This usage of Posh and DataScript combined with Reagent allows you to have a centralized application state, and to act on it from every component in your application.

The rest of the code is in the samples, but you should be able to finish (Figure 4-64) coding the application easily with Reagent and Posh at this stage.

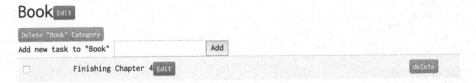

Figure 4-64. *TODO: Finish Chapter 4*

Road to Fame: Beyond Reagent

> *You don't buy a Picasso because you love the frame.*
>
> Joss Whedon

4-20. Using Re-frame
Problem

You would like to add proper events to your Reagent application, bridging an event to multiple state updates.

Solution

Use Re-frame. Re-frame adds an extra layer between the application state and events, in such a way that an event is not restricted to only one change in the application state.

How It Works

Reagent components are created as usual through the Reagent.core namespace. Data binding is now done using the Re-frame eventing system instead of the usual atom direct binding that was used up to now.

Re-frame Functions

Table 4-1 introduces the basic Re-frame functions and patterns used in application build with it.

Table 4-1. *Re-frame Functions*

Re-frame Function	Usage	Objective
rf/dispatch-sync	`(rf/dispatch-sync [:initialize])`	Dispatch an event to the event system. Many events can be dispatched in one go.
rf/reg-event-db	`(rf/reg-event-db :initialize (fn [_ _] {:time (js/Date.) }))`	Register an event in the event system. Takes a name and a function of [state, event-params] that returns the updated state.
rf/reg-sub	`(rf/reg-sub :raw-time (fn [db _] (.toTimeString (-> db :time))))`	Register the equivalent of atoms. This reads the database state and returns a value.
rf/subscribe	`@(rf/subscribe [:raw-time])`	This is like a read on an atom from Reagent components. The deref prepares the component for a rerendering depending on the new generated virtual DOM.

A Clockwork Orange

> *Initiative comes to thems that wait.*
>
> Alex – *A Clockwork Orange*

Writing an application with Re-frame is a slightly updated version of the Reagent work we have done up to now, and is easier that doing so with Posh, totally decoupling the event from the data used in the component.

   The following simple clock example shows a clock updated in real time; and, yes, if you have checked the Re-frame web site, this is a slightly shorter version of the simple example.

```
(ns simple.core
  (:require [reagent.core :as reagent]
            [re-frame.core :as rf]))

(defn dispatch-timer-event []
  (rf/dispatch [:timer (js/Date.)]))
```

```clojure
; defonce is like def, but is only loaded once to avoid
; duplicate timers on page reload
(defonce do-timer
  (js/setInterval dispatch-timer-event 1000))

(rf/reg-event-db
  :timer
  (fn [db [_ new-time]]
    (assoc db :time new-time)))

(rf/reg-sub :time
  (fn [db _]
    (-> db :time .toTimeString (clojure.string/split " ") first)))

(defn clock []
  [:div
   [:h1 "Hello world, it is now"]
   [:div.example-clock
   {:style {:color "#Q08080"}}
   @(rf/subscribe [:time])]])

(defn ^:export init []
  (rf/dispatch-sync [:initialize])
  (reagent/render [clock]
  (js/document.getElementById "app")))
```

What's the Temperature Outside?

Quite a few pages ago, you wrote many Celsius-to-Fahrenheit temperature conversion applications. Wouldn't it be nice to close this chapter like closing a circle, and write an updated version of that temperature conversion application using Re-frame? That's right, let's do it. Sorry. You go ahead and do it!

```clojure
(ns simple.core
  (:require [reagent.core :as reagent]
            [re-frame.core :as rf]))

(rf/reg-event-db :initialize
  (fn [_ _] {:celsius 32 }))

(rf/reg-event-db
  :update
  (fn [db [_ new-temp]]
    (assoc db :celsius new-temp)))

(rf/reg-sub :celsius
  (fn [db _] (-> db :celsius)))
(rf/reg-sub :fahrenheit
  (fn [db _] (+ (+ 1.8 (-> db :celsius)) 32)))
```

```clojure
(defn temp []
  [:div
   [:h1 "Temperature"]
   [:h2 "Celsius"]
   [:input {
     :type "text"
     :value @(rf/subscribe [:celsius])
     :on-change #(rf/dispatch [:update (-> % .-target .-value)]) }]
   [:h2 "fahrenheit"]
   [:div
    {:style {:color "#008080"}} @(rf/subscribe [:fahrenheit])]])

(defn ^:export init []
  (rf/dispatch-sync [:initialize])
  (reagent/render [temp]
  (js/document.getElementById "app")))
```

With this in your core.cljs file, you are all set. Notice that this is very, very similar to the previous simple example, and in fact it feels just like an expanded version of it.

You should not be surprised by the visual in Figure 4-65.

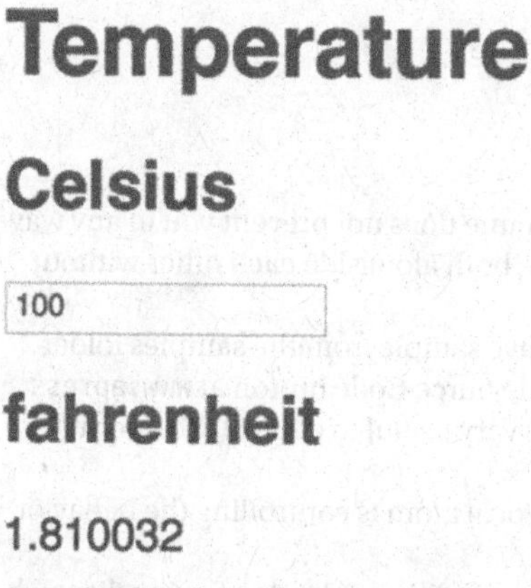

Temperature

Celsius

100

fahrenheit

1.810032

Figure 4-65. *Re-frame-based temperature conversion*

Simple but still works! To add an extra image, you could just define another Re-frame subscription:

```clojure
(rf/reg-sub :image
  (fn [db _] (let [c (-> db :celsius)]
    (if (> c 10)
      "hot.png"
      "cold.png"))))
```

And insert an image in the temperature component:

```
[:img {:width 64 :height 64 :src @(rf/subscribe [:image])}]
```

The icon updates can be seen in Figure 4-66.

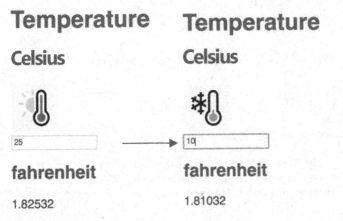

Figure 4-66. *Re-frame-based icon updates*

What About Reagent Atoms?

A quick note about using Reagent atoms: using Re-frame does not prevent you in any way from using standard Reagent atoms, and you can use both alongside each other without any problems.

Notably, if you open the Re-frame–based todomvc sample from the samples folder of this book (which you can access via the Download Source Code button at www.apress.com/9781484230084), you'll find that local atoms are very useful to control the internal state of a specific component.

In the following todo-item, see that the editing local atom is controlling the behavior and visual of each todo-item.

On the other hand, something that is application specific will be done using dispatch and the Re-frame event handling.

```
(defn todo-item
  []
  (let [editing (reagent/atom false)]
    (fn [{:keys [id done title]}]
      [:li {:class (str (when done "completed ")
                        (when @editing "editing"))}
        [:div.view
          [:input.toggle
            {:type "checkbox"
             :checked done
```

```clojure
        :on-change #(dispatch [:toggle-done id])}]
   [:label
     {:on-double-click #(reset! editing true)}
     title]
   [:button.destroy
     {:on-click #(dispatch [:delete-todo id])}]]
(when @editing
  [todo-input
    {:class "edit"
     :title title
     :on-save #(dispatch [:save id %])
     :on-stop #(reset! editing false)}])])))
```

Summary

Throughout this chapter, you have been invited to participate in the building of many examples and real applications using Reagent components, Reagent atoms, and reactive components in general.

To briefly review what was covered:

You learned how to write Reagent components using different constructs and when to use which one.

You learned how to use Reagent atoms to make those components reactive and to avoid callback hell, by artfully using those atoms at key places.

We covered how to integrate those Reagent components with pure JavaScript libraries.

How to use Reagent on the server side was also covered.

You have also written medium-sized applications like address book and painting applications, seeing how those applications can also be used natively from smartphone screens and responsive layouts.

You have seen how to use DataScript along with Reagent components so that the data used for the reactive part of the components can be based on queries.

Finally, you have seen the event handling mechanism of Re-frame, which extends Reagent with an event system that decouples the data from the rendering of each component in a clean way.

The coming chapter is about packaging all those same examples for different platforms to be able to distribute your work in various ways.

CHAPTER 5

■ ■ ■

Beyond

We must go beyond solving our personal problems to becoming solutions and answers to all the people around us.

Sunday Adelaja

This last chapter brings all your ClojureScript creations to new target environments, to platforms beyond the usual web application in a browser: hence the chapter name, Beyond. The main focus is to allow you to reuse the same real-time programming features that you have seen all along this book, so your coding interacts directly with a running application, and there is no need for reloading page or reloading application during your development life cycle.

In this light, you will see how to bring your application to a variety of platforms using three different techniques.

In Section 1, we will review how to simply bring your ClojureScript/Reagent applications to the desktop using the Electron framework, invented by github. Electron is basically a packager for a slimmed-down browser, along with your embedded JavaScript code, where the package finally generated by Electron starts and looks just like a regular native application. Quite a few applications nowadays are using this way to deliver native application to Windows, OSX, and Linux in a cost-efficient manner as well as being able to reuse code written for web applications.

In Section 2, we'll see how another packager, Apache Cordova, turns a www folder into an Android or iPhone native application. The application is a simple native template with a webview, where that view loads your compiled ClojureScript code to your main html page. This also results in simple and efficient code base, since battle-tested responsive layouts can be directly used from within your application, and thus support for many devices is vastly simplified.

And finally, in Section 3, you'll use Facebook's React-Native to enable your JavaScript to communicate with native code, depending on the target platform.

At the end of this chapter, you will be able to bring all the skills learned onto as many platforms as you need, thus bringing your work to a wider audience.

In this section, we will leave installation steps for Android, iOS to a bare minimum. This will be enough to get you running, but you may be left craving more if this is your first introduction to those development environments. (Maybe more instructions will be added into a second printing of this book!)

© Nicolas Modrzyk 2017
N. Modrzyk, *Reactive with ClojureScript Recipes*, DOI 10.1007/978-1-4842-3009-1_5

Section 1: Desktop Application with Electron

The Electron, as it leaves the atom, crystallises out of Schrödinger's mist like a genie emerging from his bottle.

Sir Arthur Stanley Eddington

As presented in the introduction, and as written on Electron's own web site:

Electron [creates desktop applications] by combining Chromium and Node.js into a single runtime and apps can be packaged for Mac, Windows, and Linux.

Chromium is the famous minimal web browser based on webkit, and Node.js is used to interact with it using JavaScript on the server side.

5-1. Modifying the Backend and Frontend

Problem

You want to run a ClojureScript/Reagent application in Electron.

Solution

Write two pieces of ClojureScript code. One is for the frontend to render the content of a browser view, and the other is for the backend, deciding on what top page to render in the main view, and communicating with the host machine.

How It Works

At this point, you should already see that two pieces of JavaScript are needed to get up and running. One part of the JavaScript is running on top of node and is managing the browser to tell it what to do. This is also the piece that interacts with the hardware the browser is running on. That script is also responsible for telling the browser which page to load.

The other part of the JavaScript, the Reagent part, is compiled for the browser, and is run from inside the browser engine itself; this would be the same as we have seen in almost every recipe since the beginning of this book.

This is illustrated in Figure 5-1.

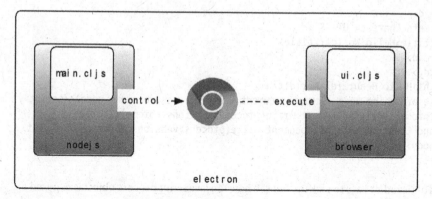

Figure 5-1. *Electron application architecture*

Getting Ready

But let's rewind a bit and review the basics.

Supposing you have Node.js already installed on your machine, you can install Electron directly using the node package manager, npm:

```
npm install electron-packager -g
```

With the Electron packager installed, you are ready for a fantastic first application that does nothing. But, doing nothing is pretty hard, and so to do nothing but doing it properly, you need the three files listed in Table 5-1 in a new folder.

Table 5-1. *Minimum Set of Files for an Electron Application*

File Name	Usage
package.json	Your application metadata, also used to find the main JavaScript file of your application.
app.js	The script to run on node, responsible for telling the browser what to do. Somewhere in the app.js code, we will tell the browser to load the index.html page. This is called the main process.
index.html	The browser base page for your application. This will be executed in the browser. This is called the renderer process.

We have the list of files; now, let's manually put something in them.

The index.html page is the easiest to understand, so let's get it out of the way.

```html
<!DOCTYPE html>
<html>
  <head>
    <meta charset="UTF-8">
    <title>Hello World!</title>
  </head>
  <body>
    <h1>Hello Beautiful World!</h1>
    We are using node <script>document.write(process.versions.node)</script>,
    Chrome <script>document.write(process.versions.chrome)</script>,
    and Electron <script>document.write(process.versions.electron)</script>.
  </body>
</html>
```

This is rather easy to pick up, but see how the JavaScript **process** object is exposed to the browser. You will see later on that this is how the browser view can communicate with the Node.js server-side process. Here, we simply retrieve different versions information about the runtime.

The Node.js application is the following app.js file (note that this is mostly taken from the Electron tutorial site):

https://github.com/electron/electron/blob/v1.4.8/docs/tutorial/quick-start.md

On the server side, we have access to the Electron library in the script and retrieve the most important **app** objects which get application life-cycle events, such as the following:

- ready: fired when the app is ready; this is in the callback of the event where you write code to set up the Window size, and load the index.html page in the new Window

- closed: when a Window has been closed

- window-all-closed: when all the Windows of the application have been closed

- activate: when the application is put in the foreground.

The rest is pretty standard Node.js code:

```javascript
const {app, BrowserWindow} = require('electron')
const path = require('path')
const url = require('url')

// Keep a global reference of the window object,
// if you don't, the window will
// be closed automatically when the JavaScript object is garbage
// collected.
let win
```

```
function createWindow () {
  // Create the browser window.
  win = new BrowserWindow({width: 800, height: 600})

  // and load the index.html of the app.
  win.loadURL(url.format({
    pathname: path.join(__dirname, 'index.html'),
    protocol: 'file:',
    slashes: true
  }))

  // Open the DevTools.
  win.webContents.openDevTools()

  // Emitted when the window is closed.
  win.on('closed', () => {
    // Dereference the window object, usually you would store windows
    // in an array if your app supports multi windows, this is the time
    // when you should delete the corresponding element.
    win = null
  })
}

// This method will be called when Electron has finished
// initialization and is ready to create browser windows.
// Some APIs can only be used after this event occurs.
app.on('ready', createWindow)

// Quit when all windows are closed.
app.on('window-all-closed', () => {
  // On macOS it is common for applications and their menu bar
  // to stay active until the user quits explicitly with Cmd + Q
  if (process.platform !== 'darwin') {
    app.quit()
  }
})

app.on('activate', () => {
  // On macOS it's common to re-create a window in the app when the
  // dock icon is clicked and there are no other windows open.
  if (win === null) {
    createWindow()
  }
})
```

Once you have the JavaScript for node in a file, we need to tell node/electron to make use of it, and this is done via the package.json file.

```
{
  "name"    : "your-first-app",
  "version" : "1.0",
  "main"    : "app.js"
}
```

To run all this, after having the electron-packager installed, you can execute the Electron command in the folder containing all your files:

```
electron .
```

The dot (.) denotes the current folder, or where the project files are located.

Quite rapidly you should see (Figure 5-2) your first desktop application and its main Window:

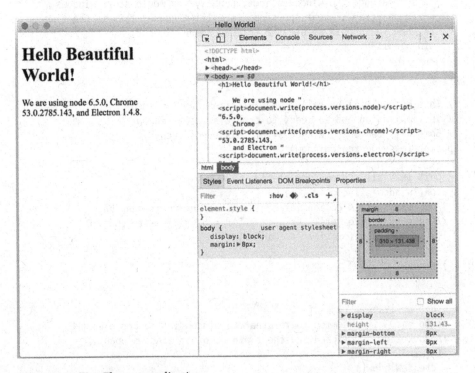

Figure 5-2. *First Electron application*

If you only have client-side code to run, you don't need much more; you can include your web site static files as is, as would be the case for simple games.

Figure 5-3 shows a simple platform game.

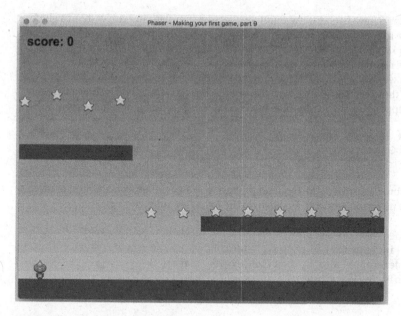

Figure 5-3. *Simple platform game*

Figure 5-4 shows 115, an open source and free Asteroids-like shooter ... packaged in Electron.

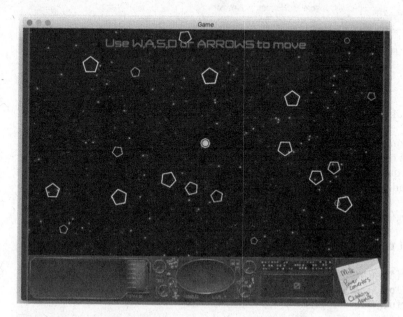

Figure 5-4. *115, Asteroids-like shooter*

Both games have been inserted into the Electron template and run without a glitch.

Now the interesting part of Electron is that it is not only a packaged browser but can also run blocks of code on the Node.js server side, using its embedded node executable, and send the result for display in the renderer view.

Say you want to send a message from the main process to the renderer. With the reference to the created Window, win, you can use the send function, as shown in the following snippet of app.js, for example in the createWindow function of the main process:

```
setTimeout( () => {
    win.webContents.send('info' , {msg:'Async hello from main process'});
}, 3000)
```

On the browser side, in the renderer process, you can embed a small script to receive the message using ipcRenderer, as shown in the following snippet:

```
<script type="text/javascript">
    const {ipcRenderer} = require('electron')
    ipcRenderer.on('info' , function(event , data){
      console.log(data.msg)
    });
</script>
```

And the message will be received and printed in the console as in Figure 5-5.

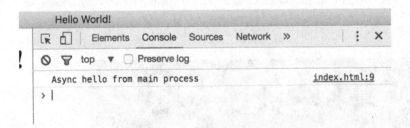

Figure 5-5. *Async message showing in the console*

Synchronous and asynchronous messages can be exchanged using the same ipcRenderer module from both the main process and the renderer process. Sync messages is quite simple.

The renderer view is set up with sendAsync:

```
console.log(ipcRenderer.sendSync('synchronous-message', 'ping'))
```

And the main process is then set up with a callback through **on**:

```
ipcMain.on('synchronous-message', (event, arg) => {
  console.log(arg)  // prints "ping"
  event.returnValue = 'pong'
})
```

The ping message is printed in the main process console, and the pong message in the developer tools console of the renderer process (Figure 5-6).

Figure 5-6. *Pong messages from the ipc channel*

Finally, you can use all of Node.js's power on the server side; obviously, the different modules to use or get native data from the host platform are also available.

To get the renderer view to display the number of files in the home folder of the machine running the electron-based application, you could send a message asynchronously to the main process, and the main process would fetch the number of files through Node.js's API and send the result back to the renderer view.

Try to do it first, using on and send on the ipcRenderer object.

See the script part of the following renderer process:

```
<script type="text/javascript">
    const {ipcRenderer} = require('electron')
    ...
    ipcRenderer.on('asynchronous-reply', (event, arg) => {
        document.getElementById("files").innerHTML =
        "You have "+arg.length + " files in your home folder."
    })
    ipcRenderer.send('asynchronous-message', 'ping')
</script>
```

And the main processes that receive the 'asynchronous-message' message and return files after a while:

```
function listFiles(sender) {
    var path = require('os').homedir()
    require('fs').readdir(path, function(err, items) {
        setTimeout( () => {
        sender.send('asynchronous-reply', items)
        }, 3000)
    })
 }
```

```
function prepareTalkToClient() {
  ipcMain.on('asynchronous-message', (event, arg) => {
    listFiles(event.sender)
  })
}
```

Reloading the application and waiting a few seconds should display a huge number of files in your home folder, and when looking at Figure 5-7, you would surely agree that it is time to do some cleanup.

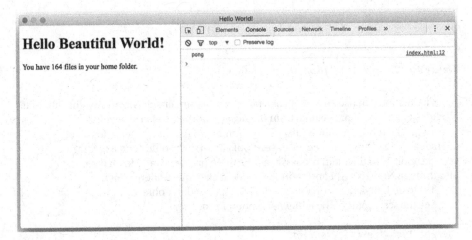

Figure 5-7. *Messaging from server process to client process*

Reagent / Re-frame Example

Here we want to package the temperature converter application to run inside the Electron framework.

The idea here is to first bring back the Boot project template we have used so far, then to compile the two ClojureScript files needed to get things running:

- one for Node.js to control Electron's browser

- one for Reagent to be rendered and used for the User Interface

The project's folder structure is shown in Figure 5-8.

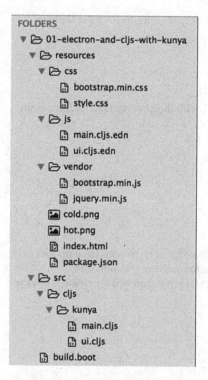

Figure 5-8. *Project file layout for Electron application*

Inside you can see

- basic CSS files, one from a vendor, one for us

- 2 cljs.edn files, one for each compilation unit, main and UI

- the index.html page, which contains our entry page for the UI

- a package.json file; this is for the Node.js part and tells the entry point for the Node.js script

- the main.cljs, which will generate main.js, the entry point for Node.js

- the ui.cljs file, which will generate ui.js, the entry js script for the browser

- the build.boot file, which will contain the build for the two scripts.

Note here that most of the files are straight copies of the Re-frame example from the previous chapter. We are adding a new file, main.cljs, and its compile settings in both the edn file and the build.boot file.

Here's the main.cljs.edn file content with the Compiler options to target Node.js:

```
{:require  [kunya.main]
 :init-fns [kunya.main/init]
 :compiler-options {:target :nodejs}}
```

Then the Node.js **package.json** file is updated, with the generated script from main.
cljs: **js/main.js**

```
{
  "name"    : "mytemperature",
  "version" : "0.0.1",
  "main"    : "js/main.js"
}
```

Now to the **build.boot** file.

Notice that the main difference between this Boot file and the ones used up to now is the fact that we are working with two cljs tasks, one for each compilation unit.

In this particular case, the main.cljs ClojureScript is not watched for changes but the ui.cljs one is:

```
(set-env!
  :source-paths #{"src/cljs"}
  :resource-paths #{"resources"}
  :dependencies '[[org.clojure/clojure "1.8.0"]
                  [org.clojure/clojurescript "1.9.229"]
                  [adzerk/boot-cljs "1.7.228-1"]
                  [adzerk/boot-reload "0.4.12"]
                  [adzerk/boot-cljs-repl "0.3.3"]
                  [pandeiro/boot-http "0.7.3"        :scope "test"]
                  [org.clojure/tools.nrepl "0.2.11"]
                  [com.cemerick/piggieback "0.2.1"]
                  [weasel "0.7.0"]
                  [reagent "0.6.1"]
                  [re-frame "0.8.0"]])

(require
  '[adzerk.boot-cljs :refer [cljs]]
  '[pandeiro.boot-http    :refer [serve]]
  '[adzerk.boot-cljs-repl :refer [cljs-repl]]
  '[adzerk.boot-reload :refer [reload]])

(deftask build-main  []
  (comp (cljs :ids #{"js/main"}
              :compiler-options {:closure-defines {'kunya.main/dev? true}
                                 :asset-path "target/js/main.out"})))
```

```clojure
(deftask build-ui  []
  (comp (cljs :ids #{"js/ui"}
              :compiler-options {:asset-path "js/ui.out"})))

(deftask dev    []
  (comp
        (serve)
        (build-main)
        (watch)
        (cljs-repl :ids #{"js/ui"})
        (reload :ids #{"js/ui"}
                :ws-host  "127.0.0.1"
                :on-jsload 'kunya.ui/init)
        (build-ui)
        (target :dir #{"target"})))
```

Finally, we can have a look at the main.cljs script. This is a ClojureScript port of the simple Node.js JavaScript code for Electron we have just seen earlier on, during the Electron introduction.

Obviously you can do more than just starting the main Window, and IPC code should be written in this server-side script too.

```clojure
(ns kunya.main)

(def electron (js/require "electron"))
(def app (.-app electron))
(def browser-window (.-BrowserWindow electron))

;; Debug switch can be overridden by :closure-defines at compile time.
(goog-define dev? false)

(def main-window (atom nil))

(defn- index-url
  "Url of index.html. Dev URL hardcoded here with dev server port"
  []
    (if dev?
    "http://localhost:3000/index.html"
    (str "file://" js/__dirname "/.." "/index.html")))

(defn- new-window
  [width height & opts]
  (->> (apply hash-map opts)
       (merge {:width width :height height})
       clj->js
       browser-window.))
```

```
(defn- init-browser []
  (reset! main-window
          (new-window 400 400
                      :autoHideMenuBar true
                      :webPreferences {:nodeIntegration false}))
  (.loadURL @main-window (index-url))
  (when dev?
    (.openDevTools @main-window #js {:mode "undocked"}))
  (.on @main-window "closed" #(reset! main-window nil)))

(defn init []
  (.on app "window-all-closed"
       #(when-not (= js/process.platform "darwin")
          (.quit app)))
  (.on app "ready" init-browser)

  (set! *main-cli-fn* (fn [] nil))) ;; see cljs.core/*main-cli-fn*
```

And all is in place! Let's quick-start the boot dev task from a terminal:

```
boot dev
```

The output from the command is slightly expanded, with one output for each script:

```
Compiling ClojureScript...
• js/main.js
...
Compiling ClojureScript...
• js/ui.js
Writing target dir(s)...
Elapsed time: 32.902 sec
```

OK, so our application is ready and hosted at the usual dev URL at http://localhost:3000. Let's check with a quick look opening our browser to the URL (Figure 5-9).

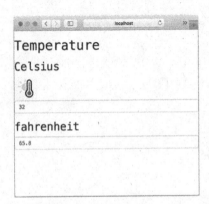

Figure 5-9. *Reagent/Re-Frame application running inside the browser*

Wait, I know, that's fun, but we are just using the browser and not really Electron at all! You are correct indeed; let's start Electron on the project's target folder of our project with the following command:

```
electron target
```

And the magic temperature Window appears within a new application; note the KuNya as the Window name in Figure 5-10.

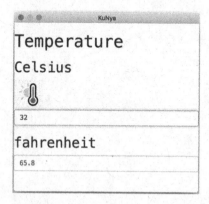

Figure 5-10. *Reagent/Re-Frame application running inside Electron*

As a reminder, the boot dev task has copied all the needed project files to the target folder so that folder contains everything Electron needs to run.

The application is a brand-new one and is entirely self-contained.

Another sweet feature we haven't lost in development mode is the ability to update code in the ui.cljs file, and see your updates still refreshed in real time thanks to the whole Boot environment setup.

Also, since we are in development mode, the developer tools Window is showing up on first load, as was written in the main.cljs file.

If you remember the two following lines:

```
(when dev?
    (.openDevTools @main-window #js {:mode "undocked"}))
```

Those are the lines triggering the rendering of the development tools Window; obviously, you could remove the lines if they get in your way each time, and you can reopen them from the application menu.

Debugging

Talking about the development Window, one feature that has not been covered yet is the debugging feature of the Chrome/Reagent/ClojureScript setup.

The Boot/ClojureScript tooling is inherently configured in such a way to match Chrome debugging feature by default, and it will allow you to debug your cljs file directly. Since cljs files are compiled to JavaScript files before being loaded, this is a tremendous addition.

The magic comes from the source map feature of HTML5, where source map files are stored along the compiled JavaScript files to link the two without affecting performance.

What that gives is that you can put a breakpoint in your cljs file, using Cmd-P or Ctrl-P to quick-open a file from the application view, and then choosing the file you want to debug, as shown in Figure 5-11.

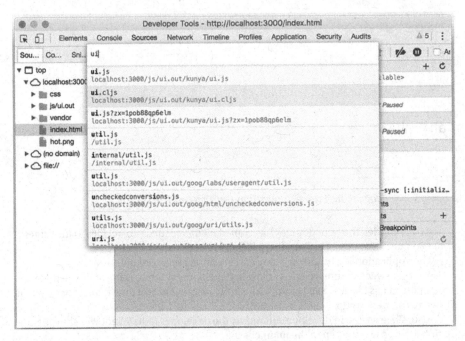

Figure 5-11. *Adding debug breakpoints: Selecting a file*

Then, put a breakpoint at your custom location (Figure 5-12).

```
35
36  (defn ^:export init []
37    (rf/dispatch-sync [:initialize])
38    (reagent/render [temperature]
39      (js/document.getElementById "app")))
40
```

Figure 5-12. *Adding debug breakpoints: Selecting a line*

And then, after hitting Ctrl-R or Cmd-R for a page refresh, you can see your application reload and stop at the given line/location in the ClojureScript file (Figure 5-13).

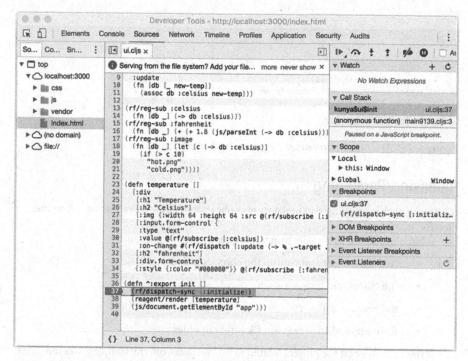

Figure 5-13. *Debugging: Application load stops at breakpoint*

Your application will look like it is in some kind of waiting mode (Figure 5-14).

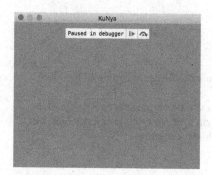

Figure 5-14. *Application in wait mode when execution reaches a breakpoint*

If you need some internal info about your namespaces, functions, and/or bindings, you can access all of those using the watch panel of the developer tool Window (Figure 5-15).

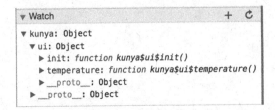

Figure 5-15. *At a breakpoint, detailed view of each of the variable values*

Releasing/Packaging

It's time to pack everything and make your application really stand alone based on the Electron framework.

What is produced by the Electron packaging command contains

- Node.js to start and control the chromium browser

- the chromium browser itself

- the resources files, css, html, and standard JavaScript files

- the compiled-to-JavaScript ClojureScript files

If you have opened the project related to this section from the samples, you may have noticed the release task in the build.boot file:

```
(deftask release  "Release build."  []
  (comp (cljs :ids #{"js/main"}
             :optimizations :simple)
        (cljs :ids #{"js/ui"}
             :optimizations :advanced)
        (target :dir #{"release"})))
```

As you can read, this compiles the two ClojureScript files and copies all the Boot fileset to the release folder.

This **does** take a significantly longer time than usual compilation times, due to the fact that we are requiring advanced optimizations on the generated JavaScript files. But even on a slow machine, you should be sorted within 1-2 minutes.

```
NikoMacBook% boot release
Compiling ClojureScript...
o js/main.js
Compiling ClojureScript...
o js/ui.js
Writing target dir(s)...
```

The content of the release folder is according to expectations with the following:

```
NikoMacBook% tree -L 2
├── cold.png
├── css
│   ├── bootstrap.min.css
│   └── style.css
├── hot.png
├── index.html
├── js
│   ├── main.cljs.edn
│   ├── main.js
│   ├── main.out
│   ├── ui.cljs.edn
│   ├── ui.js
│   └── ui.out
├── package.json
└── vendor
    ├── bootstrap.min.js
    └── jquery.min.js
```

Now to generate a binary for any of the standard platforms, you can use one of the following commands:

For Linux:

```
electron-packager release/ --platform=linux --arch=x64 --version=1.6.6
```

Figure 5-16 shows the application running on Linux.

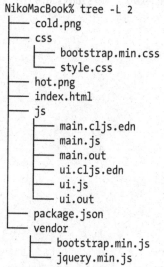

Figure 5-16. *Electron application running on Linux*

For OSX:
```
electron-packager release/ --platform=darwin --arch=x64 --version=1.6.6
```

Figure 5-17 shows the application running on OSX.

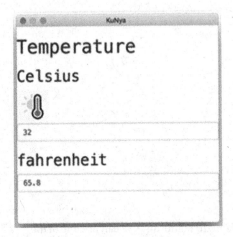

Figure 5-17. *Electron application running on OSX*

For Windows:
```
electron-packager release/ --platform=win32 --arch=x64 --version=1.6.6
```

Figure 5-18 shows the application running on Windows.

Figure 5-18. *Electron application running on Windows*

Each of the command generates a binary from

- a folder: where the project files are stored

- a platform: win32, darwin, Linux (or all)

- an architecture: x64 is the most common nowadays, but you can also use x32

- an Electron packager version, and the current version is 1.6.6 at time of writing.

From the different screenshots, you can see that the layout and rendering are very consistent between the different platforms.

One drawback to portability is the size of each binary folder; each generated folder is around 100Mb or above, and while this is rarely a problem anymore for most desktop applications , it may use a bit of your allowed bandwidth the first time.

Falling Blocks Nostalgia

Just for kicks, the very cool Tetris port hosted at

```
https://github.com/shaunlebron/t3trOs-bare.git
```

has been packaged for Electron in the examples that can be found alongside this book. Figure 5-19 shows how cool Tetris looks inside Electron.

Figure 5-19. *Tetris running inside Electron*

Maybe you should add an emergency hide mode to be able to use it at work though!

Section 2: Android/iOS Application with Cordova

Cordova is the free and open source Apache framework that as per their website creates "mobile apps from HTML, CSS & JS, target multiple platforms with one code base." If you have never heard of it, you can think of Apache Cordova as Electron used to create applications for mobile devices.

Cordova itself is a command-line tool that

- creates ready-to-deploy projects from templates

- manages target platforms for your application

- manages application plugins; understand plugin as ways to communicate with the target platform native APIs from JavaScript

- Performs some configuration managements, notably permissions

- Runs your application on target environment, providing the environment itself is available from the standard tooling for that environment (Android SDK for Android, e.g.)

Cordova prepares a template of native application for each target. The simplified life cycle for this template boils down to loading a native web view inside a native app, and then loading your page/application in that web view.

On top of this standard feature, Cordova adds a number of plugins to interact with native APIs of the device for more native and user-friendly interaction.

One of the main advantages of the Cordova framework is to be able to deploy the same application to many different devices, using simple JavaScript coding and no native APIs.

This is unfortunately also its main drawback, since JavaScript in the browser is usually quite an order of magnitude slower, and the usual native-feeling of each device tends to get lost a bit.

Still, there are many areas where you can use Cordova, and for example, using it for very fast smart device prototyping makes it quite a top-of-its-class contender.

In our case, it also means we can use the almost real-time coding feature of ClojureScript and reuse many of the components developed with Reagent and Re-frame.

■ **Note** Even if Cordova has a browser mode that could seem close to the Electron environment, it is simply exposing the rendering view of the application and cannot be packaged as a native application like Electron does.

5-2. Building a Bare-Bones Cordova Project
Problem

You want to turn a folder containing a static web application into an application that can run natively on Android or iPhone.

Solution

Use the Cordova project that can do exactly this task and more by adding native interacting to a JavaScript-based application.

How It Works

If you have followed this book and installed the different pieces of software, then Node.js is on your machine, and guess what! The Cordova CLI runs on Node.js.

Let's install it with the node package manager, npm:

```
npm install -g cordova
```

The -g flag tells npm to install the library globally; and now you already have pretty much everything needed to get started.

The plan in this small section is for you to create an application from a template, and then run it inside the browser. You will then run the same application on your Android device.

```
cordova create MySummerApp
```

Will create an application MySummerApp in the folder MySummerApp with default settings.

A brand-new project has the following file layouts, which are described in Table 5-2.

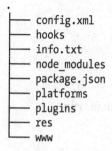

```
├── config.xml
├── hooks
├── info.txt
├── node_modules
├── package.json
├── platforms
├── plugins
├── res
└── www
```

Table 5-2. *Cordova Project File Layouts*

File/Folder	Usage
config.xml	the project global configuration, including application permissions
Hook	hooks for Cordova commands and can be left aside for now
node_modules	the folder where the Node.js plugins used by Cordova are physically located
package.json	as usual, contains name version, and library/plugins metadata
platform	project files related to each target environment
plugins	the Cordova plugins used by this project
res	resources like images, icons, etc.
www	web project location, where the index.html entry and css, JavaScript files, etc. are located

Now to run this new application, you need a target environment. This is done with the platform subcommand.

```
cordova platform
```

By default, the command shows the already installed target for the current project, as well as the available ones:

```
NikoMacBook% cordova platform
Installed platforms:

Available platforms:
  android ~6.2.2
  blackberry10 ~3.8.0 (deprecated)
  browser ~4.1.0
  ios ~4.4.0
  osx ~4.0.1
  webos ~3.7.0
```

Let's add the browser platform to test the default Cordova setup.

```
cordova platform add browser
```

Then we tell Cordova to run the project on that environment with the **run** subcommand:

```
cordova run browser
```

This will start a local web server and point your browser to open a given URL on that local server. An empty application starts: now you get the idea, it's going to rock.

See how it looks like in Figure 5-20.

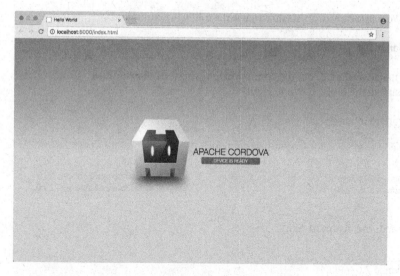

Figure 5-20. *Cordova application running in the browser*

Bare-Bones Run on Android

Let's get that very simple application running on your Android device. This is more of a list of setup operations to follow than something to fondly enjoy, but the expected result is to get the sample to run on your own Android device.

Then we will move on to work with our own application. (Temperature conversion anyone?)

The following steps show how to get the Android environment ready:

1. Install Android SDK. Go to

    ```
    https://developer.android.com/studio/index.html
    ```

    See the link to "just the tools" at the bottom of the page:

    ```
    https://dl.google.com/android/repository/sdk-tools-
    darwin-3859397.zip and then run the installer.
    ```

2. Install Android Studio (optional). If you need a full Android IDE (not used in this book) then head again to

    ```
    https://developer.android.com/studio/index.html
    ```

    And download the installer for the IDE>

3. Set up the Path. On *nix machine, the following will do:

    ```
    export ANDROID_HOME=<yourpath>/Android/sdkstudio
    export PATH=${PATH}:${ANDROID_HOME}/tools
    export PATH=${PATH}:${ANDROID_HOME}/platform-tools%
    ```

You are ready to go, if you can use the following command:

```
android --help
```

4. Install tooling. From the command line, run the following and install the tools shown in Figure 5-21.

```
android sdk
```

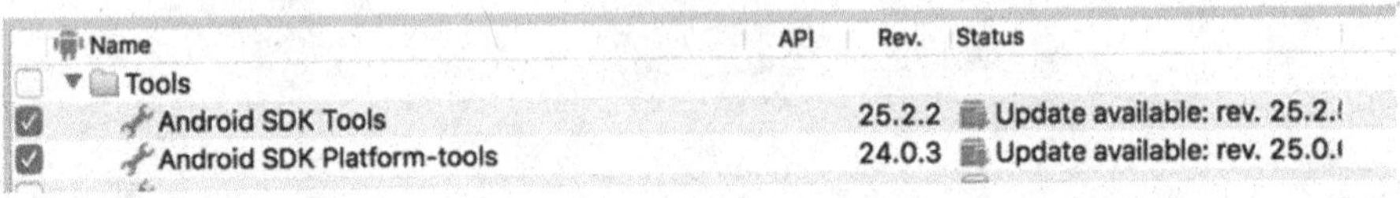

Name	API	Rev.	Status
▼ Tools			
☑ ⚒ Android SDK Tools		25.2.2	Update available: rev. 25.2.(
☑ ⚒ Android SDK Platform-tools		24.0.3	Update available: rev. 25.0.(

and the Android SDK:

	API		Status
Sources for Android SDK	25	1	Not installed
▼ Android 7.0 (API 24)			
Documentation for Android SDK	24	1	Not installed
SDK Platform	24	3	Installed

Figure 5-21. Install Android tooling

Enable developer mode on your phone. On your phone, in the view: Settings ➤ About your Phone and tap the build number seven times. The developer mode is now enabled.

5. Enable USB debugging. In Settings, go to developer. Then enable USB debugging.

6. Confirm that USB Plug and check device is available for adb, the Android debugger tool. After plugging your device into a USB port, check that the device is showing with the adb devices command.

```
NikoMacBook% adb devices
List of devices attached
QV700B1MOB      device
```

Now back to fun coding.

Your smartphone is ready; now let's put the Cordova application on it. Back to the new Cordova project folder, let's add Android as a target platform for the current application:

```
cordova platform add android
```

And check the enabled platforms list the newly added Android with the following command:

```
NikoMacBook% cordova platform

Installed platforms:
  android 6.2.3
  browser 4.1.0
Available platforms:
  blackberry10 ~3.8.0 (deprecated)
  ios ~4.4.0
  osx ~4.0.1
  webos ~3.7.0
```

Look at Figure 5-22 and enjoy a wonderful result.

Figure 5-22. Your own Cordova app on your own Android

ClojureScript on Cordova

Now this was just the beginning; obviously, you would like to bring our own application to Android, not just a standard splashscreen.

The idea here is, with the Cordova layout as a base, to insert our ever-loving Boot tooling in the project with a build.boot file, a resources folder with the index.html and related dependencies, and a src folder containing our ClojureScript code.

We will then get Boot to compile the ClojureScript code, pull in the resources files, and then output the full fileset in the www folder, which is, as you remember, the folder used by Cordova.

With the previous Cordova project, the one based on the template you just created, let's copy the resources and src folder from the temperature converter of the last section.

Then write the build.boot file yourself; it will be very similar to the usual, with a few changes.

```
(def +version+ "0.1.0")

(set-env!
 :source-paths    #{"src"}
 :resource-paths  #{"resources"}
 :target-path     "www"
 :dependencies
 '[
 [adzerk/boot-cljs    "1.7.228-2"    :scope "test"]
 [adzerk/boot-reload  "0.4.11"       :scope "test"]
 [pandeiro/boot-http  "0.7.3"        :scope "test"]

 ; clojurescript and reagent
 [org.clojure/clojurescript "1.9.494"]
 [reagent "0.6.1"]
 [re-frame "0.9.0"]

 ; REPL
 [adzerk/boot-cljs-repl    "0.3.3"]  ;; latest release
 [com.cemerick/piggieback  "0.2.1"   :scope "test"]
 [weasel                   "0.7.0"   :scope "test"]
 [org.clojure/tools.nrepl  "0.2.12"  :scope "test"]

 ; test
 [org.clojure/test.check "0.8.2" :scope "test"]
 [devcards "0.2.1"]
 [crisptrutski/boot-cljs-test "0.2.0-SNAPSHOT" :scope "test"]
 ])

(require
 '[adzerk.boot-cljs       :refer [cljs]]
 '[adzerk.boot-cljs-repl  :refer [cljs-repl start-repl]]
 '[adzerk.boot-reload     :refer [reload]]
```

```
'[pandeiro.boot-http    :refer [serve]]
'[crisptrutski.boot-cljs-test :refer [test-cljs]]])

(def host (.getHostAddress (java.net.Inet4Address/getLocalHost)))

(task-options!
 serve  {:dir "/" :port 3000}
 reload {:ws-host host
         :asset-host (str "http://" host ":3000")})

(deftask build []
  (comp (cljs)))

(deftask run []
  (comp
   (serve)
   (watch)
   (cljs-repl)
   (reload)
   (build)
   (target :dir #{"www"})))

(deftask production []
  (task-options! cljs   {:optimizations :advanced})
  identity)

(deftask development []
  (task-options! cljs   {:optimizations :none :source-map true}
  reload {:on-jsload 'cadabra.core/reload})
  identity)

(deftask dev "alias to run application in development mode" []
  (comp
   (development)
   (run)))
```

We hope you have found the differences from before by yourself; they're mostly as follows:

- We need an IP address so the phone can connect to our dev environment

- the target dir of the Boot task is set to www

Apart from the namespace, the ClojureScript code is the same as before.

```
(ns cadabra.core
  (:require [reagent.core :as reagent]
            [re-frame.core :as rf]))
```

```
(defn dispatch-timer-event  []
    (rf/dispatch [:timer (js/Date.)]))

(defonce do-timer
  (js/setInterval dispatch-timer-event 1000))

(rf/reg-event-db :initialize
  (fn [_ _] {:time (js/Date.) }))

(rf/reg-event-db
  :timer
  (fn [db [_ new-time]]
    (assoc db :time new-time)))

(rf/reg-sub :time
  (fn [db _]
    (-> db :time .toTimeString (clojure.string/split " ") first)))

(defn clock []
  [:div
   [:h1 "Hello world, on planet android it is now and running just fine"]
   [:div.example-clock
   {:style {:color "#448080"}}
   @(rf/subscribe [:time])]])

(defn ^:export init []
  (rf/dispatch-sync [:initialize])
  (reagent/render [clock]
  (js/document.getElementById "app")))

(defn reload[] (init))
```

In the resources/js folder, make sure the cadabra.cljs.end has the proper compilation options with

```
{:require  [cadabra.core]
 :init-fns [cadabra.core/init]
 :compiler-options {:asset-path "js/cadabra.out"}}
```

And now let's fire our ClojureScript development environment:

```
boot dev
```

If the compilation goes fine, we can deploy the application to the Android device, using the same Cordova command:

```
cordova run android
```

And ... yes! The oh-so-cool and unique temperature converter app is now running on our Android phone (Figure 5-23).

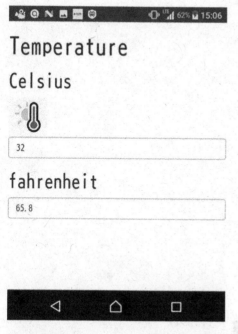

Figure 5-23. *Reagent temperature converter running on Android*

On top of that, if you are on the same network, meaning if your computer and your device can see each other, your code also updates in real time to the Android environment, just as you have been used to with the Boot setup.

Say you update the temperature Reagent component just a little bit:

```
(defn temperature []
  [:div
   [:h1 "Temperature"]
[:h2 {:style {:color :magenta}} "With Real Time Updates"]
...
])
```

Then the update shows up on your phone almost instantly (Figure 5-24).

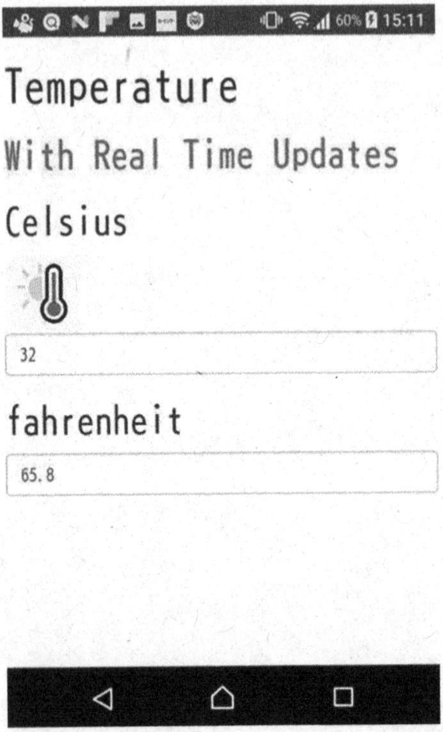

Figure 5-24. *Coding in real time on Android*

Also note that at this stage, your phone does not need to be USB plugged with your computer; the update of new code is done through the websocket opened by the Boot \ reload task!

Native APIs

Now, let's say you would like to interact with native API of your phones, say for example the phone vibration.

What Cordova does is propose plugins where the interface to that plugin is in JavaScript and the native part of the plugin is also deployed to the target platform.

```
cordova plugin add cordova-plugin-vibration
```

The plugin installed, let's update the temperature component with a vibration each time Reagent mounts the component. Let's use reagent/create-class and keep the view, while adding a **component-did-mount** callback, with the call to the vibration:

```
(defn temperature []
 (reagent/create-class
  {
   :component-did-mount
   (fn [this old-props old-children]
      (.vibrate js/navigator (clj->js [2000])))
   :reagent-render (fn []
  [:div
  [:h1 "Temperature"]
  [:h2 {:style {:color :magenta}} "With Real Time Vibrations! "]
  [:h2 "Celsius"]
  [:img {:width 64 :height 64 :src @(rf/subscribe [:image])}][:br]
  [:input.form-control {
   :type "text"
   :value @(rf/subscribe [:celsius])
   :on-change #(rf/dispatch [:update (-> % .-target .-value)]) }]
  [:h2 "fahrenheit"]
  [:div.form-control
  {:style {:color "#008080"}} @(rf/subscribe [:fahrenheit])]])})))
```

At this stage, you may have to **completely delete** the application on the Android host, before reinstalling on the device to fully update the application permissions.

Once the plugin has been added, you need to redeploy the app, since the native Android code has changed, with the same Cordova command:

```
cordova run android
```

And your phone should vibrate a few seconds on each mount of the temperature component.

Out of the box, Cordova has many, many plugins, contributed by the ever-growing community. Those can be browsed and searched at the following location:

```
https://cordova.apache.org/plugins
```

Give it a try with a few of them by deploying them on your own smartphone.

Now as you have seen, all the code you have developed in this book can be deployed almost directly using Cordova.

So go back a few dozen pages in time, and find one of the projects worked on and deploy it on your smartphone. Not complicated, and there is a small sense of achievement when you have your own code deployed on your device all the time, no?

Section 3: Reagent on React-Native

The last section of this chapter, and for that matter of this book, is about using Reagent with React-Native.

React-Native is another project that originated from Facebook labs, where components taken from the React framework are communicating with native objects from the target platform.

From a Reagent point of view, it means we can take those components, code them in ClojureScript, reuse the Hiccup DSL that we have used all along to create views and subcomponents, integrate with reactive atoms, and program for different smart devices in real time.

Learning the ins and outs of React-Native is again out of the scope of those recipes; we will focus on reusing the techniques learned so far to develop and run on target devices using React-Native.

In this section, you will see first how to get a standard React-Native project going on your machine, and then you will integrate the usual Boot tooling to the project and work on a fantastic temperature converter application.

5-3. Activating Pure React-Native
Problem

You need to get a standard React-Native project going on your machine.

Solution

There is a command-line tool to interface with React-Native that runs, here again, on node. Let's use it.

How It Works

With Node installed on your development environment, you can install the react-native-cli using npm:

```
npm install -g react-native-cli
```

With the CLI installed, we can generate a new React-Native project.

■ **Note** By the way, while there is a folder containing this React-Native example and the next one in the source files coming with this book, some of the xcode path becomes hardcoded to the machine they were generated on, so instead of trying to get it to work, you should execute all the steps yourself on your own machine.

Creating a brand-new React-Native project from the template is easy:

```
react-native init hello2
```

Because it has to pull a lot of JavaScript dependencies, this command is going to take a bit of time, and you rightfully deserve a cup of coffee at this stage of the book, so we heartily recommend that you go and get one to help finish the last few pages.

Once the command has finished copying all the files and installing the node dependencies, you should have the following project structure:

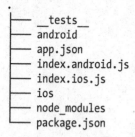

```
├── __tests__
├── android
├── app.json
├── index.android.js
├── index.ios.js
├── ios
├── node_modules
└── package.json
```

Table 5-3 describes the folders and files needed for a React-Native project.

Table 5-3. Files for React-Native Project

File/Folder	Usage
package.json	The node project metadata, with dependencies on React and React-Native
node_modules	The extracted node dependencies
iOS	The xcode project containing the application for iOS
Android	The Android Studio project containing the application for Android
index.ios.js	The JavaScript entry point for the iOS project
index.android.js	The JavaScript entry point for the Android project
app.json	The application metadata file, containing the name and display name
__tests__	Test related files to use with jtest

In case you were wondering about dependencies, you can have a look at the following **package.json** file:

```json
{
        "name": "hello",
        "version": "0.0.1",
        "private": true,
        "scripts": {
          "start": "node node_modules/react-native/local-cli/cli.js start",
          "test": "jest"
        },
        "dependencies": {
                "react": "16.0.0-alpha.6",
                "react-native": "0.44.2"
        },
        "devDependencies": {
                "babel-jest": "20.0.3",
                "babel-preset-react-native": "1.9.2",
                "jest": "20.0.4",
                "react-test-renderer": "16.0.0-alpha.6"
        },
        "jest": {
                "preset": "react-native"
        }
}
```

At the end of the **React-Native init** command, you can already see the following output:

```
To run your app on iOS:
   cd /Users/niko/Dropbox/PUBLISHING/CLJS-BOOK-APRESS/SAMPLES/chapter05-
   beyond/hello2
   react-native run-ios
   - or -
   Open ios/hello.xcodeproj in Xcode
   Hit the Run button
To run your app on Android:
   cd /Users/niko/Dropbox/PUBLISHING/CLJS-BOOK-APRESS/SAMPLES/chapter05-
   beyond/hello2
   Have an Android emulator running (quickest way to get started), or a
   device connected
   react-native run-android
```

Having a device to start hacking is not required, as you can also use either environment emulators without much problem.

Let's go with the iOS version if you are on Mac, or an Android device if you have one at hand. Once in the project, you can start the React-Native-based application **and** the React-Native packager.

The React-Native packager transforms your JavaScript code to something that can be natively run on the host platform using an extra layer, something like a mini virtual runtime inside the host, added by the React-Native framework.

Supposing your device is showing with the adb command:

```
NikoMacBook% adb devices
List of devices attached
QV700B1MOB        device
```

You can install the app on your device with

```
react-native run-android
```

If on Mac and targeting iOS, you can use

```
react-native run-ios
```

At this stage, an extra process for the packager starts, as shown in Figure 5-25.

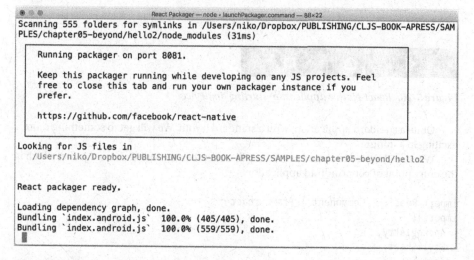

Figure 5-25. *React-Native package manager process*

Figure 5-26 shows the application as it is also starting on the target device.

Figure 5-26. *React-Native application starting on device*

Quite a standard application, with a standard layout. We will get to something more exciting in a minute.

Where did the code came from? You will remember the index.android.js file, which is the entry point of your Android application:

```
import React, { Component } from 'react';
import {
  AppRegistry,
  StyleSheet,
  Text,
  View
} from 'react-native';

export default class hello2 extends Component {
  render() {
    return (
      <View style={styles.container}>
        <Text style={styles.welcome}>
          Welcome to React Native!
        </Text>
```

```
        <Text style={styles.instructions}>
          To get started, edit index.android.js
        </Text>
        <Text style={styles.instructions}>
          Double tap R on your keyboard to reload,{'\n'}
          Shake or press menu button for dev menu
        </Text>
      </View>
    );
  }
}

const styles = StyleSheet.create({
  container: {
    flex: 1,
    justifyContent: 'center',
    alignItems: 'center',
    backgroundColor: '#F5FCFF',
  },
  welcome: {
    fontSize: 20,
    textAlign: 'center',
    margin: 10,
  },
  instructions: {
    textAlign: 'center',
    color: '#333333',
    marginBottom: 5,
  },
});

AppRegistry.registerComponent('hello2', () => hello2);
```

This is actually close to standard React components targeting the browser. The hello2 component has a render method made of a view, and three inside text components. A stylesheet is also created to style all the different components using traditional CSS directives.

Lastly, the AppRegistry class registers the component hello2 to a name and displays it at the same time.

As shown on the screen in the application (Figure 5-27), you can shake the device, and get the developer menu to show up.

Figure 5-27. *Developer menu*

Here, to get a preview of where we are heading, you can enable the "Hot Reloading" feature. This feature will make your components to update in the application's virtual dom and update the related components.

For example, if you change the text component at the top with

```
<Text style={styles.welcome}>
    I want to code in ClojureScript
</Text>
```

Then the text will be updated directly on the device after you save your file (Figure 5-28).

I want to code in ClojureScript

To get started, edit index.android.js

Double tap R on your keyboard to reload,
Shake or press menu button for dev menu

Figure 5-28. Instant updates on device

Alright, so now that you have a good idea of how to create and run a React-Native application, it is time to move on to the boot-ified version and start typing code in ClojureScript.

5-4. Integrating React-Native with Boot
Problem

You want to integrate the usual Boot tooling to the React-Native project and code your application in ClojureScript.

Solution

We will set up the usual boot-based project layout and customize it to work with React-Native a bit. You will also make use of the Boot React-Native plugins which glue things together between ClojureScript/Boot and React-Native.

How It Works

Our exercises will be based off a ClojureScript/React-Native template, and in the ClojureScript+React-Native space, there are two competing projects, as you can see on the http://cljsrn.org/ web site.

Re-Natal

Re-Natal is Leiningen based but probably has the most support in the community, as well as supporting recent versions of React-Native.

Boot-React-Native

boot-react-native, as its name implies, is based on Boot, and it hooks itself into the React-Native packager life cycle so that you can reuse the same techniques you have seen up to now, with Boot, repl programming, and hot code reloading.

The supported version of React-Native is slightly older, but this is the one we are going to use in this book. And then you can go back and send your pull request to update the React-Native version!

React-Native Boot Template

Providing that you have installed the react-native-cli already, then the dependencies are already installed. We can focus solely on the Boot/ClojureScript part.

First let's install the Boot dependencies and the sample template by cloning the boot-react-native repository:

```
git clone https://github.com/mjmeintjes/boot-react-native.git
cd boot-react-native
```

This is not required, but this makes sure you have the boot-task and the boot-sample template in sync. You can package and install the boot-task locally using the build command

```
boot build
```

This will install the Boot task jar on your local machine, and then you will reuse that jar in the sample application by adding it in the build.boot dependencies section with

```
[boot-react-native/boot-react-native        "0.3-rc2" :scope "test"]
```

Now, let's move to the React-Native application in the example/app folder and install the node dependencies for the React-Native app. This was done transparently by the command **React-Native init** in the previous section.

```
cd example/app
npm install
```

At this stage, boot-react-native needs to perform a minor patch on React-Native to plug itself in, and this is done with the following command:

```
cd example && boot patch-rn
```

That's it: you are ready, so let's get the ClojureScript code to start compiling with the (long time no see) boot dev task!

```
cd example && boot dev
```

The task **does** take a long time again to start on first run, so you can leisurely have a look at the build.boot file in the meantime:

```
(set-env!
 :source-paths    #{"src" "react-support"}
 :resource-paths    #{"resources"}
 :exclusions ['cljsjs/react]
 :dependencies '[
   [boot-react-native/boot-react-native      "0.3-rc2"    :scope "test"]
   [adzerk/boot-cljs                          "1.7.228-1"  :scope "test"]
   [adzerk/boot-cljs-repl                     "0.3.3"      :scope "test"]
   [adzerk/boot-reload                        "0.4.12"     :scope "test"]
   [com.cemerick/piggieback                   "0.2.1"      :scope "test"]
   [weasel                                    "0.7.0"      :scope "test"]
   [org.clojure/tools.nrepl                   "0.2.12"     :scope "test"]
   [org.clojure/clojure                       "1.8.0"]
   [org.clojure/clojurescript                 "1.8.51"]
   [reagent                                   "0.6.0-rc"]
   ;; [react-native-externs "0.0.1-SNAPSHOT"]
   ] )

(require
 '[adzerk.boot-cljs            :refer [cljs]]
 '[adzerk.boot-cljs-repl       :refer [cljs-repl start-repl]]
 '[adzerk.boot-reload          :refer [reload]]
 '[boot.core                   :as    b]
 '[boot.util                   :as    u]
 '[clojure.string              :as    s]
 '[mattsum.boot-react-native   :as    rn :refer [patch-rn]]
 )

(task-options! patch-rn {:app-dir "app"})
```

```
(deftask build
  []
  (comp
    (reload :on-jsload 'mattsum.simple-example.core/on-js-reload
            :port 8079
            :ws-host "localhost")
    (rn/before-cljsbuild)
    (cljs-repl :ws-host "localhost"
               :port 9001
               :ip "0.0.0.0")
    (cljs :ids #{"main"})
    (rn/after-cljsbuild :server-url "localhost:8081")
    (target :dir ["app/build"])))

(deftask dev
  "Build app and watch for changes"
  []
  (comp (patch-rn)
        (watch)
        (build)
        (speak)))

(deftask dist
  "Build a distributable bundle of the app"
  []
  (comp
    (patch-rn)
    (cljs :ids #{"dist"})
    (rn/bundle :files {"dist.js" "main.jsbundle"})
    (target :dir ["app/dist"])))
```

By this time, you will realize the difference from the usual Boot build yourself. In the
dev task, boot-react-native plugs itself inside the task with before and after cljsbuild steps:

```
(rn/before-cljsbuild)
...
(rn/after-cljsbuild :server-url "localhost:8081")
```

At this stage, the ClojureScript first compilation run should be finished. Here is the
command's full output:

```
NikoMacBook% boot dev
Starting reload server on ws://localhost:8079
Writing adzerk/boot_reload/init2372.cljs to connect to ws://localhost:8079...
Writing boot_cljs_repl.cljs...
Checking if React Native needs to be patched...
patch-rn.sh: React Native patch is already applied
```

```
Starting file watcher (CTRL-C to quit)...

Adding :require adzerk.boot-reload.init2372 to main.cljs.edn...
Adding :require adzerk.boot-reload.init2372 to dist.cljs.edn...
Boot React Native: shimming...
nREPL server started on port 55596 on host 127.0.0.1 -
nrepl://127.0.0.1:55596
Adding :require adzerk.boot-cljs-repl to main.cljs.edn...
Adding :require adzerk.boot-cljs-repl to dist.cljs.edn...
Compiling ClojureScript...
o main.js
Boot React Native: setting up dev environment...
Writing target dir(s)...
Elapsed time: 47.117 sec
```

You will also notice that the ClojureScript code is compiled to the app/build folder. Both the index.android.js and the index.ios.js files contain similar code, mostly loading an **init.js** file to share common code:

```
'use strict';
require('./init.js');
// add android-specific javascript initialization here
```

Where the init.js file itself contains a hack to transparently get Reagent to handle the React-Native DOM, require the compiled ClojureScript code, and load it, just as it would have been in the browser:

```
'use strict';
// global.window = {};
// hack: get reagent to find ReactNative.render as ReactDOM.render
global.ReactDOM = require('react-native');
require('./build/main.js');
```

OK, now we can start the React-Native packager and deploy our application to the device using the React-Native cli command from the **example/app** folder:

```
react-native run-ios
```

The React-Native packager takes a **long** time here again, so be sure to go all the way down the last output:

```
React packager ready.

[6/2/2017, 3:36:54 PM] <START> Initializing Packager
[6/2/2017, 3:36:55 PM] <START> Building in-memory fs for JavaScript
[6/2/2017, 3:36:56 PM] <END>   Building in-memory fs for JavaScript (1695ms)
[6/2/2017, 3:36:57 PM] <START> Building Haste Map
```

```
[6/2/2017, 3:36:57 PM] <END>    Building Haste Map (677ms)
[6/2/2017, 3:36:57 PM] <END>    Initializing Packager (3284ms)
[6/2/2017, 3:36:58 PM] <START> Requesting bundle: {"url":"/index.ios.bundle?
                                platform=ios&dev=true&minify=false"}
[6/2/2017, 3:36:58 PM] <START> Transforming modules
transformed 811/811 (100%)
[6/2/2017, 3:40:58 PM] <END>    Transforming modules (239740ms)
[6/2/2017, 3:44:34 PM] <END>    Requesting bundle: {"url":"/index.ios.bundle?
                                platform=ios&dev=true&minify=false"} (455850ms)
[6/2/2017, 4:03:10 PM] <START> Requesting bundle: {"url":"/index.ios.bundle?
                                platform=ios&dev=true&minify=false"}
[6/2/2017, 4:03:10 PM] <START> Updating existing bundle: {"outdatedModules":5}
[6/2/2017, 4:03:10 PM] <START> Transforming modules
[6/2/2017, 4:03:10 PM] <END>    Transforming modules (1ms)
[6/2/2017, 4:03:10 PM] <END>    Updating existing bundle:
                                {"outdatedModules":5} (63ms)
[6/2/2017, 4:03:11 PM] <END>    Requesting bundle: {"url":"/index.ios.bundle
                                ?platform=ios&dev=true&minify=false"} (185ms)
```

■ **Caution**   On a slow machine, like the author's, your application may show a red screen with an error before the packager has finished doing its job. Simply wait until the transforming phase of the packager is finished, and press reload.

If all goes well, you should see some text and reassuring Clojure colors (Figure 5-29).

iPhone 6 – iOS 10.1 (14B72)

Carrier 🜂   4:05 PM   🔋

Welcome to boot-react-native

Count: 0, click to increase

Figure 5-29. *ClojureScript with Boot React-Native*

Updated Reagent for React-Native

The ClojureScript code that generated the preceding view, while based on Reagent principles, needs a bit of new code to get things working with React-Native.

The code included in the boot-reactive-native template already has a lot of comments, but here are the few new and important things to note:

- you need to require js/React and React in a slightly obscure way

- the images and resources in general need a relative path

- React-Native components are extended to work with Reagent using: **r/adapt-react-class**

- touch interactions are done using the **touchable-highlight** component

- since there is no DOM in React-Native, the components are mounted in a slightly different way.

349

Otherwise, the code is rather standard ClojureScript/Reagent code, as you can see in the following:

```clojure
(ns mattsum.simple-example.core
  (:require [reagent.core :as r]
            [cljs.test :as test]))

(enable-console-print!)

;; we need set! for advanced compilation
(set! js/React
  (js/require "react-native/Libraries/react-native/react-native.js"))
(defonce react
  (js/require "react-native/Libraries/react-native/react-native.js"))

;; Assets need to be relative path, starting from the
;; `app/build/node_modules' directory.
;; The packager only finds images located in the 'app/' folder
;; (the directory that contains package.json) or below.
;;
;; We use 'defonce' to prevent errors on subsequent reloads.
(defonce logo (js/require "../../assets/cljs.png"))

(def view (r/adapt-react-class (.-View react)))
(def text (r/adapt-react-class (.-Text react)))
(def touchable-highlight (r/adapt-react-class (.-TouchableHighlight react)))
(def image (r/adapt-react-class (.-Image react)))
(defonce !state (r/atom {:count 0}))

(defn root-view
  []
  [view {:style {:margin-top 50
                 :margin-left 8
                 :justify-content "center"
                 :align-items "center"}}
   [text {:style {:font-family "Helvetica"
                  :font-size 20
                  :margin-bottom 20}}
    "Welcome to boot-react-native"]
   [image {:style {:width 350
                   :height 348
                   :margin-bottom 20}
           :source logo}]
   [touchable-highlight {:style {:padding 20
                                 :background-color "#e0e0e0"}
                         :on-press (fn []
                                     (swap! !state update :count inc))
                         :underlay-color "#f0f0f0"}
```

```
      [text {:style {:font-family "Helvetica"
                     :font-size 14}}
        "Count: " (:count @!state) ", click to increase"]]])

(defn root-container
  "Wraps root-view. This is to make sure live reloading using
  boot-reload and reagent works as expected. Instead of editing
  root-  container, edit root-view"
  []
  [root-view])

(defn ^:export main
  []
  (js/console.log "MAIN")
  (enable-console-print!)
  (.registerComponent (.-AppRegistry react)
                      "SimpleExampleApp"
                      #(r/reactify-component #'root-container)))

(defn on-js-reload
  []
  (println "on-js-reload. state:" (pr-str @!state))

  ;; Force re-render
  ;;
  ;; In React native, there are no DOM nodes. Instead, mounted
  ;; components are identified by numbers. The first root components
  ;; is assigned the number 1.

  (r/render #'root-container 1))
```

You'll notice pretty quickly that if you update the core.cljs file, then the Boot ClojureScript compilation kicks in and the compiled file is inserted into app/build; that folder is in turn monitored for change by the React-Native packager, and the code is hot reloaded in the native application.

For example, let's change the text of the view React-Native **text** component in the view, within the file core.cljs. You are now invited to change

```
[text {:style {:font-family "Helvetica"
               :font-size 20
               :margin-bottom 20}}
  "Welcome to boot-react-native!"]
```

351

With

```
[text {:style {:font-family "Helvetica"
               :font-size 20
               :margin-bottom 20}}
  "Time to code in ClojureScript again!"]
```

And you'll observe the immediate change in the emulator and in Figure 5-30.

Figure 5-30. *Instant coding with React-Native and ClojureScript*

Sweet. Now your own coding is needed in the coming exercise!

5-5. Using TextInput, Colors, and Atom

Problem

You want to create a React-Native TextInput field that will update a Reagent atom when text is typed in.

Solution

The Reagent atom's value will be used in another React-Native component that will output static text and have its background color according to the text entered in the first React component.

How It Works

In order for this to work, you will need to

- use adapt-react-class for the TextInput component
- update the state of the application with one more key to hold the text
- add a new input component within the root-view
- add the onChangeText attribute and add a ClojureScript function to update the state
- add a new text component within the root-view
- add a background-color attribute in the style section, where the value of background-color is the lowercase version of the related key value of the application, and, by extend, the value of the text entered in the above text input.

On the screen will be something like what you see in Figure 5-31.

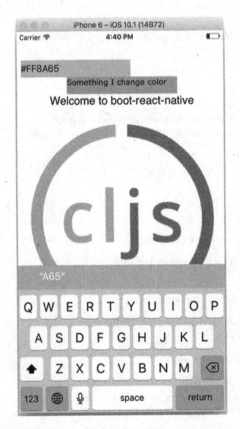

Figure 5-31. *Updates and atoms*

You should give it a try yourself here again, with the steps described in the preceding; this comes down to standard ClojureScript coding.

First, add require to the namespace:

```
[clojure.string :as str]
```

Define input, as a component extending the React-Native component TextInput:

```
(def input (r/adapt-react-class (.-TextInput react)))
```

Update the application state with a new key:

```
(defonce !state (r/atom {:count 10 :my-text "red"}))
```

Insert the input component within the view. See the onChangeText handler updating the application state, a Reagent atom, using swap!

```
[input
  {:multiLine false
   :numberOfLines 4
   :editable true
   :autoCapitalize "characters"
   :background-color "#7c7c7c"
   :max-length 48
   :onChangeText (fn[x] (swap! !state update :my-text (fn[_] x)))
   :style {:height 30 :width 200}}]
```

Finally, add a Text component after the input one, with the background-color style attribute referring to the application state:

```
[text  {:style {:font-family "Verdana"
                 :font-size 14
                 :height 30
                 :width 200
                 :background-color (str/lower-case (:my-text @!state))} }
        "Something I change color"]
```

What's the Weather Again?

This section will end with yet another temperature converter in React-Native. We will just update the previous example with the right amount of jazz to get the conversation running.

How would you do it? Here are probably the steps popping up in your mind:

- Add the images for hot and cold

- Add the input fields

- Add the key in the Reagent's atom, application state

- Add the Celsius-to-Fahrenheit conversion function

- Add an is-hot? function

- Use is-hot? in an if-statement to change the image showing in the view depending on the temperature.

Should not be too complicated, should it? Time to go ahead and code. Then, pick up a possible implementation, right after the screenshots of Figure 5-32.

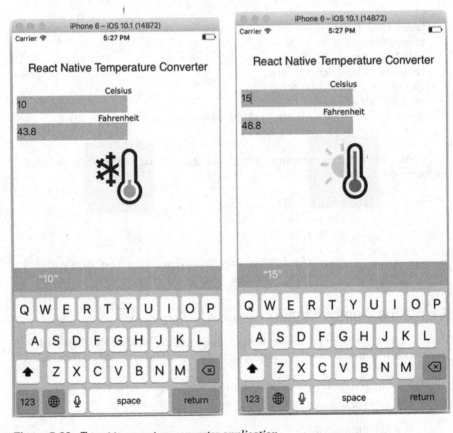

Figure 5-32. *Target temperature converter application*

```
(ns mattsum.simple-example.core
  (:require
    [reagent.core :as r]
    [cljs.test :as test]))

(enable-console-print!)

(set! js/React
  (js/require "react-native/Libraries/react-native/react-native.js"))
(defonce react
  (js/require "react-native/Libraries/react-native/react-native.js"))

(defonce hot (js/require "../../assets/hot.png"))
(defonce cold (js/require "../../assets/cold.png"))
```

```clojure
(def view (r/adapt-react-class (.-View react)))
(def text (r/adapt-react-class (.-Text react)))
(def touchable-highlight
  (r/adapt-react-class (.-TouchableHighlight react)))
(def image (r/adapt-react-class (.-Image react)))
(def input (r/adapt-react-class (.-TextInput react)))

(defonce !state (r/atom {:temperature "5"}))

(defn is-hot?[]
  (< 10 (js/parseInt (:temperature @!state))))

(defn c-to-f[c]
  (str (+ (* 1.8 (js/parseInt (:temperature @!state) )) 32)))

(defn temperature-field[title val-fn editable on-change-fn] []
  [view {:style {:margin-top 50
                 :margin-left 8
                 :justify-content "center"
                 :align-items "center"}}
   [text  {:style {:font-family "Verdana"}} title]
   [input
    {:multiLine false
     :numberOfLines 4
     :editable editable
     :autoCapitalize "characters"
     :background-color "#7c7c"
     :max-length 48
     :value (val-fn)
     :onChangeText on-change-fn
     :style {:height 30 :width 200}}] ])

(defn root-view []
  [view {:style {:margin-top 50
                 :margin-left 8
                 :justify-content "center"
                 :align-items "center"}}
   [text {:style {:font-family "Helvetica"
                  :font-size 20
                  :margin-bottom 20}}
    "React Native Temperature Converter"]

   (temperature-field "Celsius" #(:temperature @!state) true
    (fn[x] (swap! !state assoc :temperature x))))

   (temperature-field "Fahrenheit" #(c-to-f (:temperature @!state)) false nil)
```

```
[image {:style {:margin-top 100 :width 128 :height 128} :source (if (is-
hot?) hot cold)}]
])

(defn root-container [] [root-view])

(defn ^:export main
  []
  (js/console.log "MAIN")
  (enable-console-print!)
  (.registerComponent (.-AppRegistry react)
                      "SimpleExampleApp"
                      #(r/reactify-component #'root-container)))

(defn on-js-reload []
  (println "on-js-reload. state:" (pr-str @!state))

  (r/render #'root-container 1))
```

A few things to note:

- Writing our own component, temperature-field, is done in the same Reagent way as when targeting the browser.

- React-Native's TextInput component always requires a string, so the code goes back and forth between the numerical computed value and the string.

- The view component "maps directly to the native view equivalent on whatever platform React-Native is running on, whether that is a UIView, <div>, android.view, etc." as specified in the documentation https://facebook.github.io/react-native/releases/0.23/docs/view.html.

At this stage, you should probably head to the React-Native page to see the various components you can use, and how to map them to ClojureScript/Reagent:

https://facebook.github.io/react-native/

Summary

Now this is not the end. It is not even the beginning of the end. But it is, perhaps, the end of the beginning.

Winston Churchill

So, by now, you have seen quite a few ways to bring your ClojureScript/Reagent knowledge to different platforms, for different purposes.

First, you saw how to port your code directly to a browser application using Electron. This was done using a browser engine, rendering your page as if it were in a browser, and the view itself was controlled by a server-side script on Node.js, itself also included in the final bundle.

Second, and in a similar way, you saw how to port your ClojureScript/Reagent application onto a web view of a smart device using a native application running a web view again. With Cordova, your application was running as it was before in a web rendering engine and packaged to be deployed as a native application.

Finally, you saw how to use the same Reagent/ClojureScript concepts in an environment without a Document Object Model with React-Native. React-Native embeds an interpreter that was executing your code directly on the host machine through the React-Native packager and the hosted rendering engine.

And finally, this closes the last chapter of this book. The book aimed to present you the unified power of

- A build tool, named Boot, allowing you to perform the many scripting and building tasks that go along with programming without pulling your hair out.

- A platform, the JavaScript runtime, whether it is used on the browser or on the server side.

- A language, ClojureScript: a port of Clojure for the JavaScript runtime, a functional language that excels in making your code compact, simple to read once you get used to it, and with a very small core set of functions. It makes you think less about how to write in the language and more about what you should deliver or invent.

- A workflow on how to code ClojureScript code in real time either using a text editor directly or typing commands in REPL.

- A framework, Reagent, which allows you to become familiar with the concept of reactive programming, where the view and the components making the view are a direct translation of a reactive application state.

- Paths beyond, where you bring all the preceding knowledge and experience to environments in the wild.

Index

A

AJAX
  core.async, 82
    weather, 83–87
    working process, 83
  MongoDB, 87
    ClojureScript application, 91
    CORS setup, 88–89
    download page, 88
    messages, 91
    Nginx configuration, 90
    OpenWeatherMap object, 92
    platform installation, 87–88
  OpenWeatherMap
    API key, 85
    AJAX.core/GET function, 85–87
    home page, 84
    Misty Tokyo icon, 87
Animating components and MOJS, 230

B

Bare-bones Cordova project
  Android environment, 327
  browser, 327
  ClojureScript, 330
  file layouts, 326
  native APIs, 334
Boot
  ClojureScript, 25
  integrating React Native, 343
  Linux (OSX), 6
  OSX (homebrew), 7
  Reagent
    celsius-fahrenheit, 43
    dependencies array, 40
    dynamic application, 40

    states, 41
  recipes detail, 1
  REPL, 1 (*see also* Read Eval Print Loop (REPL))
  solution, 2
  supersimplistic application, 7
    Clojure application, 9
    emergency HTTP server, 11
    Java application, 8
    mp3 player, 9
  tasks
    Boot environment, 19
    build.boot file, 22
    composition, 20
    definition and dependencies, 19
    in-memory filesystem flow, 21
    interaction, 17
    sound, 24
    text files, 21
    watch, 23
    working process, 17
  Windows
    Chocolatey, 5
    manual file, 3
  working process, 2

C

CLJSJS libraries
  build.boot file, 139
  creation, 133
  deps.cljs file, 130
  dumb library, 134
  externs, 135
  jQuery, 130
    build task, 132
    dependency section, 131
    from-jars Boot task, 131

© Nicolas Modrzyk 2017

N. Modrzyk, *Reactive with ClojureScript Recipes*, DOI 10.1007/978-1-4842-3009-1

CLJSJS libraries (*cont.*)
    jar file, 132
    JavaScript script location, 131
  MyLib library, 138
  working process, 130
ClojureScript project
  bare-bones Cordova project, 330
  Boot
    compilation options, 31
    development workflow, 29
    Hiccup syntax, 38
    page autorefresh, 33
    REPL, 33
    structure, 26
    text files, 25
    turning reactive, 37
    working process, 26
  closer-asynccode (*see* Core.async)
  DOM API
    button insertion, 52
    element creation, 51
    events and event handlers, 53
    find, update and delete
      elements, 50
    innerHTML, 52
    input events, 53
    insert nodes, 52
    JavaScript functions, 51
    modification, 51
    mouse event detection, 53–54
    removeChild function, 53
    Window object, 54
  features, 49
  manipulation of DOM
    access and modification DOM
      nodes, 64
    creation and modification, 72
    elements and properties, 60
    energetic and running cat, 59
    event handling, 64
    handling events, 62
    project preparation, 55
    sliding, 69
    SPA, 55
    triggering animation, 71
    working process, 55
  Quil
    Boot setup, 106
    ColorJoy, 114
    quilax 1, 109
    reactive Quil, 116

    real-time coding, 110
    superposition effects, 111–112
    trailing effect, 111
    working process, 106
  reactive streams, 93
    Beicon, 93
    core.async, 99
    Google's Firebase, 94
    working process, 93
  rules/trigger events and React, 101
  TODO list applications, 50
ColorJoy, 114
Cordova
  advantages, 324
  bare-bones (*see* Bare-bones Cordova
    project)
  command-line tool, 324
Core.async
  AJAX (*see* AJAX)
  button events, 80
  channel interaction, 77
  concepts, 77
  counters increases, 82
  counting milk boxes, 78
  elasped time updates, 82
  Firebase channels, 99
  last milk boxes, 80
  project's components, 76

■ D

DataScript, 284
Debugging, 317
Desktop application, 304
Dommy functions, 67–68, 75
Dynamic donut-shaped charts, 233

■ E

ECharts
  atoms and watchers, 148
  bar chart, 145
  bar charting, 146
  beautiful charts, 142
  ClojureScript-based configuration, 147
  JSON-based configuration, 142
  pie, 144
Electron, 304
  backend and frontend
    Asteroids-like shooter package, 309
    application architecture, 304–305

async message, 310
ClojureScript code, 304
createWindow function, 310
debugging, 317
desktop application, 308
falling blocks nostalgia, 323
files, 305
folder structure, 312
index.html page, 305
life-cycle events, 306
Node.js code, 306–308
package.json file, 308
platform game, 308–309
pong messages, 311
reagent/re-frame, 312
releasing/packaging command, 320
renderer process, 311
renderer view, 310
server-client process, 312
shooter, 309
Tetris, 323

■ **F**

Functional reactive programming. *See* Reagent

■ **G**

Google's Firebase, 94
application content, 95
custom data, 96
dashboard, 95
distributed application persistence, 99
get-in function, 97
in-browser real-time, 96
reactive flow, 98
synchronized app, 98

■ **H**

HTML5 location, 226

■ **I**

Integrating React Native Boot, 343
boot-react-native, 344
ClojureScript, 349
re-natal, 344

template, 344–349
updated Reagent, 349

■ **J, K, L**

JavaScript
CLJSJS libraries (*see* CLJSJS libraries)
ClojureScript (*see* Node.js)
JavaScriptProblem, 140
animation (TweenJS), 149
ECharts, 142
HTML5 creation engine (*see* Pixi Engine)
oboe, 140
working problem, 140
linking parts, 119
Paho and Mosquitto, 172
PhaserJS, 176
physics engine, 164
timezones (jQuery), 119
ClojureScript setup, 120
compilation flow, 129
error messages, 128
event handling, 127
extended compilation flow, 129
JSON file and DOM elements, 122
mode problems, 127
toggling element, 121
working process, 120

■ **M**

Movie catalog application
detailed view mode, 273
list view mode, 272
smart device, 274
template, 270
working process, 270–272

■ **N, O**

Node.js
auto reload express app, 196
back to boot, 191
compiling ClojureScript code, 189
express notes, 194
namespaces (fs module), 192
REPL, 191
third-party modules, 193
working process, 189

■ P, Q

Paho and Mosquitto
   ClojureScript showcase, 174
   connection, 174
   distributed MQTT messages, 172
   setup, 172
Painting application
   controller parameters, 280
   core-async go-loop, 281
   drawing board, 283
   event handler function, 280
   homemade smiley, 282
   option-bar component, 282
   update-function, 283
   web framework, 279
   working process, 279
PhaserJS
   animation manager, 180
   games, 176
   layout, 177
   MQTT-driven animation, 188
   phzr, 184
   reacting-user events, 182
   Sprite adding mode, 179–180
   Spritesheet function, 181
   websockets and Sprites, 185
Physics engine
   clicks and shapes, 167
   colored circles, 169
   equilibrum, 170
   free-falling wire-framed boxes, 165
   FrictionAir, 172
   gravity effect, 167
   same shape and different forces, 171
   setting up, 164
Pixi Engine
   animate loop, 159
   event listener, 161
   HTML creation, 156
   resource loading events, 158
   Sprites, 162
   stage, 157

■ R

React-Native project, 336
   adb command, 339
   command-line tool, 336
   developer menu, 342
   folders and files, 337
   index.android.js file, 340–341
   init command, 338
   instant updates, 343
   manager process, 339
   package.json file, 338
   project structure, 337
   target device, 340
Read Eval Print Loop (REPL), 1, 12
   Boot environment, 14
   Clojure code, 13
   network, 15
   working process, 12
Reagent
   address book application
      add and delete buttons, 274
      contact application, 277
      contact subcomponent, 275
      friends list, 278
      functions, 275
      internal database, 274
      removing contacts, 276
      resulting application screen, 277
      toggle-sort function, 277
      update-contacts, 276
      working process, 275
   animating components, 230
   applications, 269
   atoms
      ClojureScript atoms and HTML, 210
      HTML, atoms and cursor, 214
      user interactions, 209
      working process, 209
   celsius-fahrenheit, 43
   components, 201
      function, 204
      input fields, 202
      life-cycle events, 209
      map of functions, 206
      React root, 203
      rendering function, 202
      static nodes, 203
      temperature component, 201
   dependencies array, 40
   DOM tree resulting, 200
   dragging and dropping
      components, 263
      code, 263
      comments, 265–266
      Dragula library, 263
      result, 264
      working process, 263

dynamic application, 40
donut-shaped charts, 233
exercises, 218
HTML5 location, 226
local storage
　code, 221
　comments, 222
　result, 222
　working process, 221
mini audio player, 248
　ClojureScript, 249
　comments, 251
　HTML, 249
　louder music, 253
　result, 250
　smart device, 251
　web audio player, 250
　working process, 249
movie catalog application
　detailed view mode, 273
　list view mode, 272
　smart device, 274
　template, 270
　working process, 270–272
painting application
　controller parameters, 280
　core-async go-loop, 281
　drawing board, 283
　event handler function, 280
　homemade smiley, 282
　option-bar component, 282
　update-function, 283
　web framework, 279
　working process, 279
recipes, 199
Re-frame
　atoms, 300
　clockwork orange, 297
　functions, 297
　temperature
　　outside, 298–300
　working process, 296
server-side code, 266
　comments, 269
　express part, 267
　node setup (Package.json), 267
　Reagent part, 268
　Reagent rendering, 269
　result, 269
　working process, 267

single page application and
　multiple pages
　code, 223
　comments, 225
　result, 224
　working process, 222
sortable table
　browser error console, 220
　code, 219
　comments, 220
　creation, 218
　elements, 218
　result, 220
　working process, 218
states, 41
SVG (*see* Scalable Vector Graphics
　(SVG))
TODO application
　application overview, 287
　categories panel, 293
　connection and
　　insert data, 284
　dashboard view, 294
　DataScript, 284
　DataScript queries, 292
　deleting data, 286
　insert/upsert, 285
　menu.cljs, 294
　namespaces graph, 289
　opening, 296
　Posh, 287
　pulling data, 286
　queries, 285
　reactive database
　　queries, 289–292
　tutorials, 287
　updates, 295
　working process, 284
TypeAhead HTML input box
　ClojureScript, 246
　comments, 248
　HTML, 246
　result, 247
　value selection, 248
　working process, 245
video player
　ClojureScript code, 253, 255–257
　code, 254
　result, 254
　w3.org player, 257

Reagent (*cont.*)
   web workers, 238
      ClojureScript, 239, 241
      comments, 240
      HTML, 238
      Parallel.js, 238
      result, 240
Re-frame
   atoms, 300
   clockwork orange, 297
   functions, 297
   temperature outside, 298–300
   working process, 296

■ S

Scalable Vector Graphics (SVG), 258
   ClojureScript, 259–260
   comments, 263
   CSS, 260–261
   elements, 258
   result, 262
   rotating carousel, 262
   sweet sunshine, 259
   working process, 258
Single Page Application
      (SPA), 49, 222
swap-cat-dommy function, 66–67

■ T, U, V, W, X, Y, Z

TextInput, colors and atom
   onChangeText, 355
   React-Native component, 353

target temperature converter
      application, 356
   temperature converter, 355
   updates and atoms, 354
   working process, 353
TODO application
   application overview, 287
   categories panel, 293
   connection and insert data, 284
   dashboard view, 294
   DataScript, 284
   DataScript queries, 292
   deleting data, 286
   insert/upsert, 285
   menu.cljs, 294
   namespaces graph, 289
   opening, 296
   Posh, 287
   pulling data, 286
   queries, 285
   reactive database queries, 289–292
   tutorials, 287
   updates, 295
   working process, 284
toggle function, 66
TweenJS
   animation, 149
   ClojureScript code, 150
   ClojureScript function, 150
   composition, 154
   easing functions, 155
   framework, 153
   rotating cat, 153
   square shape, 152

Get the eBook for only $5!

Why limit yourself?

With most of our titles available in both PDF and ePUB format, you can access your content wherever and however you wish—on your PC, phone, tablet, or reader.

Since you've purchased this print book, we are happy to offer you the eBook for just $5.

To learn more, go to http://www.apress.com/companion or contact support@apress.com.

Apress®

Printed in the United States
By Bookmasters